WHY TIME BEGINS ON OPENING DAY

Books by Thomas Boswell

WHY TIME BEGINS ON OPENING DAY

HOW LIFE IMITATES THE WORLD SERIES

Thomas Boswell

WHY TIME BEGINS
ON OPENING DAY

DOUBLEDAY & COMPANY, INC.
GARDEN CITY, NEW YORK
1984

Chapters 7, 9, 10, 12, and 19 first appeared in *Inside Sports.* Copyright © 1981,
1982, by Inside Sports Magazine, Inc., Evanston, Illinois.
Chapters 4, 8, 13, and 18 first appeared in the Washington *Post.* Copyright ©
1977, 1981, 1982, 1983 by the Washington Post Company.
Chapter 15 first appeared in *Playboy.* Copyright © 1983 by Playboy.
All are reprinted with permission.
Library of Congress Cataloging in Publication Data

Boswell, Thomas, 1948–
Why time begins on opening day.

1. Baseball—Addresses, essays, lectures.   I. Title.
GV867.B65   1984   796.357
Copyright © 1984 by THOMAS BOSWELL
ISBN Number: 0-385-18409-3
Library of Congress Catalog Card Number: 82–46029
Printed in the United States of America

First Edition

To my parents
Elizabeth and Paul

CONTENTS

WHY TIME BEGINS ON OPENING DAY

1.
BALLPARK
WANDERER

I am a ballpark wanderer.

Sometimes I think I am as attracted to the parks as I am to the game. When your job takes you to a hundred games a year, hopscotching among two dozen cities, you become aware of how baseball is diffracted by the town and the ballpark where it is played. Each city and stadium draws out the hidden flavors of the sport; by a nice symbiosis, the game also illuminates the places where it is played.

American baseball may be one nation, indivisible, with free agency and juggled tax depreciations for all; but from Yankee Stadium and Fenway Park to Chavez Ravine and the Big A, it doesn't seem that way. Each major league park is persistently and confidently unique. Does baseball, like a liquid, take the shape of its container? In every case, the stadium, and even the seat, seasons the game. Consequently I imagine that each park has one best place to perch.

That's why the first three innings are *mine*. Each day, to keep my taste buds alive, I follow my whims in search of that game's best spot. If that means a stroll to the bleachers or a visit to the scouts with their radar guns in the box seats, then that's what I do; if the sundown, all crimson and lavender, seems more promising than the game, then I hike to the upper deck and watch them both. I've even been known to sit above the dugout and bench-jockey players in what I hope is an unidentifiable voice.

In Detroit there's a cozy seat at the railing in the second deck where you can lean forward and hear the swish of the bat when the on-deck hitter swings. When there's an argument at the plate, you don't have to ask the players afterward what was said. This is the best spot I've found to grasp the central aspect of the sport, the tense business being conducted between the pitcher and the hitter. It was here that I suddenly said to myself, "So *that's* 'changing speeds.' " One night the Tigers' Jack Morris made me feel Warren Spahn's dictum—that hitting is timing and pitching is destroying timing.

From that seat, I finally realized that Morris' forkball—if properly set up—simply could not be hit. No, not even if the hitter looked for it. Human reflexes, unconsciously synchronized to an excellent fastball, could not react to a slower pitch thrown with the same motion. Until then, I'd assumed change-ups were pitches which only worked if they took the hitter by surprise. Surely anyone who guessed correctly on Scott McGregor's silly sixty-mile-per-hour slip pitch could hit it. Don't all cutie-pie pitchers live in a world of danger?

But from that spot in Tiger Stadium I sensed the paradoxical physics of pitching. It's as physically difficult to hit a slow pitch after *seeing* a fast one thrown with the same delivery as it is hard to hit a laser-beam heater. That's why these guys so seldom get their comeuppance; their success isn't predicated on their savvy but on the hitter's synapses. Changing speeds isn't a trick. Once mastered, it's a dependable basic. Whitey Ford said he had the hitter's front foot on a string and could jerk that lead foot off stride whenever he wanted. In Detroit from that seat you can feel what he meant.

The game's only comparably close seats are in Fenway Park and Wrigley Field. The Boston boxes are so near ground level that you look up at the mound. Checked-swing fouls arrive at light speed; you're closer to the bat than any infielder.

This is where you learn the truth about big league fastballs. In high school, where I was a nondescript player, I once lined a double off a kid named Tom Bradley, who later won fifty-five games in the majors. I got it in my head this meant major league pitchers didn't throw that much faster than the best high school and college pitchers: sure, better control, better breaking balls, but I thought I'd seen respectable fastballs.

Then, from the Fenway boxes, I saw Goose Gossage pitch to Carl Yastrzemski with a pennant in the balance. What Gossage was throwing was not a baseball; it was a quark, something out of a different, smaller dimension. On my best day I wouldn't play catch with Goose Gossage, not with all the world's equipment. Nor would I get in the on-deck circle. In fact, sitting in those box seats, you suspect that you're already too close to him.

When faced with the incomprehensible, like Gossage's fastball, it's comforting to return to the familiar. That's why we often spend almost as much time looking at the people around us as we do in studying the field. Parks may teach us as much about towns as they do about the game.

Detroit is baseball's city of lowered expectations. Tiger fans savor small blessings. They don't snipe sardonically at their fate, like Cub fans, nor rage with Sophoclean passion like betrayed Bosox believers. The slightly threadbare Tiger followers no longer expect Ty Cobb or Prince Hal; they'd settle for one relief pitcher who didn't look like a sideshow freak.

Ushers in Tiger Stadium bear the mark of the baseball connoisseur; they're almost as interested in the *visiting* team as they are in the Tigers, viewing the home team with a hint of dispassion.

"Tom Brookens looks pretty steady at third base," one elderly Tiger usher said to me probingly.

"He's awful," I said. "In fact, he's worse than if he were bad. He's just the kind of competent nice-guy who clogs up an important power position for years and keeps the Tigers a peripheral contender but never a winner."

"That's what I really thought," said the usher.

In Milwaukee I stand in line to get the bratwurst, even if it means paying for the same thing that's free in the pressbox; the smoked meat smells better in the autumnal stands, and the Germanic crowd, in ruddy wool sweaters and hunting jackets, is redolent of a nineteenth-century-American health and self-confidence.

"In heaven, there ain't no beer," says a homemade sign in the County Stadium stands; "that's why the Brewers play here."

For some, Milwaukee baseball is synonymous with the Clockwork Orange gangs who turned twenty blocks of downtown into a riot corridor during the '82 Series. The cops watched the urban circus from a judicious distance. What's a little restaurant demolishing, bar trashing, window smashing, bottle throwing and random brawling between friends? Just excitable boys.

These incidents weren't so much Milwaukee as they were the latest installment in our new American tradition of turning any citywide sports "celebration" into a sociopaths' convention. Motorcycle gangs and punks of every persuasion instinctively spot their chance to play Visigoth while the town's hair is down; legions of glazed adolescents wander sheeplike into what they think is a good-natured beer bash—until they end up in the hospital. You're safer spending the night in San Quentin than walking the streets of a town that's just won a pennant.

To me, Milwaukee isn't warfare at the intersection of State and Wisconsin, but a baseball-addicted cab driver who calls himself the Red Baron.

During that '82 series, the Baron and I accidentally hooked up two days in a row and had a grand old time gabbing on the way to the park. The Baron's a bouncy, earthy, fiftyish street-corner philosopher whose wife has been in a wheelchair for years. He saves up, takes her on vacations all over the world.

Although he's the defiantly optimistic type, the Baron thinks the world is a pretty hard place, the kind of place where your young wife gets paralyzed in a stupid little traffic accident and you never figure out why. As usual in such cases, I told him more about myself in half an hour than I've told some friends in half a lifetime; the basic strangers-on-a-train syndrome. On the third day, the Baron and I met again in front of the hotel. This time, however, there was a free press bus that three of us were going to take to the park. "Sorry, Baron," I said, "can't waste the ten dollars."

"What the hell, get in," he said to us. "I'd rather talk than make a buck."

So we talked Brewer baseball all the way to the park. The

Baron wouldn't even take a tip; instead he gave us directions to his favorite restaurant.

"A cab driver who won't take money," said my colleague Dave Kindred, dumfounded. "Only in Milwaukee."

In Boston I always make an excursion to the infamous Fenway bleachers to see if the inhabitants still look like refugees from the interplanetary bar scene in *Star Wars*. Beam me up; set phasers to stun.

The Fenway bleachers are either the best, or the worst, place in baseball.

At its best, this tower of Bosox babel, with its 7,420 seats, is a curious blend of rabid Red Sox excitement and laid-back relaxation. The folks who chant so vociferously for the Boston pitching hero of the day—be he Bill Lee, Luis Tiant or Dennis Eckersley— are usually doing their bellowing with their shirts off, their suntan oil on and a twenty-four-ounce beer in hand.

"New England has three great things that everyone agrees on from birth," a former Springfield College catcher named Tim Duquette says: "sitting in the bleachers at Fenway, vacationing at Cape Cod and I've forgotten the third."

"Ah, it's a grand way to spend a summer," says ex-cop Mike Doughery. "Smuggling in beer under the sandwiches and chicken in a big cooler. About ten of us came to every game for years and sat out there. Everyone had their special section and their favorite days."

Nothing in baseball approaches the crush in Lansdowne Street when the Yankees are in Boston. The bleacher lines start forming at sunrise, fifteen hours before the first pitch. By noon, four thousand people are queued for the twenty-five hundred game-day tickets. The endurance, and persistence, of Boston fans is legendary. "What can we do?" says veteran usher Ken Miller. "You see a grappling hook come over the top of the wall in the rightfield corner and before you can get there, the guy has blended into the mob. If he wants in that bad . . ."

No known discomfort will dissuade the Boston bleacherite. On weekends when the temperature never dips below 98.6, people sit elbow to elbow in this human barbecue pit. "Get your cup of water here. Only fifty cents," cry vendors, knowing that much of the lukewarm liquid will end up being poured over heads.

The caverns under the stands look like a prison scene from *Les Misérables*. Thousands of people at a time flee the burning bleachers to collapse under the stands between innings, lying on the concrete or standing in lines forty people long to suck a little water from fainthearted fountains. Many of the folded and fried fans only leave their shady underworld to dash up the ramps into the stands when the Sox get men on base. Thus the bleachers seem to breathe, inhaling and exhaling thousands of human specks as Boston threatens to score or goes out with a whimper. "It's an ape house," a Red Sox official once told me. "You can get high from the pot smoke just walking through the stands . . . We learned that the liquor store a block away sold more 'miniatures' of liquor than any store in Boston. People tape them under their arms and walk in with their arms akimbo. One guy came in with his arms practically out like wings. He had eight of those 'nips' under each arm. And he was coming in free on a clergyman's pass."

It takes a certain Wild West appetite to sit in the Fenway bleachers. Some, like usher Miller, a former BU football player, relish it. "There's nothing like a Yankee series. It's fantastic," he said to me one memorable night. "We've had eight fights already and the game hasn't started. They've been working on the beer and pot for three hours.

"To be an usher out here, you got to enjoy it. We're a select group chosen to go out and break heads . . . I got hit in the back with a beer bottle two weeks ago . . . but I nailed that guy the best punch I ever hit a fan. We were all down wrestling in the aisle, me and Danny, the supervisor, and this guy's about six foot five. I got him in a headlock and hit him in the mouth as hard as I could. They get calm real quick with a few loose teeth.

"Hey, don't get me wrong," says Miller. "This guy was wearing a Yankee hat."

Ironically, this same Fenway Park probably attracts the most analytical, devoted and informed fans in the game. One of the best ways to measure a city's baseball fascination is to see how many baseball writers it nurtures.

The litmus test on Boston is that it sustains a large first-rate group of scribes at the Lowell *Sun,* the Worcester *Gazette,* the Lawrence *Eagle,* the Quincy *Patriot-Ledger,* the Lynn *Item* and a half-dozen other small-to-middling papers. And they're nuts. For years, whenever Carlton Fisk pulled a line drive narrowly foul, several pairs of pressbox eyes would meet, words would be muttered and heads nodded. These reporters kept a running tally of how many extra-base hits the pull-hitting Fisk lost by a yard or less; that bizarre Fisk foul count was kept continuously for years until the number of barely lost doubles and homers was well over a hundred. Fisk, of course, was kept apprised and periodically agitated about his tormenting batting flaw.

For a sportswriter, Boston's the best audience going. No statistic is considered too obscure, no potential trade or signing too remote, no flight of poetic enthusiasm too purple, no indignation too intemperate, no controversy too small, no bench warmer too obscure to have his life story set in type. The only sin in Boston is lack of passion. Tell us, these lovers of the Red Sox plead, do the Blue Jays have a promising AA infielder whom we might land in an off-season waiver deal? Everybody knows we need infield depth at Pawtucket.

"When the Yankees come to town, I even have to put the *Harvard Crimson* in the bleachers," public relations director Bill Crowley once said of his jammed pressbox. One journalistic visitor, however, has Crowley stumped. "He claims he's from the Agence France-Presse and is filing dispatches to Cuba," grumbles Crowley. "I'm sure he's lying, 'cause he only shows for the Yanks. Every year I make him send me documentation from all over the world. But somehow he gets in and he's now eating one of my steaks."

Nothing galls the Red Sox front office worse than freeloaders they can't shake, whether they are surgeons, politicians or just gate-crashing geniuses. "Anybody can wrap six cameras around his neck and say, 'Jeez, I lost my pass,' and try to fake his way through the gate," said Crowley. "But one guy has beaten me for twenty years.

"One year he has phony tickets from another team. The next it's credentials from a bat company. Somehow he even gets in our dressing room. Twice I've seen him standing on the sidelines behind a Super Bowl coach. He even got in the background of a Carling Beer commercial.

"So when I see him in our locker room at the '75 World Series, I grab him by the neck. He turns around and darned if his credentials aren't issued and signed by Bowie Kuhn himself.

"He looked me in the eye and said, 'Whaaddya think of that, Irish?' "

Naturally, in a city that has at least a million self-appointed general managers, there's no lack of confident grandstand opinion. After every game, the Boston press corps must expose itself to this *vox populi* as it mills down through the stands to get to the locker rooms; there's no ritzy-phony elevator in this joint.

On one such night, Bob Ryan of the Boston *Globe* and I drifted through the crowd when suddenly a foghorn voice bellowed, "Hey, Ryan!"

Without looking at the source, Ryan said, "Just keep moving."

"Hey, Bob Ryan, I mean *you*. I'm *talkin'* to *you*," said the fan, standing up to his full considerable height and pointing at us.

Ryan turned to face the firing squad. "Yeahwhatisit," he shot back.

"Nice story this mornin', Bawby," boomed the fan, giving the "okay" sign.

That could only happen in Boston.

The proper counterpoint to the cultivated connoisseurship of Boston is the tough, tart viewpoint that reigns in baseball's more hard-boiled burgs, the parks where Philip Marlowe or Sam Spade would feel comfortably ornery. That means Wrigley Field in Chicago, Veterans Stadium in Philadelphia and, above all, Yankee Stadium in the Bronx.

Each of these towns has a different sort of knuckle.

Wrigley Field fans go in for resigned sarcasm; it befits a franchise whose top-level incompetence has been a marvel of consistency since World War II. Here the devoted but disillusioned bleacher bums cross the street to Ray's Bleachers and The Cubbie Bear Lounge to drown sorrows in Old Style beer and mourn along with the honky-tonk dirge "After 'Sweet Memories,' Play 'Born to Lose' Again."

The Cub fan not only knows in advance that his club will fail pathetically, but he knows *why;* he can provide the etiology of defeat at the drop of a pop-up. The immutable first cause, of course, is that the miscreant is a Cub, and therefore damned perpetually. Nevertheless, all the *particulars* of his offense are subject to endless autopsy.

Once, as Jerry Martin came to the plate to pinch-hit in Wrigley, a fan with a Suma wrestler's build brayed, "Sit down, Jerry. You're too hurt to *play.* Your knee's sore. You could walk up and down Rush Street last night, but you can't start the next day."

After Martin had completed his Cub mission—striking out on three pitches—the fan bid his hero adieu with the farewell advice, "Limp, Jerry, limp."

Such a nice blend of bitterness and whimsy might be beyond the grasp of a Philadelphia fan.

Is it possible for a particular city to breed a virulent strain of fan with a hair-trigger boo? My intuition is that there's precious little difference between curmudgeonly Phillie fans and hero-worshiping Yankee fans except that Philadelphia went its first ninety-seven years without a champion, while the Yankees have been in the World Series thirty-three times since 1920. Every fan brings a certain quotient of big-city wrath into the park with him. In Philly, you learn to dump it on the Phillies; in New York, you try to verbally eviscerate the visiting team.

There's no park as feared as Yankee Stadium. In no other place do ballplayers talk openly about their fear of being rocked in the outfield or assaulted in the parking lot or sapped and robbed in their posh hotels. From the time a team leaves the Sheraton on Seventh Avenue until it pulls up safely at the Stadium's entrance, ballplayers sound like a bunch of maiden aunts who are certain that they're about to be hijacked to Yemen.

These fellows, in their gold watches and diamond Series rings, are scared. As the bus rolls through a hundred blocks of Harlem, it's clear they aren't in the habit of driving their Porsches through the poor sections of town when they're back home. No, not the black and Latin guys, either.

The Yankees know their environment intimidates foes. The '78 Dodgers spent so much time moaning about getting out of the

Bronx without having their suntans slashed that they forgot to show up for the Series; the Angelenos arrived with a two-game lead and went back to Hollywood just one game from being eliminated. The Bronx Zoo got 'em.

Once, the Yankees even imported a box-seat terrorist, flying a 329-pound fellow named Boot Buttrey in from Canton, Ohio, for a pennant-race series against the Red Sox. When this giant wasn't bench-jockeying the Sox from the first box-seat row, he bit the tops off beer cans, set off firecrackers in his mouth, ate an entire pizza in seventeen seconds and generally turned himself into a true New York City folk hero.

"You bums ain't in Fenway Park any more," Buttrey began yelling in batting practice when the Sox long flies died in the Stadium's Death Valley.

"I just bite the tops off 'em, then chug 'em down," explained Buttrey, quaffing his first of fourteen beers. "Thurman Munson loves to see me do that. He's my best buddy. We've known each other since we were eight years old. Thurm told Mr. Steinbrenner that getting me here was what the team needed. The Yanks are picking up my whole tab."

Throughout the game, Buttrey would celebrate by lighting one more small firecracker and letting it explode between his lips. Afterwards, Buttrey was a minor celebrity in the appreciative Yankee locker room. "I've never been in Yankee Stadium before," said Buttrey. "I'm just a guy from Canton who likes to set off firecrackers in his mouth. Ain't much I can't do, 'cept swallow the tops of these cans after I bite 'em off."

Munson, by way of thanks, crept up behind Buttrey and set off an air horn in his ear.

Most parks have their special lessons, their familiar perversities, which give the game a quality unique to that place or which accentuate something that is present everywhere but almost never noticed. Anything which brings brains, judgment or daring into the game is good. And in almost every case, idiosyncratic parks, or novel wrinkles in apparently conventional ones, serve that purpose.

For instance, Fenway Park presents enormous problems in

player evaluation to the often befuddled Bosox brass. The lesson of the Fens is that we must always measure a player's statistics in light of his home park. Of course the Red Sox know this. But they can't seem to bring themselves to act on it.

Throughout the late '70s, the Sox wanted to know why they were a poor road team. One reason was that several members of their Over the Wall Gang—Fred Lynn, George Scott, Dwight Evans and Butch Hobson—were much less dangerous hitters outside Fenway. The club refused to face the fact that on the road they were a slue-footed team with good, but not great, power. Much of their clout evaporated when they left Fenway.

While Red Sox fans and brass always tended to overestimate their hitters, they have, conversely, tended to judge their pitchers too harshly. When you find a Boston starter with an ERA under 4.00, you should treat him like solid gold. Yet the Sox have repeatedly let pitchers like Fergie Jenkins, Bill Lee, Luis Tiant and even Rick Wise and Reggie Cleveland slip out of the organization before their usefulness was done. Familiarity, and a few dozen cheap flyballs off the Monster, breed contempt.

Perhaps most important, the Sox have always been impatient with young pitchers, letting them sink or swim in pennant-race deep water. Of course, with Fenway's aid, they sink time and again, their fragile confidence in tatters. Bosox brass always wants to compensate for past disappointments by bringing along the next phenom too fast. Beware, Oil Can Boyd and Rogers Clemens. The contrast to the agonizingly patient Orioles is total and explains almost entirely why, in the past fifteen years, Baltimore has done much more with less.

By contrast, the Yankees seem always to have accepted the lopsidedness of their stadium and worked hand in hand with its bias in favor of both left-handed pitchers and left-handed power hitters. What other team has won 103 games in a season with its first four starting pitchers all left-handed and without a single right-handed batter with fifteen home runs, as the '80 Yankees did? Well, the '81 Yankees came back and went to the Series with (again) four left-handed starters and (again) no right-handed hitter with more than thirteen homers.

As if more examples were necessary, the '78 Yanks won a world title without a single right-handed hitter with more than *six* home runs. So much for the hallowed theory that a great team must have left-right balance in both its pitching and slugging. One lesson unlearned.

Baseball is just discovering that in the spacious new turf parks of Kansas City, St. Louis and Houston, conventional statistics are as suspect as numbers produced in bandboxes. Speed is inordinately important in these places for one crucial, complicated and hidden reason: many of the things speed does never show up in the box score. And all of these speed-factor occurrences happen more often on turf. The Royals, Cards and Astros have, all since 1980, reached the playoffs with teams almost as totally geared to swiftness as the sprint-relay clubs of dead-ball days.

For instance, how will anyone ever measure how much three new players—Lonnie Smith, Ozzie Smith and Willie McGee— meant to the '82 world-champion Cardinals? Their arrival transformed the club in every aspect. Their defensive range significantly improved every pitcher on a mediocre staff. Their speed on the bases made every St. Louis hitter more effective, because they gobbled extra bases in a dozen disguised ways. As an example, these guys routinely turned potential inning-killing double-play grounders into successful inning-making sacrifice bunts, because they were running on pitches that were grounded to the infield.

"Unfair" parks are one of baseball's greatest charms. It's one of the central reasons that a 162-game season remains interesting. A team's range of abilities and inabilities is only properly shown when it must play many games in many types of parks. You gotta love those goofy yards. They test the wits and patience of everyone who encounters them.

Even the smallest variance from the 330–380–400 norm can make a park individual. In Oakland, the vast foul territory turns an absolutely typical park into a distinct pitcher's paradise. One or two extra outs a game, over 162 games, is a large cumulative factor. Baltimore's Memorial Stadium appears to be boringly uniform. Yet you should notice those 309-foot signs in the two corners. The Orioles do. Their hitters make a study of finding ways to get pitches to pull, while generation after generation of excellent

O's pitchers live by the maxim that fastballs on the outside corner will be hit for long outs in the power alleys.

Chicago White Sox hitting coach Charlie Lau is pained whenever he watches batting practice in Baltimore. "Our guys hit tape-measure homers in BP, and long fly outs in the game," said Lau a couple of years ago. "Their guys hit fly outs in batting practice, then hit homers into the corners in the game. They must hit fifty homers a year more than we do, but we have more players who can hit the ball farther. Maybe we hit better, but they *think* hitting better."

Detroit is the exact opposite of Baltimore. The corners are deep, but the alleys shallow. Though the total acreage of the Detroit outfield is larger, the curious net effect is that Baltimore is a pitcher's park, while Tiger Stadium will always be a home-run heaven. The reason? Mankind has not yet devised a theory of pitching that prevents solid flyballs to the alleys.

Two of the most crucial ballpark factors are in a sense invisible to the average fan: the wind and the length of the infield grass. Around dugouts and batting cages, there's more discussion of the breeze and the thickness of the infield vegetation than about deferred payments or long-term contracts.

The best ballparks—the truest ones—change their identities every day, depending on the direction and force of the wind. Fenway and Wrigley Field may be the coziest of hitters' parks, yet on a day when the wind is blowing in, they suddenly become the two best pitchers' parks in the game, better even than the Astrodome.

If the wind belongs to God, then the infield grass belongs to the home team's manager; if he's any good, he knows its length to the sixteenth of an inch. In an apparent paradox, Dodger Stadium is statistically both a better-than-average pitchers' park, and a better-than-average sluggers' park, because while the fences are near, the grass is far—far too long, that is. Detroit's the same. Tommy Lasorda and Sparky Anderson have good pitchers, but merely average defensive infields; this combination calls for knee-high, grounder-eating weeds.

At the other extreme, one of Earl Weaver's first bright acts as a young manager in '69 was to order his long infield grass shaved to the nub. "For weeks I'd watch our infield of Brooks Robinson,

Mark Belanger and Dave Johnson make nothing but routine stops while the other teams were robbing us blind," recalls Weaver. "Finally, I realized that our great infielders didn't need the help. Only the other teams were benefiting from the high grass. So we mowed it low. All of a sudden our guys were making the great plays and the other teams couldn't quite get to the ground balls.

"My first three [full] years, we won over a hundred games every year," says Weaver, "and cutting the grass might have been the only smart thing I did."

Any park which replaces the grass with turf, or eliminates the wind by completely enclosing the park, has done itself a major disservice. If the turf were velvet, the stanchions made of gold and the girders studded with diamonds, baseball would still be poorer without these two natural elements.

Baseball, however, is not merely in danger of losing its elements, but of squandering some of its sense of dimension as well. To a degree, distance is being eliminated from the game. Once, the truly long home runs—the *upper-deck* home run, the over-the-roof home run and the (hold your breath) tape-measure home run —were a central part of the game's lore.

Now where have they gone?

Fact is, the typical modern park swallows up the difference between the routine homer and the 475-foot monster. The best old parks accentuated it.

When the new Yankee Stadium made its rooftop façade unreachable, the place may have been physically enlarged, but it suffered emotional shrinkage. What good fan doesn't know that Lansdowne Street runs behind Fenway's Green Monster, or that Waveland and Sheffield are the avenues (beyond the bleachers in Wrigley Field) where traffic accidents have been caused by bouncing home runs?

Hard as it is to believe, of the twenty-six parks now standing, only five have ever had balls, or ever will have balls, batted entirely off the premises and into the public domain—Fenway, Wrigley, old refurbished Comiskey Park, Memorial Stadium and Tiger Stadium. If Babe Ruth returned today to duplicate his 602-foot home run, it might well go unremarked, swallowed up by the gargantuan, insatiable, million-row centerfield upper deck of some

monotonous football coliseum. To what extent is it a coincidence
that these remaining "small" parks are among the most distinctive and beloved in the sport? Three of them in particular—Wrigley, Fenway and Detroit—are the very best. Yankee Stadium,
Chavez Ravine and Royals Stadium would get votes too, but no
other parks are allowed on the ballot. Preserve diagrams of these
six, burn the rest and, in 3001, if we're of a mind to put parks on
Mars, nothing much will have been lost.

Unfortunately, some modern parks tell us nothing about the
game and reveal as little as possible about their towns. These
flashy cylindrical stadia are handsome outside, antiseptic inside
and aesthetically inhospitable to baseball; in fact they are football
theaters where baseball is also played.

Such parks—particularly in Cincinnati, Pittsburgh, Philadelphia, St. Louis, and Atlanta—almost completely annihilate any
traditional sense of place. Once you're in one of these mutant oil
filters, you might as well be in any of the others. Like glass office
buildings and eight-lane cloverleaves these parks are sources of
inordinate civic pride only because people haven't grasped yet
that every other town has one.

One crucial test for ballpark architecture is simple: when you
glance around, do you know instantly where you are? Each year it
seems fewer parks pass this test.

Of all the modern parks, only five are distinctive in the same
sense that all old parks were. Three of these—Los Angeles' Chavez Ravine, Royals Stadium in Kansas City and the Minneapolis
Metrodome—are distinguished by their beauty and individuality;
they are heirs to Fenway and Wrigley. By contrast, the Houston
Astrodome and the Seattle Kingdome are singular in their un-
redeeming ugliness; someday they'll take their wrongful place beside Cleveland's old Municipal Stadium—the Mistake by the
Lake.

From the promontory of Chavez Ravine, the City of the Angels
sprawls at night beneath Dodger Stadium in all directions, a dia-
dem of colored lights. The rubies and emeralds of traffic blinkers,
the neon diamonds of a thousand midnight burger joints, create a
twinkling crown around the Dodgers' fortress. Dodger Stadium is
a blue palace on a hill, a Spanish stucco place of clean colors and

sharply defined heroes. It stands outlined against the night sky, beckoning to the city below with muffled roars that roll down the gorges like thunder.

Royals Stadium and the Metrodome, each in its way, demonstrate that the sport's two most disturbing stadium trends—toward symmetrical fields with artificial turf and toward domed stadia—don't have to be disasters.

Royals Stadium may be symmetrical, but it sure isn't bland. If you aren't certain of a club's overall team speed, its basic athletic gifts, then watch it when it plays in Kansas City. For instance, one could not properly appreciate the limitations of such an apparently strong team as, say, the '77 to '82 Orioles, until they were seen in all their ignominy in Royals Stadium. For years, Earl Weaver's many relatives and in-laws in the Midwest would not accept his free tickets to games in Kansas City, because they knew the Orioles would be humiliated and Weaver would be horrid to postgame company. So great was his aversion to the place that Weaver once calculated that if it weren't for all the games he lost in Royals Stadium he would have had the sport's second-highest career managerial winning percentage instead of being merely third.

If K.C.'s waterfalls, sloping grass banks, gaudy scoreboard and light towers as well as its cozy seating plan are positive proof that a modern park can be a classic, then the low-budget Metrodome gives hope that a domed park need not resemble a prison. All earlier experiments in the roofed genre have been dingy, oppressive baseball abominations. The Astrodome and the Kingdome should be the sites for the World Wreckingball semifinals.

The Metrodome hardly brings a lump to the bleacher poet's throat, but at least the seats are painted a bright blue and are close to the field. At least the dome is made of lightweight translucent material so that, until sundown, light actually fights its way through the roof. At least the outside temperature is reflected to some extent indoors, instead of that eternal flat 70 degrees.

If some climates necessitate domes—and who says that baseball was meant to be played in such infernal places—then let the new monsters resemble the airy, light, almost cheerful Metrodome.

To an enlightened American, few things are more depressing than Montreal in general and Olympic Stadium in particular. It's everything many of us wish an American city and crowd would be —stylish, intelligent, civil and spontaneously jubilant. Wandering through the cavernous beer gardens, restaurants and shops of Olympic Stadium, it is impossible not to wonder how fifty thousand people from a fairly broad cross section of the city's society could have a ball together without any hint of friction. During the playoffs of '81, for instance, I meandered throughout the stands during a chilly two-hour rain delay. Everybody was laughing, singing, cheering and flirting, but nobody was conspicuously drunk or stoned. Everybody was friendly, like a gigantic family. Nobody ran on the field. Nobody booed or chanted. Nobody complained. My true American reaction was "Something is terribly wrong with these people."

When a fifth game of that playoff was postponed from Sunday to Monday—a workday, when thousands of these people would have to give away their expensive tickets or throw them away— not a boo could be heard. The thirty thousand souls who remained in the park after the interminable delays quietly walked out and rode their spanking-clean subway back home. No wonder economists say Montreal is a dying city and predict its doom. The place is too good to exist.

In fact, Canadian baseball fans in general seem too good-natured to believe. And too cherubic not to take advantage of. When it comes to slightly perplexed, novice fans, lovely, polite Toronto wins all the awards. Blue Jay crowds are notoriously quiet, uncertain what they should cheer or when. However, one day in 1981, with a gang of nearly thirty thousand on hand, a group of fans behind the dugout of the visiting Baltimore Orioles got itself into a rhythmic-clapping tizzy which spread throughout the park as the Blue Jays built a rally.

As crusty Oriole manager Earl Weaver stalked angrily back from the mound, he glared up into the stands above the dugout and screamed, "Shut the hell up!"

"The fans who heard Earl were shocked and did shut up, then the ones next to them shut up," testifies Orioles pitching coach

Ray Miller, "and in just a few seconds the whole park was quiet again.

"We've laughed about that for years. I've tried it myself. I'm not as good as Earl, but anybody can cut the noise in that park in half just by lookin' mean and cussin' at 'em. They're not used to us Americans."

To the ballpark wanderer, airports and motel rooms may become monotonous, but "getting to the yard" remains magnetic and fresh.

Of our other massive architectural adventures—our attempts on a heroic scale—how many can claim to have a natural, innate size? A ballpark's grandeur—the easy, royal way it eats up several square city blocks, not to mention its seignorial cape of parking lots—is never pompous; rather, it's in the order of things. The size of the park is ordained by the limits of human strength: four hundred feet to center field is what the species currently requires; even the remoteness of the farthest bleacher seat is defined by the strength of the average fan's eye.

Our cathedrals and capitals have an arbitrary majesty; they are built to the dimensions of a man's or a nation's ego. Even a ballpark as grandiose as Yankee Stadium has an innate appropriateness; it was conceived first for function. (That's not to say one wouldn't be curious to see what Christopher Wren could have done with the Astrodome contract.)

A town's taste is tested by its ballpark too. Bostonians threatened a noble insurrection when philistine part-owner Buddy LeRoux hinted that Fenway Park might be tinkered with to suit his wallet. When an equally callow chap, that well-meaning bull-in-a-china-shop Dallas Green, began intoning "lights for Wrigley Field," the populace raised a hue worthy of the Chicago fire.

On the South Side of town, the White Sox' new owners proved their worthiness by spending millions to restore marvelous Comiskey Park, the oldest stadium in the majors; the Gold Anniversary All-Star game in 1983 turned into one long testimonial to their wisdom. Not only had a compact, forty-three-thousand-seat heirloom been polished to a fresh luster, but the grass field had been retained and home plate was moved eight feet closer to the outfield fences.

What could eight feet mean? To those who know the game, a great deal. Since World War I, when Big Ed Walsh (a pitcher) advised architects on how to build Comiskey, the park has been a graveyard for hitters. Now, with a tuck here and there, the fences are finally placed propitiously for the modern age. Pitchers still have a slight edge, which is meet and right, since the White Sox have marvelous young pitchers. However, truly powerful sluggers are no longer discouraged. And who happens to have just that sort of hitters? Why, the Sox. It's called marrying your park to your team, and eight feet can do it.

As an unexpected bonus, that eight feet was just enough to bring the Comiskey roof within range of two White Sox bombers, Greg Luzinski and Ron Kittle. Five times in 1983 the Windy City was buzzing with discussion of the "roofers" hit by those muscle men; what used to occur once a decade was suddenly happening once a month. Luzinski even posed for a color poster standing on the roof. It's doubtful that any of the '83 homers would have reached the old roof. And nobody notices a near miss.

Perhaps the strangest quality about ballparks is their peculiar power of attraction. Veteran players, coaches and managers, as well as reporters, are mystified by the way they seem to reach the yard a little earlier each season, as though the relaxed authority of the place had drawn them against their will. Perhaps humanity has a homing device for monuments—the civil servant drawn to the marble halls of his office building, the curate who haunts the sacristy.

In the case of ballparks, however, it is not mere lazy habit which binds us.

We live in a time when one of the most common experiences of American travelers is a sense that urban life is acquiring a deadly, homogeneous dreariness. Our sense of place, of region and accent and local tradition, is ground down in the face of identical, toneless, expressionless Eyewitness Anchorpersons whose duty is to make Cincinnati or Oakland the identical bland equal of Chicago or New York. From the airport to the shopping mall, from the neon gas-and-gulp thoroughfares to the gaudiest clerestory lobby of the ritziest hundred-dollar-a-day hotel in town, the distinctions between one city and another, between one region and another, are disappearing.

The more you travel, the harder it is to remember where you are.

Sometimes, if you still have a vestigial appetite for vivid detail, for the human face as it runs through the spectrum of emotions, it might be wise to head for the ballpark. Yes, head for the bratwurst line in Milwaukee or the bellicose brogue of the Boston bleachers, or the trendy satin-to-punk fashions of the box seats in L.A. Whether it be a crusty debate among weathered ushers in the Motor City or a mob of pretzel munchers in the belly of Comiskey Park, the ballpark is still the place to go if you want to see people as they are.

Here we find that we are still a nation of countless shades and shapes, heartening and hearty. Orwell's fears have made little headway at the ballpark. There we still find it easy to remember where we are and why we came.

2

BRED
TO A HARDER THING
THAN TRIUMPH

Beneath a mist of World Series victory champagne in the locker room of the Baltimore Orioles, Mike Flanagan stood gazing upon the giddy scene before him with all the lenient bemusement appropriate to his New Hampshire stock.

Before him wobbled John Lowenstein, on his way to a new major league record for sucking back a magnum of the bubbly. "Am I waxed!" Lowenstein murmured contentedly. Rick Dempsey was on the phone nearby, quipping with the President. Joe Altobelli, tears in his stinging eyes, said he was too exhausted for joy and just wanted to get back to Rochester and play grandfather. Rich Dauer, feigning disgust, said, "Now we gotta go home and ride in that stupid parade."

Flanagan, almost melancholy from too much bliss, said quietly, "Several times this season, I watched the highlight film of last season. I'd remember it all and enjoy it, until, near the end, I'd realize that I already remembered the last part too well. And I'd turn it off. I never could watch it to the end.

"Now we've got what we all wanted. A highlight film with a happy ending."

For the lifelong fan, the most abiding pleasure may be cleaving to one club for years and studying it well. Our most engrossing delight comes when that team gets into a tough pennant race. At last all our attention and affection pay off. We sense how every twist of luck or heroism interacts with every wrinkle of providence that has gone before it. In the year when history calls the team to its accounting, we share the club's extremities of joy and anxiety.

If we have a thread of the artist in us, we can even flirt with a higher satisfaction. By keeping a pane of private glass between ourselves and the action, we sometimes fancy that—thanks to this fragile emotional buffer—we understand the club just a shade better than it understands itself.

How do we watch one team, our team, in a pennant race?

Doesn't the adamant fan crave the raw evidence of the past so that he can draw analogies to his team in the present? What wouldn't we give for entrée to the dugouts of the '51 Dodgers or Giants? If we knew them, and other such teams, more thoroughly, mightn't we watch the pennant contenders of the future with a deeper comprehension?

Let's visit a classic pennant race of the recent past—one which proved to have a resonance beyond its own moment—and view it from the inside.

No, not Baltimore's triumph last season. After all, the Birds clinched their division a week early, then dismissed the White Sox and Phils in the playoffs and Series in just four and five games respectively. Instead, let's look at the pennant race of '82. *That* was the engine which drove the Oriole machine in '83. That was the experience which galvanized a team so powerfully that it seemed preternatually resistant to crisis the following year.

Often, great disappointments beget great achievements. Just as the past-their-prime Phillie and Dodger champions of '80 and '81 were soldered and strengthened by their repeated post-season failures in the late '70's, so the Baltimores were tempered to steel by defeat.

The Chase of '82 in the American League East was surpassingly special. The last six weeks of that struggle between the Orioles and Milwaukee Brewers had all the best qualities of any excellent race. The dynamics of pressure baseball were as close to the surface, as open to inspection, as we are likely to see.

Before approaching the subject in detail, let's have a taste of synopsis.

On August 20, Baltimore trailed Milwaukee by 7½ games. By September 20, one torrid, 27–5 month later, the Orioles had seen their hopes, their fantasies, even their most preposterous whims, become reality. The final thirteen days of that season were delightful madness. Three times, the Orioles seemed dead. Each time, they rose. On the last day of September, Baltimore's margin of error was down to nothing. In the last hour of the month, three Orioles came to bat assuming that if they made outs, the race was over. All three got RBI hits.

At sundown on October 1, the Orioles returned home for four games in the season's last three days, all against Milwaukee. If Baltimore won all four, they'd win the division by a game. Lose any game and they were eliminated. Less than twenty-four hours later, the O's had won three times. Total score: 26–7. With one more victory, they could complete the greatest last-week comeback in the history of the sport.

"It feels like it *must* happen," said owner Edward Bennett Williams. "Does that mean it's going to happen?"

Baltimore sent the hottest pitcher in baseball—thirty-six-year-old Jim Palmer, on a 12–1 streak—to the mound. For preposterous garnish, that Sunday was also the final game of his career for manager Earl Weaver, the retiring legend.

In fantasy, the Orioles would have won; the crowd would have cheered till every eye was wet. In fact, the Orioles lost. But, to illustrate that we are sometimes better creatures than we suppose, the crowd roared anyway, for a quarter of an hour, until the Orioles returned to the field to weep and blow kisses and, finally, join in the joyous innocent spelling of their team name.

Every excellent team has its own signature.

The '70–'76 Reds were thoroughbreds; Cincinnati meant talent. The '76–'81 New York Yankees were gritty, gamy, nasty, hellbent. Those Yanks meant guts. The Los Angeles Dodgers of '77–'81 were ritzy, dapper and disciplined. Dodger Blue meant baseball breeding.

The Orioles of '79–'83 meant—and still mean—brains. They

play in a working-class town in a glamorless brick ballyard before middling-size crowds in a television market offering modest profit. Other clubs may be more exciting, controversial, wealthy and talented. But nobody matches the Orioles for smarts. How else could a team that has never signed a free agent for more than two-hundred-thousand-dollars a year win more games than any team since the advent of free agency in 1976?

Baltimore intelligence takes forms which sometimes shock the newcomer. Each spring, as was the case in '82, some newly acquired Oriole looks perplexed. How can the players insult Weaver? And he them? How can the team, in fact, mock Weaver to his face with squawking imitations of his laugh ("Whaaaa . . . whaaa") just seconds after he's chewed them out during a losing streak? How can the manager's only rebuttal be "Whaaa . . . whaaaa, yourselves."

Why are there so few cliques? Why do most of the players live in Baltimore in the off-season, not Southern California? Why is race seldom an issue? How can rookies feel welcome almost instantly, even become team leaders? Why is the locker room so relaxed after a loss? How can players talk so freely to reporters? How can one pitcher read John Updike in the clubhouse, while another talks about his published poetry and his gourmet restaurant?

Why does everybody work willingly on boring fundamentals? Why have players cut off contract negotiations at a salary under what their agents tell them they could get if they pushed harder? How can the owner and general manager wander about amid an aura of respect, just as old-timers say it used to be before baseball's labor wars? Above all, how can a big league team prosper when it not only shows respect for, but actually encourages, intelligence, humor, eccentricity and dissent?

"When new players get here, they're so used to dealing with jerks that they have to get readjusted to real people," says Ken Singleton. "I enjoy watching them as they sit there and figure out one little piece of the puzzle after another. This team knows it's going to win and it's just going to have as much fun doing it as possible. We win them over to our way of doing things."

The Oriole way starts at the top, with owner Ed Williams, trial lawyer, prominent liberal Democrat. It's delighted Williams to discover that he accidentally bought a team in '79 which already embodied many of his values. He's become far more addicted to the sport, the team and the town than he expected. "EBW" had plenty of jet-setter in him. However, he reformed enough so that he came to see the Orioles (as long as they don't cost him money) as a community trust, an indigenous part of the genteel, old-fashioned Baltimore ethos.

Williams had the wisdom to take a crash course in baseball from his employees. General manager Hank Peters and Weaver did the talking, Williams the listening. Revolutionary, for an owner. Williams learned the O's tradition of building from within, emphasizing scouting, then teaching young players well, while only trading or buying free agents when a certain piece looked perfect for the puzzle.

The core of the club is homegrown, nurtured and tutored from the first day at Bluefield, in the Appalachian League. The Birds have their Book, with theories on everything. Other clubs buy pitching. Baltimore teaches it: in '82, the O's introduced their latest prodigy, George (Storm) Davis, twenty, then the youngest player in the majors. True to the mold, he was poised, an assured fielder, able and willing to throw strikes. "Looks like a duplicate of Palmer," said Mike Flanagan. "Guess that means he's not a Storm. He's a Cy-clone."

No one person or policy is responsible for the sense of moderation, tolerance and decency that runs through the Orioles. Partly it's sequestered Baltimore. Partly it's the fifteen-season influence of Weaver, who, beneath his saltiness, is a cracker-barrel philosopher and a concerned man. Partly it's dumb luck.

Also, before signing a scout, coach, manager or player, the front office considers temperament as well as talent. Perhaps this single commitment has brought the Orioles their consistent excellence. Some teams talk about having Dodger Blue in their veins, or possessing Pinstripe Pride. But the modest, make-do Orioles, the team that has won more games than anybody since 1957, would never make such grandiose claims. They're too smart for that.

As you entered the 1982 clubhouse, the first Orioles locker you saw belonged to Floyd Rayford, a young utility man who stood five foot ten and weighed a great deal. The team called him Fat Floyd and Honey Bear. When the O's first saw Rayford in spring training, Palmer asked innocently, "Excuse me, Floyd, how many people are trapped in that uniform?"

Rayford, the least important Oriole of '82, was nonetheless typical of the team. Like many Orioles, he seemed underqualified for his duties; yet Weaver could expound at length on the bizarre potential advantages of having this Rayford creature, who could catch, play third, pinch-hit or even pinch-run. Weaver'd never seen this exact combination; it fascinated him. Rayford provided Weaver with his most precious managerial commodity: "Moves." The existence of this smiling Buddha allowed Weaver to pinch-hit for catchers, rotate infielders or use a pinch hitter in an unconventional spot. Mind you, in none of these circumstances would Rayford actually play. His existence was an emotional insurance policy so Weaver could wheel and deal.

Rayford, the butt of jokes, was usually the winner in repartee and found ways to earn his letter. He had more courage than skill and he played without fear of failure. As Martin Luther would have wished, he went and sinned bravely. If Ron Guidry struck him out, Rayford glared at him as though Lou'siana Lightnin' had just bought himself trouble down the road. Because of his indefatigable bearing, Rayford's mistakes never unnerved his mates the way the jittery errors by another sub—the more talented back-to-Rochester Bobby Bonner—always did.

Once, the Honey Bear slid into second, then stood up in the face of the shortstop turning a double-play pivot. The throw hit Rayford in the head, shattering his helmet; the ball landed in the on-deck circle on the fly as the winning run scored. When the groggy Rayford told his buddy Eddie Murray that they were taking him to the hospital to X-ray his skull, Murray said, "They must have a new machine."

When Rayford hit his first career home run, the Orioles gave him such a polished silent treatment that Rayford sat alone, convinced no one would congratulate him. Then players began fainting and being revived with towels. Finally, all engulfed Rayford and tried to pound him to mush.

Rayford's other home run of the season was a sudden-death game-winner in Memorial Stadium. The Yankees fainted.

Next to Rayford sit Eddie Murray and Ken Singleton. They've been the offensive heart of the team for five years, averaging a hundred RBI a year. Murray, twenty-six, is close to his peak; Singleton, thirty-five, is past his. They couldn't be more different.

Murray finds it natural to live by the motto on his necklace: "Just Regular." However, Murray is often suspicious of anyone who is not part of his blood family (he's one of twelve children) or his baseball family. Three of his older brothers played pro ball; none made the majors. Murray grew up hearing hard-boiled stories about the realities of big-time sport.

"We had a lot of little downfalls," says Eddie's brother Leon. "Eddie avoided them."

"Some people just got to get hurt. You can see it. They either run into walls on the field, or they run into 'em off it," says Murray as his brother listens. "The easy way is the only way. Avoid problems. I might be the weakest of the five brothers, but I didn't run into the problems they did. You gotta push things away in the game that bother you and upset you and keep you from your goal. It almost happened to me, I think. I got mad the year I wasn't sent up to triple A when I thought I should. It was hard to swallow, 'cause it's your pride. But sometimes you got to swallow. Otherwise you'll get on the club's bad foot. And that's the beginning of the end."

That's a long Murray monologue, probably only delivered so his brother could hear how well he'd learned their hand-me-down wisdom.

"Eddie has no problems, no wife, no children,'" says Leon. "He's only got one boss—our mama. What she says goes. There are no hard heads in our family. None of us has ever been wild or bad."

Murray regards notoriety as poison and ducks the limelight as religiously as Reggie Jackson courts it. Murray firmly believes what old Lee May told him as a rookie: if you have talent, fame can't help you, but it's an even bet to ruin you. To hawk his personality like some public commodity is, he suspects, a perfect way to be robbed of his sense of self. Murray's weakness is that, like Hank Aaron, he's a leader only by example; little fire, only efficiency. He lacks the charisma of the last Oriole leader, Frank Robinson. The Birds accept Murray for what he is. Just your run-of-the-mill future Hall of Famer.

Singleton is the most emblematic Oriole. Like the Birds, he is consistent but seldom spectacular. "We're persistent," says Terry Crowley. "You know how sometimes you stick your key in the front door but it won't open. You say, 'I know this is my key,' so you just stand there jiggling that key in the lock until it opens. That's how this team is in a close game."

Like Singleton, a slow runner never burdened by great expectations, the Orioles have the mixed blessing of limited talent. Each spring they are the underdog against some more glamorous collection of stars. They are often excused, and even pitied, if they come up short after gallant attempts. To the degree that this near-miss perception infects the team—giving it a Noble Loser Complex—it constitutes a sort of defeatism.

The Orioles' weakness is their lack of a fierce athletic wildness; they almost never throw a knockdown pitch, crash into walls, spike opponents, get into bench-clearing brawls. Their only forms of intimidation are mental: bench-jockeying, Weaver's mind games with umpires and the sense which they transmit to other teams that they have some unseen, inexplicable edge because they understand the game better. Like Singleton, the Orioles are hard-nosed, but not pugnacious; they'll play hurt, but they won't hurt you. Everybody respects Baltimore; but nobody fears them.

Filling out the row of lockers against the left wall is the real substance of this and any other Oriole team—the pitching stars. They have their chairs in a row, the better to discuss their common craft. Nicaraguan Dennis Martinez and Coloradan Tippy Martinez come first; they sit together so they can confuse media types who don't know that they're not related and that Tippy, a third-generation American, doesn't speak any Spanish at all.

Next come the club's Cheech and Chong—Sammy Stewart and Mike Flanagan.

In the bullpen, Stewart practices juggling a baseball, Globetrotter style, bouncing it off all portions of his body, catching it in the crook of his elbow and finally making the ball disappear into thin air. He's convinced that someday, in a World Series, the national TV cameras are going to be focused on him; he wants to be ready. The righty also works on his sweeping left-handed curveball—taught to him by the devious instigator, Flanagan. Stewart's already used it once. "A lot of managers might have gotten real upset about that pitch," drawls Stewart, called "the Throwin' Swannanoan," after his North Carolina hometown, "but Earl lived right up to my expectations. He said, 'That's why I still enjoy comin' to the ballpark. You never know what the hell you might see.'"

Stewart serenades his teammates with bluegrass ("In the pines . . ."), rock 'n roll ("I'm not your steppin' stone . . .") and the latest punk rock. One evening in Yankee Stadium he spotted punk leather queen Joan Jett, whose album had hung in his locker for a year. He introduced himself, used his "A" material on her, then was shattered to discover that Jett had come in hopes of meeting Jim Palmer. "It's not fair," said Stewart. "She ain't seen me in *my* underwear."

Flanagan is New Hampshire's wry, hidden child—world-leery and cryptic. The '79 Cy Young winner is a third-generation professional pitcher, yet he describes his job as "fool on the hill." Under his uniform, he always wears a T-shirt that says "Dead Goat Saloon." "If I weren't a baseball player," Flanagan says, "I think I'd make an excellent killer bee." His nickname is Dr. Large, but you could call him the Samurai Southpaw.

Everything about his appearance is deliberately and defiantly styleless. He forgets to shave. He's sweaty. His uniforms are baggy, as if they were borrowed from his dad's era, when Sal Maglie was the epitome of pitching style. He never displays emotion, never shows up an opponent, never plays to the camera. When he won a Series game, he barely tipped his cap.

Flanagan is a gamer, an Iron Mike who pitches hurt. Once, he went 155 turns without missing a start. He has paid a high price for following the tough-it-out code of his father, his state and his manager. By ignoring various discomforts, Flanagan has seen his status shrink from superstar to that of the gut-it-out fifteen-to-eighteen-game winner. He lost a couple of feet off his fastball somewhere along the way and will probably never get it back.

Finishing the row are the team's class acts: Scott (Dr. Small) McGregor and Jim Palmer; they appear antithetical—a choirboy and a sex symbol. Actually, they're entries 1 and 1-A in the clean-living sweepstakes. Each, however, has a hidden quality.

McGregor's pitching soul is made of ice. "He'll stand out there with nothing but those cold eyes and never give in," says Singleton. "You shouldn't be able to win twenty games with his stuff. Cold eyes, man." McGregor probably has the sport's best change-up and one of its most intuitive minds. He also has an athletic audacity that comes from a rare source: serenity. Before games, he'll sit for forty-five minutes in the dugout during batting practice, absolutely unmoving, staring before him. Is he meditating? Psyching himself up?

"I just think it's beautiful watching the park fill up and the evening approach," he says. "I'm just sitting there getting peaceful."

Once, in a 1–0 victory, McGregor struck out Reggie Jackson three times on nine consecutive pitches. "They were all fastballs right down the middle," said McGregor. "I couldn't understand why he didn't hit every one ten miles. But he didn't. So I kept throwing 'em."

Palmer appears to be a similar placid portrait; actually, the club watches this all-time great out of one corner of its collective eye to see what quirky, bizarre, compulsive thing he'll do next. Think of him as one-half Mr. Perfect and one-half the Hyperactive Hypochondriac. Doug DeCinces once said of Palmer, "We're a club with twenty-four team players and one prima donna." Palmer has not, in recent years, been completely a part of the team. He's considered a freakish special case who, the club seems to have agreed, will never unduly annoy or distract them. "We try to bring him down to the same level as the rest of us," says Singleton.

Tucked among these more or less fabled hurlers is the Future— Cal Ripken, Jr.

In April of '82, he was a twenty-one-year-old third baseman trying to get his batting average over .200 and struggling to crawl out of the small shadow cast by his father, the third-base coach. By October, Ripken was the Rookie of the Year shortstop, a slugger with twenty-eight home runs and ninety-three RBI. Though even Weaver could hardly believe it, the kid was also the closest thing the club had to a team leader during its pennant fight.

When Little Cal is mentioned, it is with an affection few rookies will ever know. Partly, it's because many have known Jr. since he was a child. Dauer recalls looking behind him during batting practice in Asheville, North Carolina, years ago and seeing a thir-teen-year-old catcher snagging the best stuff that Double-A pro pitchers could bring to the plate. "We've known for a long time that he was going to be special," says Dauer. Doug DeCinces, traded to make room for Ripken, went further: "I'm just playing between legends—Brooks and Rip." Once, a crazy kid was firing a rifle from a hill down at the Asheville diamond and DeCinces scooped up Little Rip and dove into the dugout with him. Palmer even remembers Ripken as a three-year-old playing at the park back at Aberdeen in '64.

Mostly, however, the affection around Ripken has to do with his father. Little Rip is Big Rip's reward for all the BP he has pitched, all the towering foul pops he has fungoed, all the pitchers he has warmed up, all the buses he has ridden in twenty-five years in the Oriole organization in Phoenix, Wilson, Pensacola, Amarillo, Appleton, Little Rock, Leesburg, Aberdeen, Ken-newick-Richland-Pasco, Rochester, Miami, Elmira, Dallas-Fort Worth and Asheville.

When outsiders pester the senior Ripken with questions about his son, he says, "I've never been able to watch him at any level, even Little League. Why should I start talkin' at him now? He's got his job. I've got my job . . . Am I proud of him? Well, sure, I'm proud of him as my son. But as a ballplayer, ask in fifteen years."

Now we've reached the back wall of the locker room. The general tenor of literateness and quick repartee continues. John Lowenstein holds down one end of the row. He's Brother Lo, the aging hippie with indoor sunglasses and a perm. He's the native of Wolf Point, Montana, who's a backpacker, white-water rapids shooter and wilderness worshiper. He's the college grad with a degree in anthropology. He's the husband of a former Las Vegas dancer and lives in Sin City.

A veteran, Lowenstein is the quintessence of a Weaver player. Lowenstein has nightmares about left-handed pitchers and loves being platooned. He considers it providence that in his baseball old age (thirty-five), he was sent a manager who not only believes in his ability but also believes in free speech and couldn't care less what he says or thinks. One member of the '82 Orioles batted .320, hit twenty-four homers and led the major leagues in slugging average. It was Brother Lo. As his teammates reminded him, "Man, you picked one helluva year to go from being a [career] .245 hitter to doing your Babe Ruth imitation." His contract was up and he became a free agent.

At the other end of the back row is the perfect bookend for Lowenstein: pitching coach Ray (Rabbit) Miller, the club's resident school-of-hard-knocks sage. Miller has the first seat by the entrance to Weaver's office; like the man who sat there before him —George Bamberger—he is a genial, funny, widely-liked man who, beneath his tall tales, knows and sees everything within the club's small world. Like Bamberger, he knows as much as anyone about the players' lives, their motives, their private problems. When Weaver needs to know something in the Heart and Soul Department, Miller tells him.

Miller has the burrs from fifteen years' worth of bush-league briar patches. His spitball, his knockdown pitches and his gentle, buck-toothed smile never got him past a lot of AAA strikeouts. When the burly, six-foot-three Miller wasn't pitching for off-season teams like Federal Storage or Buffalo Sand and Gravel, he was working as a coal miner in Pennsylvania, a street sweeper in Portland, a shipping clerk, a rental cop, a house painter or an electrician. "I learned that it's better to get shocked on the back of your hand than the palm, and I saved enough money so my wife and I could build our dream house. I'm proud that I did it before I got to the majors." On the wall of their New Athens, Ohio, home is a letter of congratulation on their wedding from J. Edgar Hoover. "That gets some double takes," Miller says. "I met my wife when she worked for the FBI. I tell people she was investigating me."

A typical Miller tale comes from his winter ball days as a

twenty-eight-year-old pitcher, coach and manager in Venezuela. "I'd visit the pitcher on the mound, send myself to the bullpen, warm myself up, visit the pitcher again, replace him with myself, pitch, visit with myself, signal to warm up a lefty 'cause I was in trouble, call a coach out to calm me down, give the ball to the new pitcher and send myself to the showers. Then the other guy would get shelled worse than I did, and I'd have to explain afterward why I couldn't pitch, coach, *or* manage."

Between Lowenstein and Miller sit a handful of folks who fall under the generic term "good baseball men." Cal Ripken, Sr., Ralph Rowe and Jimmy Williams are reliable, contented career coaches. Among them sit catcher Joe Nolan and outfielder Jim Dwyer, both of whom frequently compare the awkward clubhouse life of their various former teams with the easy pleasures of being an Oriole. Nolan escaped the regimentation of the Cincinnati Reds ("like being in the Army"), while Dwyer was a graduate of the Boston Red Sox' pre-Houk institute of cliques.

Now, as we come to the right-hand side of the O's smallish, eight-by-twelve-pace inner sanctum, the tone becomes more that of Any Team, U.S.A. Here we have your basic, well-adjusted, the-major-leagues-are-heaven jocks. Al Bumbry, Tim Stoddard, Terry Crowley, Gary Roenicke, Rich Dauer, Benny Ayala and Rick Dempsey read the sports page first. They are blue-collar ballplayers and proud of it. They don't fire off quips or make headlines; they believe in team spirit and live by it. None of them find baseball an easy or secure life. None has signed a million-dollar contract.

The grinning, needling Bumbry is a small, overachieving bundle of muscle, work and worry. If he could lay off the letter-high fastball, he'd have made a half-dozen All-Star teams and be as rich as he is popular. "It's like chocolate cake," Bumbry once said of the pitch. "I see it and it looks so good that I swing."

A Bronze Star platoon leader in Vietnam, Bumbry's bearing is military, as is his inner self-discipline. On the road, the Bee wears three-piece suits—and on a club given to jeans. Bumbry may lead all of baseball in one category—charity work. He goes everywhere, does everything. Bumbry is basically shy and once had a bad stutter. By meeting people, speaking in public, he has his speech under control most of the time, though when he feels strong emotion he reverts.

Perhaps only an Oriole would understand why the five-foot-seven Bumbry and the six-foot-seven Stoddard—the smallest black and the largest white—would have adjacent lockers and be friends. Forget the high-priced sociology. On the Orioles, it just never applies. Stoddard and Bumbry are friends because Stoddard started at forward for the NCAA championship North Carolina State basketball team in '74, and Bumbry thinks he could have too. Probably right. Their bond is ball. One reason for the Orioles' chemistry is that half the team is addicted to basketball. Ask these grown men, making hundreds of thousands of dollars a year, what they'd *really* like to do and Stoddard, Bumbry, Murray, Stewart, Ripken, Palmer, Flanagan, Dauer, Crowley and a half-dozen others would say, "Play pickup basketball."

Every team has to have a couple of hardnoses and an old pro. In Baltimore, Dauer and Dempsey are the former, while Crowley is the latter.

When Dauer graduated from USC, after being an All-American on back-to-back national championship teams, he easily overshadowed teammates like Fred Lynn, Steve Kemp and Roy Smalley. Dauer set new NCAA records for hits, RBI and total bases. And he broke USC's season records for homers. When he hit .336 in AAA, the O's assumed he'd be at least as good a hitter as Bobby Grich or Don Baylor.

Nobody's figured out what happened to Dauer, who is a lifetime .261 hitter with no power. Unless . . . Few players have ever had such a traumatic baptism in the majors. Touted as a potential batting champion, Dauer arrived in September of 1976 as a finished product of twenty-four with more than enough seasoning and no available excuses. He went four for thirty-nine. The next spring, still tagged as a phenomenon, Dauer didn't get a hit until May 13 and was one for forty-one entering *June.* Think of it. Three *months* in the majors and only *five* hits. An .063 batting average (five for eighty) and a terminal case of shattered confidence. Dauer went into a shell of being a no-ego team player, erasing all those predictions of greatness from his self-image.

As though trying to squash high expectations, he's begun seasons with slumps of oh for twenty-two, three for twenty-eight, two for twenty-seven and eight for fifty-four. Dauer bats defensively, often seeming content to slap the ball somewhere in play early in the count. He's unselective, seldom walks, never looks for a pitch to hit for power, and when the game isn't on the line, hardly seems to care, giving away at bats carelessly. As a hitter, he lacks ambition as well as discipline. Every O's batting coach has wanted to strangle him. By contrast, he's a good clutch hitter.

Dauer's nickname is Wacko.

The only time the too-humble Dauer has expressed frustration was when his major-league record of eighty-six consecutive error-less games was broken by Manny Trillo. Dauer, who has the highest fielding percentage of any second baseman in history, felt the record was virtually stolen, since Trillo plays on perfect-hop turf and he plays on grass.

"Look at it this way," said his roommate, Flanagan. "It took three guys to break your record."

"Three?" said Dauer.

"Sure," said Flanagan. "A Trillo."

If Dauer is called "Wacko," then Rick Dempsey really is wacko. His parents were a vaudeville act. So is Dempsey. During rain delays, he has stuffed pillows under his jersey, turned his hat sideways and brought thirty thousand people to their feet with his "Baseball Soliloquy in Pantomine." After starting with a parody of Babe Ruth's called-shot home run in the '33 series, Dempsey takes a belly-flopping trip around the tarpaulin-covered infield, pratfalling over every base, then sliding face-first through the rain and puddles to home plate. Other players are in awe of Dempsey's stage presence and *joie de vivre*. To know Dempsey is to be reminded of a British diplomat's evaluation of the exuberant Theodore Roosevelt: "You must always remember that the President is about six."

Dempsey is about five. He climbs the backstop screen for foul balls and loves home-plate collisions. "Dempsey loves pain," says Weaver. Once, Dempsey and Weaver threw shin guards and a chest protector back and forth at each other. Since it was Dempsey, nobody took the incident seriously.

The battle between the two was constant. Dempsey always

wanted to play, Weaver always wanted to platoon him. Weaver cited as evidence the case of a game in which Fergie Jenkins struck Dempsey out four times on twelve pitches, all sliders low and away. Dempsey missed them all, and finished each at bat by spinning in a small circle, wrapping the bat entirely around his body. Weaver considered pinch-hitting him on the fourth appearance, but as Weaver said, "Everybody wanted to see if he could do it again."

In '82, Dempsey decided, at thirty-two, to become a switch-hitter. In the end, by much diligent labor, Dempsey turned himself into the worst left-handed hitter in history. Including pitchers. Weaver humored Dempsey, though he finished spring training on an oh for nineteen. Weaver even let Dempsey bat southpaw on Opening Day just so, once and for all, he'd make a fool of himself and be done with the damn project forever. In his first at bat, Dempsey got a broken-bat pop-fly hit. It took Weaver the rest of April to get Dempsey to stop batting left-handed.

In spring training one year, a Japanese firm was peddling electronic gloves that allowed a manager to give signals to his pitcher or catcher.

"Great, dial-a-pitch," said Dempsey. "Now Palmer can blame you instead of me."

"I just hope," said Weaver, looking at Dempsey with paternal concern, "that you don't electrocute yourself."

Dempsey, in his never-ending attempts to one-up Weaver, once allowed his hair and beard to grow for the entire winter. On the first day of camp, Dempsey showed up looking like a Miami drug dealer, complete with red bandana, motorcycle boots, sunglasses, gold chains and diamond rings. Dempsey paraded past Weaver's nose as the manager tried to figure out whether to call the police or just hit him over the head with a bat and bury the body.

"Who the fuck is that and how'd he get in our clubhouse?" hissed Weaver.

"This is your fucking catcher, Mr. Genius," exulted Dempsey.

The next spring, Dempsey arrived with his hair short, no mustache and dressed in white shorts. "Tennis, anyone?" he trilled, prancing through the clubhouse.

Dempsey's great moment of '82 came in September in Yankee

Stadium. New York owner George Steinbrenner had been discussing shortening the left-field fence and moving the stone monuments to Yankee greats which stand beyond that fence. Dempsey said he thought the new fence would make it easier to hit home runs, but it would be a shame to move those graves.

Someone related the grave story to Weaver but wouldn't identify which player had said it.

"Aww, gimme a hint?" said Weaver. "Is he the only one who plays in foul territory?"

Decidedly.

The care and feeding of the beloved Dempsey is entrusted to his roomie, Terry Crowley—the Crow, the King of Swing. It's like putting a walking mare in the same barn with a skittish thoroughbred; it's hoped that some of Crowley's genial sanity, his patience and his sweet compact swing will somehow rub off on Dempsey.

Now we come to the short front wall of the locker room. Here, as though drawn together by their similar concerns, are the season's most tormented players: Disco Dan Ford, Lenn Sakata, Ross Grimsley and Don Stanhouse.

The Japanese-Hawaiian Sakata is a stone-silent little infielder who can bench-press four hundred pounds. Sakata has soft hands but tight muscles, a gentle disposition but a tightly wound, athletic physique. If Sakata's muscles and mind were less taut, less prone to nagging pulls and tormenting strains, he'd be a starting infielder instead of a quality utility man. A natural second baseman, he was given the shortstop spot for half of the season but couldn't hold it. The shortstop requirements—the mental alertness to relay both signals and throws, the verbal cockiness to be a take-charge guy—weren't part of Sakata's makeup. By July, Sakata played himself back to the bench and often seemed happier there, contributing nicely around the edges, not being asked to play beyond his own, limited vision of his abilities.

Next to the sober Sakata sit the club's two zanies: Don (Stan the Man Unusual) Stanhouse and Ross (Skuzz) Grimsley. Both were once fine pitchers in Baltimore. Both left for free-agent millions. Both became hurling disasters and pariahs on their new teams—Grimsley with the Indians, Stanhouse the Dodgers. Both were released outright after '81, told to take their bags of money and stop cluttering up the roster. Both still had $400,000-a-year contracts with years to run. Neither needed to pitch to be rich. But both decided pitching was what they did best. They'd do it for nothing. So they worked out all winter, came to Miami for a tryout and finally regained their professional dignity by making the Oriole team as mop-up men. All year, there they were, pitching a half-decent inning or two to help save the bullpen's arms. They were proud to be on a team in a pennant race.

Weaver, judging them by their dedication to task, not their eccentricities, referred to them as the Unusual One and the Mystic. Stanhouse is prone to primal-scream therapy and for years drove a black hearse to the park; a toy gorilla sits in his locker and is periodically fed beer. Grimsley, a greaseballer, has spacey, pale-blue *Village of the Damned* eyes and long, curly hair that looks like you'd have to measure its oil content with a dipstick. On most teams, Stanhouse and Grimsley would be tagged as bad actors, veteran subversives. In Baltimore, they were seen as boosters of morale, just straight-talkin' fellas.

Even on the Orioles, though, there are limits to broad-mindedness. For instance, Dan Ford. If ever a player was meant *not* to be an Oriole, it was Ford. He arrived from the Angels, traded for DeCinces, with a bad rep. The previous year, he'd been suspended for using a corked bat, started two brawls, posed nude for *Playgirl,* and was criticized as a self-centered, moody player. Weaver dismissed this, saying that he'd had his best minor-league season using a corked bat, that he'd had a few fights himself and that he'd just posed in his underwear for a TV commercial with Palmer. Why was everybody breaking out into a rash?

Ford proved an acceptable fellow; it wasn't his personality, just his fundamentally atrocious play that bedeviled Ford. When he was confronted with his flaws, Ford managed—in his good-natured way—to put at least half the blame somewhere else. That just made DeCinces' stats as an Angel look even better. Ford needed to be back in Anaheim, where baseball illiterati play with a beach ball during the late innings of tied games. There, like Ford, they don't even know what a cutoff man *is.* And they don't care. They cheer one-handed catches, enjoy a smile after an error and think two runners trapped on one base is cute.

In that slack atmosphere, Ford could relax and let his natural talents—slashing first-pitch hitting and speed on the bases and in the outfield—express themselves. To Ford, Baltimore was an uptight town; the place taught him, for the first time in his career, the dangers of thinking, of worrying, of playing for the team. Ford tried to change himself from an open-hearted good-time ballplayer into a Weaver player. The result was a mess.

Rock Bottom and Rebirth

Ford was also upsetting because he seemed symbolic of the gradual erosion of the ambience which provincial Bal'mer called "Oriole Magic." In '79 and '80, the O's seemed to be in a comely state of grace; where was the bell jar big enough to cover this team and preserve it from harm? Many a time Weaver must have wished he could put his team in suspended animation and protect it from the world and time.

In bilious economic times, the Birds showed that the game could be played properly. Yet even the Oriole brass suspected that this flash-powder paradox of a team would eventually find itself in jeopardy. Nothing good can stay. By August of 1982, the bell jar seemed shattered. Rust never sleeps, not even in baseball. Slowly the O's returned to dismal, everyday reality; they became as testy, as prone to second-guessing, as given to bonehead plays as a run-of-the-mill team. The process by which the pastoral idyll on Thirty-third Street turned sour was familiar and drab.

To summarize a season in a sentence, the '81 Birds were put off their feed by the strike and played disinterestedly by September. In the off-season, the worried front office discovered that many players had no market value whatever. The winter meeting consensus was that the Orioles had irreversible dry rot; the club apparently had neither the farm system nor the cash to save itself. Peters and Williams kept the old gang together because they had no choice. Ironically, the Ford-DeCinces trade was their attempt to placate fans.

For five months of '82, the O's imitated '81. Their capacity for avoiding significant accomplishment was astonishing. Every rubber game of a series or a road trip seemed to go against them, usually in some ugly fashion. This knack for futility became a bitter team joke. Oriole Magic was turning Oriole Tragic.

Touchingly, the team clung to its sense of itself as indefinably special. But first their foes, then their fans, became aware that the Birds' clean economy of play was deteriorating; this club could go south in a hurry, and stay there for years, as the Cincinnati Reds already had. Finally, after nearly two seasons of treading water, the club admitted its deep, almost sorrowful concern. Once, McGregor was told, "You play your next dozen games against the worst teams in the league." "You mean," said McGregor, "we get to play ourselves." Dempsey, the soul of enthusiasm, said, "We may be watching the end of an era."

When the Orioles flew to Boston in August, owner Williams went too. "Damage-control mission," he said bleakly. The next day, on Weaver's birthday, he gave his best summation-to-the-jury pep talk. "I asked him how he ever lost a case," said an impressed Palmer. That afternoon, the Orioles won when a throw to home plate in the tenth hit a rock and bounced sideways. "The road back! We may never lose again!" crowed Dempsey.

Weaver was relieved: "I asked Ed not to do it. Those pep talks scare me to death. *What if you lose?* Then what do you do next? Glad I was wrong."

But Weaver wasn't wrong. The next morning, the Orioles' born-again chapel speaker was Charles Colson. An hour later, the Red Sox got *nine* consecutive batters on base in one inning—the most by Boston since 1901.

Then things really went bad. In Minnesota, the Orioles led by a run in the tenth inning with two outs. "Dauer's playing third," said Weaver, "and we yell at him to move closer to the line. He does. The batter hits a grounder right where we placed him. The ball goes right between his legs into the corner. Two runs score. We lose. We were in shock. The next night, in the first inning, they scored six runs before we got anybody out. That was the low point. It was just unfuckingbelievable."

One rule of watching baseball is that a team is often most slapstick just before it goes on its longest win streak. Teams get more and more disgusted, bedeviled by minutiae until finally a genuinely fantastic misadventure pushes the club over the edge into a harmony of indifference. Suddenly they laugh, they relax, they say, "That's unfuckingbelievable." Before they know it, they've won three in a row.

A team will frequently slump until it embarrasses itself so thoroughly that its whole collective system is purged by the shock. Weaver has never hidden his instinctive relish in horrid, error-filled defeats. Take the cure in a couple of big, gulping doses, not in a dozen one-run sips of defeat.

For the O's, the Minnesota nadir proved the springboard for the hottest streak in the club's history. "When we got to Texas, there was a revolt on the team," said Dempsey. "We were revolted with ourselves."

Another hidden revolt took place in Texas. It went on in Weaver's mind. He finally decided that he would manage the club more the way the team and coaches wanted it managed. All season, Weaver had been criticized by his players more sharply than ever before. In July a coach told me, "I may quit. Earl won't listen to anybody. He's got an autobiography and a biography out at the same time. He's retiring. He's on every TV show. He's carried away with himself. I've made a million suggestions and he hasn't taken one."

The bill of particulars against Weaver makes dull history. Every team in every season has squabbles concerning ambiguous questions of dicey baseball judgment. In a sense, only the team cares about them and only the team knows how important they are. The Orioles' gripes were typical of how every team's inner gears grind. Weaver faced many questions.

Should Cal Ripken play third or shortstop? Should Ford be benched against right-handers? Should Gary Roenicke play outfield full-time? Should Bumbry, nursing leg injuries, be benched against left-handers? Should Singleton, in a two-year slump batting right-handed, be benched against left-handers? Should Tim Stoddard's arm be treated more gently? (At one point, Weaver had Stoddard warm up twenty consecutive days.) Should rookie Storm Davis be used more, both spot-starting and relieving? Should the exasperating comedy team of Stanhouse and Grimsley continue to be brought into important long-relief situations? Should pinch-hitters Terry Crowley and Benny Ayala play more?

This is the kind of scuttlebutt which saturates most contenders, since the smallest move affects several players.

Starting in Texas, Weaver began shifting his tactics, changing the ingredients in his managing brew: less Bumbry, more of rookie John (T-Bone) Shelby; less Singleton and more Ayala; less Ford and more Roenicke; much more Cyclone Davis and almost no work for the Unusual One and the Mystic; Ripken every inning at short and plenty of the walk-drawing third baseman Glenn Gulliver, but less Sakata; less manic warming up in the bullpen; less stubborn insistence that Palmer work his way out of late-inning jams.

This was a hard potion for Weaver to swallow, particularly because, in his last seasons, Weaver developed a strange flaw. Throughout his career, he insisted the key to managing was making impersonal, team-first decisions. However, Weaver became increasingly hurt by the denunciations of veterans when he finally had to cut their professional throats. Weaver's need not to hurt those who had helped him—and conversely, not to be hurt by their howls of betrayal—became obsessional. Frequently Weaver cited his desire "not to hurt people anymore" as a reason for retiring. Outsiders scratched their heads, never dreaming Weaver was being honest. His patience with Bumbry, Singleton and Ford drove Williams and Peters bananas. Even in the last week of the season, Weaver was still agonizing over "what Kenny [Singleton] and Al [Bumbry] must feel like" on those occasions when he benched them.

On that night in Minnesota when the Orioles hit bottom, when the club, after two years of resistance, finally shrugged its shoulders and admitted that no act of will power could reverse their course, nobody could have foreseen that the team would win seventeen of its next eighteen games.

In retrospect, several basic baseball-watching factors were involved.

First, the depth of the team's depression was a perfect psychological juncture for a total reversal of form: streak to streak.

Second, the team's awful play prompted the manager to make shifts that were overdue but hard to accept. Nobody takes castor oil *before* his belly aches.

Third, the American League's schedule came into play.

For a century, schedule-studying was a waste of time, because schedules were well made. Now that's changed. In 1977, the AL voted to expand to fourteen teams so each owner could grab a couple of million dollars as his slice of the expansion fees paid by Toronto and Seattle. These "fees" are the bribes baseball requires to get into its monopolistic social club.

The league found, to its shock, that neither man nor machine could create a rational schedule out of a fourteen-team league. The increase by just two teams had complicated the matrix in ways no one had dreamed. The results have been an annual embarrassment.

For instance, on July 26 in '82, the Brewers began a streak of thirty-eight games in which thirty-six of their opponents were among the league's losing teams. On the *same* date, the Orioles began twenty-three straight games against winning teams. Later, the worm turned. Baltimore played thirty-four straight games against losers, while Milwaukee closed the season with twenty-nine games in a row against winners. That was one central explanation for the ebb and flow of the '82 race—that goofball schedule. By no coincidence, of the twenty-seven wins in Baltimore's 27–5 comeback, twenty-six came against losing teams.

The cumulative effects of such a schedule are even greater than most would imagine. The more losers you play, the less abuse your pitching takes, the more confidence is built and the more rested the bullpen becomes. By the same token, a team's hitters tend to get their kinks worked out when they go weeks without seeing the front-line pitchers on contenders.

Finally, losers know how to lose—dramatically. During their comeback, the Orioles got sudden-death homers from five players. Such shenanigans make a team think it's pixilated. The opposite effect is equally strong. If you play winners for a month, your pitchers lose confidence, your bullpen is worked to the bone, your hitters get demoralized and "momentum" drains.

The Orioles, like several teams in recent years, have proved to be preternaturally suited to "streak and sweep" baseball. In '79–'80, the Orioles—like the Reds and the Pirates in earlier periods in the '70s—made a shambles of any theory of baseball probabilities.

In those years, Baltimore *swept* thirty-two series, while being swept only three times; their total record in all *swept* series was 91–9. In all other games, 111–110. Chew on that. It should give palpitations to the too-serious gambler.

To tell the truth, the Orioles litmus test didn't come in the month when the public was drooling over their historic rush. Only one of the Orioles was aware of both the schedule pattern and the team's knack for rattling off series sweeps. Weaver, naturally. "Of course, you have to look at the schedule," he growled. "You never know *how* you're really playing until you look at *who* you're playin'."

By Labor Day, the Birds knew they had, with some luck, righted themselves once more. The sense of revived spirits and restored faith was as sudden as the deterioration of that confidence had been slow; the damage done in two years seemed fixed in two weeks. Perhaps that's the real mark of team character. "Over the years, we've crawled out of more coffins than Bela Lugosi," Weaver snorted.

That Labor Day weekend provided one tableau which captured the redemptive mood which surrounded the team. Enormous fireworks filled the sky above Memorial Stadium, exploding until their tracers seemed to fill the bowl of the ballpark with their colorful splendor. "God Bless America" filled the air—loud, clear and poetic enough so that even Baltimore's Francis Scott Key couldn't have begrudged the selection. Beneath the canopy of sight, the panoply of sound, a cannonade of bomb bursts ripped into the night. Beside the third-base coach's box, the Orioles, still in uniform and fresh from a victory minutes before, sat on the grass with their families and watched the show. This fireworks display had been scheduled for May but, symbolically, was rained out. In September, with the team finally making fireworks, the rescheduled exhibition had rolled around just in time.

Pleasures deferred are all the sweeter.

Into the Fire

Some teams have Bat Day and Cap Day. 'Round the Ides of September, the Orioles had Divine Intervention Week.

Five times in four days the Birds beat New York in Memorial Stadium before delighted congregations of Yankee-haters. In each of the first four games, Baltimore had to come from behind, overcoming a dozen runs' worth of Yankee leads. In those four increasingly dizzy games, the winning pitchers were named Mike Boddicker, John Flinn, Storm Davis and Don Welchel. All had been at Rochester in May. Sometimes reporters had to request maps to find the previously uncharted auxiliary dressing rooms where these gentlemen donned uniforms bearing numbers in the fifties.

Kids, kids, kids! Everywhere you looked, the Orioles were trying to steal a pennant from the Brewers with a bunch of children. If it wasn't those infant pitchers beating the Yankees, then it was Ripken—always Ripken—hitting a home run or making an intuitive play at short. As the mean age of the Oriole heroes got younger and younger, it seemed the club found its natural field leader: the six-foot-four, two-hundred-pound rookie. His blossoming could be traced to two simple factors.

First, in the depths of a May slump, Ripken accidentally got identical pieces of advice on the same day from two people he respected—his father and Reggie Jackson. Both told him to stop trying to be a pull hitter (Weaver's influence) and revert to his normal, all-fields, line-driving hitting. From that day, he hit over .300.

Next, in August, the kid was having his problems in his first month at shortstop. Coaches were moving him and shading his position on every batter, almost every pitch. Weaver told him, "Play short just like you did in high school. Do whatever feels right. Stop looking in the dugout."

So Ripken did. Gambling and guessing, shading and leaning as his instincts told him, the big, polished kid with the strongest arm on the team began materializing on the grass in short centerfield to turn grounders-through-the-box and bloopers into outs. Twice, and only twice, Ripken guessed wrong and looked foolish as routine grounders hopped through his normal position as he was caught flat-footed and couldn't reverse his direction.

By his twenty-second birthday, in August, Ripken was the oldest head in the infield. It might be his first season in the bigs, but he'd been a Ripken much longer.

The appositeness of these contributions from the team's infants could hardly be overstated. They came just when it seemed the pitching staff was unraveling.

First, Stoddard slipped in a Manhattan eatery and disabled himself for the season; Big Foot wasn't drunk, just hungry and, as usual, clumsy. Next, McGregor came down with shoulder tendonitis and won only one game in the final seven weeks. Finally, Palmer pulled his monthly prima donna stunt, taking himself out of a game in Cleveland after seven innings, despite a 2–0 lead and a two-hitter in progress. Palmer, observing that the bullpen was rested, deduced that he should take a powder and informed the five-foot-seven power structure of this decision before retiring to the warm water. The bullpen blew the lead, then the game. "If I were one of Palmer's teammates," said Weaver, "I'd punch him in the mouth."

In the face of such miseries, minor miracles were mandatory. And they were delivered forthwith. In one win over the Yankees, the blithe Stewart was told to warm up in a hurry. "I got tickled at something [bullpen coach] Elrod Hendricks said and I laughed so hard that I swallowed about half a can of snuff," said Stewart, who came in to get the save. "I didn't pitch too bad for a sick guy. I was so dizzy warming up that I saw four bullpen catchers."

To this the pitiless Orioles responded, "Way to 'snuff out' that rally, Sammy."

By September 16, the Milwaukee lead was down to one game. The Orioles, caught up in the pennant-race thrall, believed themselves possessed of mystic powers. During one Yankee game, the Oriole dugout alternated their late-inning cheers, half the time yelling, "Come on, Tippy," and half the time hollering, "Come on, Lance." The Yankees understood the Tippy part, since Tippy Martinez was pitching in relief. But who the heck was Lance?

Well, you see, Weaver not only tolerates scoreboard watching but loves it, insisting, "We're supposed to *enjoy* this." Since Weaver believes in every conceivable superstition, he often picks out a scoreboard hero—some player he senses will beat the team that the O's hope will lose. This day, Weaver's choice as Orioles helper was Detroit catcher Lance Parrish. So the whole dugout picked up the idea. What the Birds couldn't believe was that, within minutes of leaving the field with another victory, Dan Ford burst into the locker room and shouted, "Lance did it! Two-run homer in the eleventh. Milwaukee loses, four to three."

Stunned? Oh, yes. But not too dumfounded to start screaming, *"Thank* you, veeery much," and "Thank *you,* very much," and "Thank yooooou, very *much,"* and all the other readings of those four silly words.

When we are children, we're fetched toward baseball by the game's romantic fiction—the fables about characters like the young High Pockets of John R. Tunis making his way through the minors to the majors. No florid excess of plot can be omitted. There comes a point when a beat writer has to admit to himself that there's a substantial difference between the reality of a major league race and the fictions of childhood. There's no escaping the fact that . . . well . . . the real thing is much better. Actual pennant races are more melodramatic, improbable and all-purpose purple than fiction dares to be. Every first-class pennant race puts the excesses of pulp fiction to shame.

Take "Thanks Earl Day."

As a minor league player, Weaver was a small, slow, tough, short-on-power second baseman who hit and ran, seldom struck out, made the double-play pivot in the face of spikes and hardly ever made an error. That also describes Dauer, who is the embodiment of the big leaguer Weaver never quite got to be. So, in the tenth inning of a 2–2 game against Cleveland, Dauer stepped to the plate as 41,194 fans asked him to give Weaver a present that would surpass all the gifts and garlands that he'd received before the game. Dauer once went without a home run for more than a calendar year and became known as the Hostage, because, as Flanagan put it, "Richie's been kept inside the fences longer than the hostages were held in Iran."

This time, Dauer launched the first and only sudden-death home run of his whole, six-season career. In a strange, fitting sense, Weaver got to see himself hit the game-winning home run on his own retirement day.

Want something even cornier?

Who pitched all ten innings on Thanks Earl Day but Flanagan? Before the final game of the '79 Series, Flanagan's wife, Kathy, had a miscarriage. Five months later she had another miscarriage. Doctors told the couple that she should have a hysterectomy; they should adopt children. No news could have hit the couple, both from the same small New Hampshire town, harder; both define themselves in terms of kith and kin. Flanagan refused to allow the operation, saying they would wait and hope some new medical process would be discovered.

For nearly three years, Flanagan seemed a changed person, less active, less motivated, deeply troubled, as though his major league success, even his $2.5 million contract were some kind of vicious joke when balanced against personal disappointment. The Flanagans bought the house overlooking a small lake in Amherst, New Hampshire, the one they had always wanted; but in a way it was an empty house.

Flanagan's pitching mirrored his state of mind. Star-crossed and often injured, he pitched just badly enough to lose, where he'd once pitched just well enough to win.

In July of '82, Kathy and Mike Flanagan made world news. They became the fourth couple in history to have a "test-tube baby" through artificial insemination. The new process that Flanagan had insisted would be found had been found.

When their daughter was born, Flanagan's record was 8-10 for the season. Within a week of the birth, Flanagan started his longest winning streak since his Cy Young season, of '79. Over the last three months of the season, he lost only one game. And on Thanks Earl Day, Flanagan won his seventh game in a row. Afterward, in the locker room, he held his two-month-old daughter in his arms as his teammates dropped by to inspect the miracle.

To illustrate that such excess, once underway, knows few limits, the next night Baltimore won in the bottom of the ninth when a Lowenstein flyball hit the top of the rightfield fence and bounced into the stands momentarily. The Tigers' Sparky Anderson stormed, "At no time did that ball leave the park." "I don't know if it left the park or not," retorted Weaver, "but I'm goin' to."

Those back-to-back sudden-death homers by Dauer and Lowenstein were both the crescendo of the Orioles' streak and the end of it. No sooner had the Orioles reached this strange, uncharted world where fantasies were granted nightly than they were reintroduced to reality, losing their next three games 11–1, 10–5, and 15–5. Not only did the pitchers allow thirty-six runs, forty-nine hits and 8 homers in just three nights, but the defense chipped in with nine errors.

GM Hank Peters, a dignified man occasionally mentioned as a possible commissioner of baseball, summed up the three days pithily: "We can play some real horseshit baseball."

Many an Oriole knew the genesis of this collapse. It began, as so many twists of a pennant race do, with one pitch—this one thrown a thousand miles away. On the night of Lowenstein's sudden-death homer, the O's gathered in the clubhouse to listen to the final outs of what they supposed to be a Red Sox victory over Milwaukee. They listened as the Brewers, down a run in the ninth, made one out, then two. Down to the last hitter. Then, down to the last strike.

The Birds called on their best voodoo. "Pop one of those balloons," snapped a coach, and one of the balloons in Elrod Hendricks' locker had a pin jabbed at it. Then Dennis Eckersley decided to end the game with a high fastball. And Ben Oglivie decided to hit it into the bleachers to tie the game. "When we heard Oglivie's home run over the radio," said Weaver, who was on his way home, "my brother-in-law almost drove us off the road."

That home run, and the winning run which the Brewers eventually pushed over in the eleventh, hit the Orioles in the solar plexus; the Brewers weren't planning to cooperate in this matter of the Great Baltimore Comeback. To the O's, a team much given to omen-pondering, it seemed to demand that they lose horridly three times in a row.

The first two losses, to the Tigers, were bad enough, but the third was a horror, since it came in the opener of a three-game series in Milwaukee. The Brewers' greeting to the Orioles was nothing less than bloodthirsty. In just six innings, they put twenty-two runners on base and scored fifteen runs. The parade of

Oriole relief pitchers should have been driven from the bullpen by ambulance, rather than Toyota.

The Orioles could have been devastated by that evening's charade. Yet Weaver's reaction was the absolute opposite. He was in a genuinely upbeat, cheerful mood. Weaver loves to get slaughtered, certain that the thrashing will, in the long run, do more good than harm.

So four games behind with nine to play, with his pitching staff in tatters, Weaver put on one of his best postgame performances. "This is the way we like it. Tough as nails," rumbled Weaver. "A two-game winning streak and we're just two games out. No wonder we're closin' in on 'em. We've won twenty-seven of our last thirty-five and I'm proud of these guys who have done it."

Peter Pascarelli, of the Philadelphia *Inquirer*—a cigar-smoking wise guy who covered the Orioles with distinction in the previous year for the Baltimore *News American*—walked up behind Weaver. In his best gravelly Earl-imitation voice, Pascarelli read back the preposterous quote: "This is the way we like it. Tough as nails."

Weaver snorted so hard, trying to keep from laughing, that he choked on his postgame cold cuts. Then Weaver rolled his eyes like a little boy. No, not this tough.

The next evening at sundown, Weaver, in the dugout, said out of the blue, "What I want to know is, what the hell are we doing in this race?"

Weaver didn't get his answer, but he got his wish. On Saturday, Palmer beat Milwaukee with almost disdainful ease, getting the last seventeen outs on twenty-seven pitches. His victory seemed to say, "What's so tough about beating Milwaukee?"

The next day's pitcher, Dennis Martinez, had been watching. "They are a very hungry team for fastballs, and they will follow them out of the strike zone," he said. "Look at Jimmy and learn." If Martinez was watching Palmer, then every Oriole was watching Martinez. Exactly one week before, Martinez had learned that his father had been killed in a traffic accident in Nicaragua. Martinez flew to the funeral. Teammates scrutinized him closely on his return. "This might be the most interesting game Dennis ever pitches," said one Baltimore veteran. "He's never been able to concentrate as well as he should. He's never wanted to win as badly as some pitchers. But he's going to want this win for his father. We keep waiting for the New Dennis, the Mature Dennis. Maybe this will bring it out."

On national TV, the right-hander pitched one of the guttiest, most intense games of his career; he was, in a hard-to-define way, everything that he had not been in his first five seasons. Crises seemed to invigorate him, call out the best in him, whereas, often in his career, difficulties had ruffled him, as though the unstylish job of pitching with men on base was beneath him.

Thanks to the best Orioles throw of the season—a peg to the plate from center field by Shelby in the eighth inning to gun down the tying run—both Martinez and the Orioles had their victory.

"Shelby wasn't aware of the urgency of the moment," appraised Lowenstein. "Otherwise he'd have thrown the ball waaaaaay over Dempsey's head and askew to the right. Sometimes it's better to have an unconscious rookie than a seasoned veteran."

Now two games behind with a week to play, Weaver looked like a bullheaded little tough-as-nails prophet. In September a manager's most vital job may be fine-tuning his team's mood by his choice of public and private words. He can't determine how his club will react, but he can certainly shade it, lead it, help it arrive at a useful composite of feeling. Language, as well as strategy, is a manager's medium. Picking the right tone of voice, the proper gut response to events, is an art. Perhaps it is, finally, more a product of experience, trial and error than intelligence.

Weaver's strongest suit in a pennant race may have been this knack for sensing the flow of a season the way a riverboat pilot might once have sensed the twists of the channel. He was acutely aware that a team's direction could easily be reversed in only two or three days; that's all the time it takes for a rested, synchronized pitching staff to get shot to hell; that's also how long it takes a bedraggled staff to catch its breath, become strong again.

"Every team carries nine or ten pitchers. That's always the wrong number," said Weaver. "Either six is too many, or twelve ain't enough."

When the world is going well, six pitchers are too many, because there is only enough work for the four starters and one short reliever. So the rest of the staff gets rusty. Eventually, of course, the starters all get tired—often at the same time—and all have a bad turn. That's when twelve pitchers aren't enough. The starters get shelled by the third inning day after day; the long relievers haven't worked in two weeks, so they're lousy. The whole staff gets crucified, the process feeding on itself.

In the same way, batting lineups tend to get hot together, then go into slumps together. The process repeats itself eternally for every team in every season. First a couple of off-key hitters get hot. This puts men on base, damages the opposing pitcher's confidence, excites the whole offense, creates myriad opportunities for every other sort of tactic. Marginal hitters glow in the reflected light of larger stars. The cliché "hitting is contagious" is a basic truth with predictable lines of causality.

Conversely, the "cooling off" of just one or two hitters has the reverse ripple effect throughout a lineup. Word of who's hot and who's suddenly not goes quickly through the pitching grapevine.

Almost every major league game has these elements in play. In a pennant race, it is essential that a manager know the true reasons behind his team's play, rather than retreating (even in his own mind) behind catch phrases like "we have momentum" or "my guys are choking."

Weaver saw his team clear and whole, reached valid conclusions, not emotional ones, and took strategic steps that had a concrete, rather than a superstitious, connection with events. Where another manager might, as a desperate joke, pull his batting order for the day out of a hat, Weaver would try a specific ploy, like batting the team's coldest hitter in the No. 2 spot in the hope that just one day in front of Singleton, Murray and Ripken would let him see a diet of fastballs instead of curves.

"You're never as good as you look when you're winning," said Weaver, "and you're never as bad as you look when you're losing." And the shifts from one to the other can be so sudden, part of a cycle that is so quickly repeated, that a team can get terminal vertigo.

Perhaps that's why, as the Orioles left Milwaukee in an exultant mood, Weaver was a worried little prophet. Before the Birds and the Brewers could end their showdown with four games in Baltimore, each had to play three dangerous road games: the Orioles in Detroit, the Brewers in Boston. Weaver, who had in a week seen his team go from hot to cold and then back to heroic, was worried that the roller-coaster syndrome, once started, might be hard to stop.

"Now's the time that their two-game lead really helps them," said Weaver, sitting in raw, autumnal Tiger Stadium. "They don't *have* to win every game in Boston." The Orioles' euphoria on leaving Milwaukee was separated only by a thin membrane from potential panic in Detroit. Again Weaver was painfully correct. The Birds and the Bengals played fierce, taut games before small, disinterested crowds in that big old park. It was a textbook case of a team going nowhere trying to ruin the season for a contender. The first evening, it was Lance Parrish turning a Detroit defeat into victory with a late-inning home run. The next night, John Wockenfuss hit a tie-breaking home run to beat the Birds again. Both nights, Milwaukee won. Their lead was back to four and seemed like forty.

Monologist Sparky Anderson, baseball's master of the double negative, summed up this annual baseball slice-of-life nicely. "I don't like the taste. I make sure I walk real slow when I come out of the dugout. I don't want the Orioles sayin', 'Look at Sparky. He thinks he's doin' something.' I remember what I used to think about those 'spoilers' when I was managin' the Reds. Believe me, they ain't nice things. I hope none of my players says they're enjoyin' this, 'cause I'm not . . . Back with the Reds, lousy teams would beat us in September and say, 'We blocked 'em [from clinching].' Man, that made me hot. Where were they in April-May-June-July, when it was on the line and we were sweepin' 'em six in a row? Then, when the pressure is off 'em, they start talking about 'blocking' and 'spoiling.' No spoilers don't collect no checks."

Thus ended the sermon and, it appeared, the Orioles' season. Nothing in baseball is quite so depressing as losing a long, hard pennant race. A club bleeds to death collectively, one tiny nick of fallibility after another, its chances draining away until finally the last cut feels more like a decapitation than a scratch. Wockenfuss, a swarthy, hairy fellow who would look at home with an ax in his hand and a black hood over his face, was a fine choice as executioner. As the fellow referred to by Weaver as "Wochenfutch" circled the bases and was engulfed by the brazen Tigers at home plate, the Orioles' gopher of record, reliever Tippy Martinez, remained at the base of the pitcher's mound, slumped in an abject crouch, a small, unmoving man suddenly shrunk to toadstool size.

So low had the Orioles sunk that, by the next night, they had completely changed their goals. Instead of thinking about the World Series, they were disgustedly determined not to be swept in Detroit. The same idea sprouted in several heads; all had visions of "how awful it would be to go back home for three sold-out dates and not have the games mean anything." If all else was lost, the Orioles decided to win one for the spite of forcing the Brewers to clinch in Memorial Stadium.

With two out in the Oriole ninth and the Tigers ahead 5–3, even survival seemed remote. Down to the last out, Ripken singled a run home. Then Jim Dwyer singled to tie the score on the next pitch. Finally Gary Roenicke hit a pathetic shattered-bat bloop that floated over the mound and eluded the gloves of two diving Tigers by inches as the winning run scored.

When the Brewers blew a lead and lost in Boston, the Orioles quickly began refiguring their arithmetic. Instead of being eliminated, they were suddenly three behind with four to play. The odds against sweeping such a series from the Brewers to steal the division flag were one in sixteen—a 6 percent solution.

Weaver saw matters differently. "Our magic number is four," he said.

What the Orioles faced following their victory in Detroit was completely against the nature of the human constitution, but completely true to the nature of pennant races. After midnight, the Orioles flew half the width of the country, getting into their own Baltimore beds before sunrise. Then, excited but also exhausted, they tried to get a few hours' sleep before meeting the Brewers three times in less than twenty-four hours. Yes, three games in a day, since the Friday twi-night doubleheader was followed by a day game. Baseball makes everything as fair and orderly as possible on the field and as unfair and chaotic as possible off it. The sport is as much a test of self-management as a test of skill. So many days, so many ways to beat yourself.

If those three games in twenty-four hours were difficult for the O's, they were impossible for the Brewers. The Birds had adrenalin, fresh hope and a home crowd, as well as the residual anger from their Tigers losses. The Brewers had nothing. Milwaukee had played winning teams for a solid month. They, too, had flown at night, but flying along with them to Baltimore was the champagne they'd wanted to uncork in Boston—a bad omen. Worse, the Brewers' pitching was on the edge. Reliever Rollie Fingers had been disabled nearly a month earlier and the whole staff was overworked, from sore-armed starters Pete Vuckovich and Mike Caldwell to a bullpen full of convicted arsonists. The Brewers' everyday players were worn close to the nub after 158 games. Playing in front of fifty thousand fans who were screaming, "Sweep, sweep," and shaking brooms at them didn't help.

In one harrowing Day of the Orioles, the Brewers lost 8–3, 7–1 and 11–3.

A four-game lead on Thursday night was a no-game lead by Saturday. The Brewers had gone from total security to total anxiety in forty-two hours. What befell the Brewers was more like a series of natural disasters than baseball. The Orioles released a season of hostilities in those three games, putting fifty-eight men on base in just twenty-four innings.

"Every break went our way, every close call, every ball in a gap," said Flanagan. "The only thing we had to guard against was overcheering."

A collective psychodrama was running its course. The Orioles didn't have to search for the proper analogy as they gazed at a Brewer team that looked like twenty-five Daniels searching for a friendly lion in Baltimore's deafening den. For proper comparison, the Orioles only needed to think of themselves in the final three games of the '79 World Series. Perhaps nothing in baseball is so fascinating, so morbidly riveting as watching an excellent team caught in the riptide of such events. With each inning, the Brewers seemed to be pulled farther from the safety of shore.

By sundown Saturday, one word described the scene.

Perfection.

After six months of mutual torture, the two teams with the game's best records (94–67) would meet one last time on the final day of the season to settle their differences. Such a last-day winner-take-all game had only occurred three times in 113 years. The pitchers would be those posterity might prefer—263-game-winner Palmer, winner of 13 of his last 14 decisions, against 257-game-winner Don Sutton, the Brewers' million-dollar late-season pennant insurance, acquired from Houston in a trade.

Rarely do teams know, down to the marrow, that they cannot escape becoming part of their sport's history. If Baltimore won on Sunday, it would gain five games in the final four days of the season—the greatest last-week comeback in history. The Brewers had a much different sense of history. History repeating itself concerned them. For weeks both teams had become increasingly aware of an exotic leitmotif running through their struggle.

Back in June, Milwaukee catcher Ted Simmons thought that a John Lowenstein strikeout had ended an inning, so he casually flipped the ball in the general direction of the umpire as he jogged toward the dugout. Before Simmons realized there were only two outs, a pair of Baltimore runners had advanced a base. The next man singled home two runs, instead of just one. The game ended in a 2–2 tie instead of a 2–1 Milwaukee victory. Then rain arrived after nine innings. But for that tie, which was replayed as part of the Friday doubleheader, the Brewers would have clinched their flag before they ever got to Baltimore. Baseball historians will instantly note the similarity to the famous Merkle Boner of 1908 when Fred Merkle cost the New York Giants a victory over the Chicago Cubs when he forgot to touch second base after a teammate's apparent game-winning hit. Instead of a victory, the game went down as a tie, and the Giants, forced to replay the contest at season's end, lost the pennant to the Cubs by a single game.

Simmons, asked if he was aware of the parallel with Merkle, said, "I've only thought about it *every day* since it happened."

The levels of pressure in baseball and the reaction to that pressure sometimes seem to follow immutable laws that operate just far enough beneath the surface that we cannot quite fathom their basic principles or predict their results. Yet as soon as a thing is done, it acquires in hindsight a quality of inevitability so that it seems we knew the outcome all along, but couldn't recognize it until the instant of its completion. This tantalizing, addictive "of course" is at its strongest in pennant races. Many a midseason game seems ruled by caprice. But when every player feels himself to be on a psychological and physical rack, the sense is strong that we could foreknow the outcome if only we knew the participants well enough.

Meet a veteran player or a manager before some "ultimate" game, and it's hard not to say, "So what's going to happen?" There is a shared sense that if somehow our senses were just a trifle better, we could see the shadow of the future.

There are times, however, when even the immediate future seems a mystery. The path to the present moment has been so full of twists and doublings back that, though we assume some line of causality runs through the proceedings, we have long ago given up trying to figure it out. That feeling that we have no idea what will happen, but that it may well be wonderful, is the ideal concluding note for a pennant race.

Twice in recent years a season came to that. The mystery reaches a point where the path to the present is overgrown with incident, so that we give ourselves up entirely to the moment. The event is richer than our imaginations. The last days of such a pennant race are like the living equivalent of a dense detective yarn where finally, our heads aching, we forsake deduction and say, "Surprise me."

In 1978, when the Yanks and the Red Sox met in a playoff for the American League East title, both teams seemed caught in the hands of the event, as though the game were playing them. No one on either team claimed to have an intuition of what would or should happen. No one was crass enough to predict.

That sense of being suspended in midair, caught on the high wire of the moment, also existed before the final Oriole game of 1982. Even driving to the park on that crystal October morning was a sharp pleasure, as though all days in paradise would be freighted with such high-spirited, innocent anticipation. And such certainty of a resolution.

Before the seventh game of the World Series, or the last game of a pennant race, the players barely know what they feel and cer-

tainly don't want to discuss it. Not only are the stakes self-evident, but in a few hours all pregame thoughts will be rendered
irrelevant by the game's outcome. Often a player will just grin and
shake his head involuntarily as though saying, "So here we are."

On Saturday, Milwaukee's team leader, home-run champion
Gorman Thomas, stood by the batting cage, irritated and antsy,
and said, "This shit has gone far enough. We better win today,
'cause nobody wants it going down to Sunday." On Sunday, by
the batting cage, Thomas had lost that case of nerves. He was
quiet, observant, dignified. Like thoroughbreds in almost every
field, when it was genuinely important that he perform, Thomas
had the capacity to be at his best. "Feel fine," he said, while
talking about the reassuring particulars of his craft—the shifting
of the wind, the white-shirt-sleeve background of the upper deck.

Actually, only a handful of plays from that game retain a particular vividness. Each told enough of the tale so that much of
what was to come after seemed to follow obediently.

Robin Yount, the second batter of the game, hit a flyball to the
opposite field that sliced into the bleachers for a homer. That
loosened the Brewers' shoulder blades and proved to both dugouts
that Palmer didn't quite have the fastball he needed.

In the bottom of the first, with the bases loaded, rookie Gulliver
ran through a stop sign at third and was thrown out at the plate
by forty feet to end the inning. The next batter would have been
Jim Dwyer, who had reached base thirteen consecutive times,
three short of Ted Williams' all-time record. After a portent like
that, you could have played "Dueling Banjos" on the tensions
lines of Weaver's forehead.

All the breaks and blessings which, mixed with talent and grit,
had enabled the Orioles to beat Milwaukee five straight times in
eight days suddenly switched their allegiance and came to the
rescue of the equally deserving Brewers. Yount homered again,
then Cecil Cooper went deep, firing his fist in the air. Sutton
pitched well, helped by the Orioles' gradually tightening nerves.
"They bought the gold goose," said Lowenstein of Sutton, "and
today he gave them the golden egg."

In the final act, Oglivie made a sliding catch at the foul line in
left to end the O's last serious rally. Milwaukee scored five runs in

the ninth, a useful conclusion since it made the final score a deci-
sive 10–2, thus aborting the usual blame-casting postmortems.
History and drama lost that day, but perhaps justice and generos-
ity won. Many in Memorial Stadium capsulized the day in four
clean, consoling words: "The better team won."

Tears and Cheers

From '78, I remember the marvelous silence which fell over
Fenway Park for several minutes after the last Red Sox out; a
gentle, sad organ calliope played over the public address system;
that moment was so vivid that no one in the park wanted to move,
to hie himself to some lesser place.

From '82, I remember that morning drive to the ballpark and
the bittersweet sensation of wondering what prevented all days
from being so urgent and full.

And all for a "meaningless baseball game," as the proper modern conventions tell us—forgetting to mention what does mean
something. Even the players would admit that this game was only
one slice of a career; just, finally, one more manageable, digestible,
expendable day at the park.

Yet the sense of accumulated life, of past days all packed into
the precarious teeter-totter of one present hour, is intoxicating.
We move very slowly, appreciate every detail and sensation, just
as we might feel gratitude for every detail of every day, were we
better.

When the final Orioles out had been made—some flyball to the
outfield, it usually is—the Baltimore crowd did what no crowd in
American sports has done. The throng, spontaneously and immediately, decided to reverse the outcome of the game. They found
defeat unacceptable, unworthy of both themselves and their team;
so they decreed a victory. After all, joy and sorrow are often
arbitrary, largely states of mind; nowhere is it written that joy
must accompany victory and sorrow defeat.

Had the Orioles won, spelling would certainly have been in
order. So, in defeat, the crowd began to spell "O-R-I-O-L-E-S." It
started loudly and then became gargantuan. "When they started

spelling 'Orioles,' " said Ted Simmons, "you'd find yourself yelling it along with them out of self-defense."

When they weren't spelling, they were chanting, "Earl, Earl, Earl." So Earl came out, looking as small and vulnerable as we visualize ourselves in our dreams. He was a mess, his hair mussed, his gray undershirt on lopsided. Tears ran down his face and he let them; he blew kisses to the crowd, but especially to the loyal loonies in Section 34 in the rightfield upper deck. He joined with the team's mascots in leading the spelling, using his body to mime the letters.

Finally, Weaver called the team out, and they came. All in various stages of emotional undress, their faces torn between the deep disappointment that they felt, the sense of self-betrayal, and the delight they took in the crowd's standing ovation. Finally, one by one, the players broke the rules of sport-for-money and began smiling, laughing, joking with each other in disbelief. Gradually, they understood. The crowd had decided that they had won. After a quarter hour of cheers, they decided to concur.

In the Boston locker room in 1978, the Red Sox looked as if they had died and were sitting in some anteroom of hell waiting for the barge to take them over into damnation. In the Baltimore locker room in 1982, the Orioles smiled and drank their beer. No one blamed or was blamed. No one was downcast. As they left, the Birds shook hands and made plans—for the first winter basketball game, perhaps. Rich Dauer, grinning, wandered around giving handshakes. "It's a weird feeling," he said. "I can't wait for Opening Day." Weaver thanked the team, told them they couldn't have thrilled him more if they had won the World Series. Then, all baseball to the end, he said brusquely, "Win a hundred and five for the new guy." (Little did he know that in 1983 the Orioles would win 98 regular-season games, 3 in the playoffs and four in the Series: exactly 105.)

For once, defeat had no funereal overtones. The crowd and its team had finally understood that in games, as in many things, the ending, the final score, is only a part of what matters. The process, the pleasure, the grain of the game count too.

3

TRADER JACK, WHITEY THE RAT AND OTHER GOOD IDEAS

When young, we are fascinated by deeds. As we age, we learn to prefer ideas.

The particular catches our fancy first, but eventually it is the principle which runs through events, promising a shadow of coherence, which holds us.

This is even apparent in the link we feel with baseball. As children, we are captured by the spectacle and energy of the ballpark, by the heroism of a leaping catch and by the fanciful prospect that we might do such things someday in such a place. The players themselves are everything to us, their least gesture magnificent, their smallest failure a cause for childhood tears. Such creatures as managers and pitching coaches, general managers and farm directors barely exist for us.

Sometime, perhaps in late adolescence, it is common to say we have "outgrown the game." What we mean is that we are no longer enchanted by every home run. Gradually we realize the sport is distinguished more by its contemplation than its action. Then, one summer, the game grabs us again. But usually it does so in a new way. The simple thrills of the sport aren't dead, although perhaps they are muted. What's changed is that something unexpected has been added. As adults watching other adults, we start to realize the game is not something outside our everyday world, but merely a heightened and focused form of our common experience.

Our system of weights and measures begins to change. We watch the technique of the great catch, appreciating that this fellow has worked on such plays for fifteen years; his act is not so much heroism as rugged craftsmanship. We watch the players as men who come before us out of a particular life history and with specific personalities and problems which shade the way we feel about their accomplishments. We see the insignia on their uniforms less, their faces more.

Of all our forms of adult second sight, one in particular is a sure sign that we're gettin' older. Only grown-ups talk about "team building."

On the day when, hot dog in hand, we lean back and, instead of screaming at the ump, say to our companions, "What makes some teams so good every year, while others stay so lousy?" it's as certain a sign of age as a receding hairline.

As our frame of reference increases, as we catch ourselves saying, "This lineup is almost as good as the late-fifties Yanks," we become increasingly captivated by the game's key adult question: What makes winners and losers?

Why are some teams always contenders, others always offenders? Why do the same off-the-field figures—the same small group of managers, GMs and team presidents—always seem to be at the heart of the pennant race? When Whitey Herzog or Harry Dalton changes cities, why does the pennant follow him? Why do folks who learn their trade in the Dodger or the Oriole chain always seem two steps ahead of those who wear the stamp of the Indians or the Cubs?

As a starting point, let's note that few things are rarer than a good idea.

If one thread runs through most successful organizations, it is the ability to conceive a simple idea of what kind of team is desired and then doggedly stick to that plan. The nature of that guiding idea is not nearly as important as the courage to carry it forward through hard times.

The common denominators of winners are patience and planning.

Few franchises realize that no team, not even the richest, has everything. All organizations, even the most consistent of the past quarter century—the Orioles, Dodgers, Yankees and Reds—have losing seasons. The key to victory isn't creating a team without weaknesses, but constructing a club with concentrated strengths that outweigh its flaws.

The '27 Yankees lacked speed, and the '75 Reds had mediocre starting pitchers. Recent champs in the '80s like the Dodgers, Cards and Orioles had obvious defects. Los Angeles had lousy defense in the middle infield and next to no speed. St. Louis was last in the majors in homers, had no starter with sixteen wins and used two nondescript rookies in its rotation. Baltimore had "Three Stooges" in its batting order. The key is for a club to identify the players that suit its park, its tastes and, in these free-agent days, its wallet.

There is no better example of the vagaries of team building than the contrasting styles of two of the most successful managers of recent years. For fifteen years, former Baltimore manager Earl Weaver loved "[starting] pitching, three-run homers and fundamentals," while putting less value on team speed, depth of relief pitching and high-average, all-fields hitting. When he retired, Weaver boasted he could have managed two more years, gone winless (0-162) both seasons, and still ended his career more than one hundred wins above .500. So the Earl of Bal'mer had the best idea, right?

Wrong. Weaver just had *an* idea.

In both Kansas City and St. Louis, Whitey Herzog's success was built on (guess what?) overall team speed, depth in relief pitching and high-average slap-hitting. And what areas did Herzog choose to neglect? That's right. Exactly the three things Weaver worshiped: starting pitching, three-run homers and brainy fundamentals. Both team builders were eminently successful because each had a concept that suited his stadium, his club's resources and his own baseball tastes and intuitions.

The Orioles play in a pitching-oriented grass park where, because of short, slanted walls in the corners, outfielders can pinch the alleys. The park has always killed batting averages. The result is that walks and down-the-line power are theoretically the best style of offense. A line-drive, gap-hitting team, such as the late-'70s Royals, would be at an offensive disadvantage there. Their grounders wouldn't scoot through the soft infield, their base stealers would be a step slower on dirt than phony turf, and their doubles in the gaps would be singles or outs.

On the other hand, in Royals Stadium, the Orioles were an embarrassment for years. Their long flies were just outs. And their pitchers' routine grounders and infield chops suddenly became hits that opened up K.C. innings. To show how this infects every corner of the game, almost every pitch, consider that pitcher's friend, the change-up. Oriole pitchers love it and watch it produce double plays; in K.C., the O's have, as a staff, almost abandoned the pitch, because it consistently produces those exasperating chop hits.

Almost without exception, winning teams gear their squads to their parks. The '76 to '81 Yankees were, without question, built on George Steinbrenner's checkbook. However, he did what many other rich owners couldn't do: he spent his money fairly wisely. Those Yankees were based on left-handed power hitting and left-handed starting pitching, thus making use of the Ruthian porch in right.

The early-'80s Houston and Oakland clubs which reached the playoffs understood that they played in the best pitchers' parks in their respective leagues. So they built around their pitching staffs. The Astrodome is a singles-hitters' park, so Houston wisely went for line-drive hitters and ignored home runs. Oakland realized its huge foul territory and grass infield were the reasons for low scoring, but that there was no reason home-run hitters couldn't prosper. So, like the Oakland champions of '72–'74, the '81 A's selected power hitters with good walk totals and actually won their division, despite having an infield and bullpen of triple-A quality.

Ironically the Astros (put together in the late '70s by GM Tal Smith) quickly forgot their winning formula as soon as Smith was fired by owner John McMullen. With Smith gone, Houston denuded itself of base stealers—the heart of what little offense the team had—in the winter of '81–'82. The next season, the Astros went from being a contender to being a loser. It's easy to forget the ideas that got you to the top.

Conversely, the common denominator of clubs that can't seem to get into serious contention, such as the Giants, Indians, Rangers and Cubs, is an inability to settle on a coherent theory of team building. Sticking to a plan usually means hanging tough with the same general manager, manager, farm director and head of scouting long enough so the entire organization has a feeling of continuity from rookie league to major league.

"Even when you've got the nucleus of a good ball club, you have to be constantly tinkering with parts, parts that don't fit, parts that wear out," says Baltimore general manager Hank Peters. "But you should never overhaul. The teams that overhaul are the ones who are in trouble."

The regression of the '82 Yanks is a good example. "They were a power team and then all of a sudden they said, 'Hey, let's become a speed club,' " analyzes Peters. "Then, in midstream, they decide New York fans don't like it, they're not winning games, and they want to change. That's when you start bouncing off walls. You require your players to play in a certain style and then you change your mind, and the result is a mess."

When franchises, such as Cleveland and Texas, constantly move their fences in or out (or, like the Yankees, talk about it), it's a giveaway that the club has, in its indecision, constructed a team that can't even play in its own park. Ever hear the Dodgers talk about a new wall for Chavez Ravine?

Of course, as every fan knows, several basic factors have always correlated closely with long-term team success. As Branch Rickey first proved decades ago with the Cardinals and the Dodgers, few things beat a fine farm system, especially a farm system that specializes in teaching one thing well.

The Orioles, the Mets and the Dodgers have traditionally emphasized pitching and defense in the minors. Somewhere, tucked in their scouting systems, are folks who know a pitcher when they see one. The Reds, the Pirates and the Giants always have been noted for producing hitters, although the Giants usually trade theirs, just as the Mets can't seem to hold onto pitchers. In fact, the research of Bill James *(Baseball Abstract)* indicates that the Giants actually produced more talent from 1958 to 1978 than any other club in baseball, but traded it to the four winds.

Expensive farm systems are nice, but, as the Yanks discovered, it isn't the quantity of good minor leaguers that matters, but the occasional superstar—the Mike Schmidt or Robin Yount—who defines a franchise's fortunes. Teams are built on a foundation of stars; supporting-role players are a dime a dozen (if you know what you're looking for).

If free agency has taught anything, it's that the game's two greatest wastes of money are 1) a farm system needlessly overstocked with "prospects" and 2) the purchase of multimillion-dollar free agents who are good but not great.

What's more misleading than a farm system that boasts of winning several bush-league pennants every season and of having "fifty top prospects"? The wise team knows it's lucky to have five real prospects at any one time: the minors exist to move these few forward. The club that can't discriminate among its own prospects—read the Steinbrenner Yankees—might as well save its money. Clubs like the Dodgers and the Orioles which correctly spot their Valenzuelas and Saxes, their Ripkens and Murrays, then advance them boldly and make room for them confidently, are rare.

Few teams have the judgment to isolate their future stars from all the minor-league chaff. In some cases, one man makes the final calls, the way Paul (the Pope) Owens made critical personal decisions that revived the Phillies in the '70s as the Reading-to-Eugene-to-Philadelphia pineline produced Schmidt, Luzinski, Bowa and Boone. More often a club's ability to evaluate young players is a test of its collective intelligence: if a team gets superficial reports from its unseen rank and file—from its Class A manager, its roving minor-league coaches, its Instructional League director, its Eastern Seaboard bird dog and many others in its informational grapevine—then it's garbage in, garbage out.

In part, that's why the transformation of a perennial loser into a winner, or the deterioration of a winner into a loser, is usually so gradual. It takes years to assemble all the hidden people in a club's chain of command, and then it takes years to tear that infrastructure down. Free agency has made it easier for a franchise to cover its lack of collective wisdom with a quick fix of dollars; but when the cash runs low, the truth will out. To build for the long haul, build from the bottom, not the top.

"We try to judge every decision in the organization by the same standard—whether it's a new manager, a minor-league trade or a new usher," says Peters, whose Orioles so often rise from their own ashes. "We ask, 'Is this change a plus for us, or a minus?' If you want to stay on top, then over the years you better make a lot more plus moves than minuses."

This methodology, epitomized by Baltimore, is a time-honored baseball practice. For generations, fine organizations like the Cardinals and the Brooklyn Dodgers believed detail was enormously important because ultimately detail created ambience. No detail, not even the tone of voice of the person answering the phones, could be overlooked.

That old, civilized atmosphere still exists in the Dodgers' communal dining room in Vero Beach, where the amenities are preserved so gently but unpretentiously that the richest player and the newest secretary bring their families to the same table. A World Series buffet in Memorial Stadium's Bird Feed Room might be the best cuisine in a food-loving town; even the Orioles' annual Information Guide is a book-length work of patience, intelligence and taste. The offices in Fenway Park are as friendly and old-shoe as they are cramped; crusty, cuddly old Tom McCarthy still roams the pressbox passing out scorecards, just as he did to Ring Lardner and Grantland Rice.

These and other vestiges of a sweeter time remain, but a change has taken place in recent years. Baseball's innocent old-school-tie clubbishness has given way to corporate thinking. When a fellow who's made his millions in sprockets buys a club as a toy, then a get-there-in-a-hurry, conglomerate mentality can take hold.

Which brings us to $500,000-a-year utility infielders.

Since '75, baseball has been prodigal in its bids to ordinary free agents. New owners have dreamed of building their organizations from the top down. Buy star players, win the Series, then worry about laying the boring foundation for a perennial contender. This mindset has made wealthy men of Wayne Garland, Rennie Stennett, Dave Collins, Claudell Washington, Al Hrabosky and others who, in 2001, will be forgotten.

Every general manager should have a sign on his desk which says, "Will the free agent that I want to buy end up in the Hall of Fame: Yes, Maybe or No."

If the answer's "yes," pay anything for the fellow, regardless of age. Pete Rose and Reggie Jackson were bargains at three and four million dollars.

If the answer's even "maybe," then you probably better grab the guy, if he fills a weakness. Gentlemen like Catfish Hunter, Don Sutton, Tommy John, Fred Lynn, Dave Winfield, Rollie Fingers, Goose Gossage, Nolan Ryan and Carlton Fisk tend to make their employers happy.

However, if the answer's "no way," then double-lock the company vault. Most free agents are just such dross, yet some GMs can't make distinctions that any stat-conscious fan could manage if you asked about a player's chances for the Hall. On the day they became millionaires, did anybody think that Bill Travers, Doc Medich, John Curtis or Oscar Gamble had a chance at a bronze bust?

Of course, this method's sketchy. George Foster was a "maybe," yet he burned the Mets. Don Gullett looked like a "yes" when the Yankees first got him. And some "no's" have done nicely. Still and all, the best teams know you spend millions only for greatness. Then, if you're strong in trumps, you can finesse at the edges. Witness the anonymous Orioles, who always seem to be playing over their heads.

"Not everybody can be Mickey Mantle. You have to be satisfied with players who have one or two tools and make the most of them," theorizes Weaver. The O's '82 leftfielder, a three-headed platoon creature, had baseball's best power stats: 41 homers, 123 RBI. In '83, left field produced 35 homers and 130 RBI. The Birds got John Lowenstein for the waiver price, Benny Ayala in a minor-league trade and Gary Roenicke as a trade throw-in. Yet for two years they might have been the AL's MVP: that is—Most Valuable *Position.*

To these notions about wise free-agent money management, there's one dramatic exception: the New York Yankees.

In this wide-open period, no sport has been as receptive to scheming, bold, piratical thinking as baseball. In a sense, these are baseball's early Wall Street days, when speculation is rampant and the rules of the game are poorly defined. To wit, meet George M. Steinbrenner III.

Sometimes the fossil of a prehistoric fish is discovered in mint condition, because the creature, aeons ago, ran aground in a shallow backwater where it was perfectly preserved by the mud that trapped it. Such may prove to be the case, ages hence, with Steinbrenner. Social historians of a future time may gasp with pleasure and say, "Here we have the ideal example of the American capitalist who saw himself as a romantic hero."

Seen against the wide and various world, Steinbrenner is a corporal of industry who ships grain on the Great Lakes, owns a sliver of Tampa, feeds some thoroughbred hayburners and has friends in politics. However, as Steinbrenner says, "No one pays attention to a shipbuilder." So he's gone public with the business habits that are tantamount to his worldview.

Steinbrenner alone recognized that the moment in baseball history had come when an unregenerate Social Darwinist might flourish—that is, if his team played in New York, if his team won, if he got huge local TV contracts and big crowds, and if he cashed in on the bonanza of postseason play. Steinbrenner used all of his club's financial power to take advantage of a marketplace biased as never before toward wealthy franchises.

Only one other team had the market and the money to try the same stunt: the Dodgers. But the O'Malley family, raised in baseball, couldn't stomach what in poker would be called a no-limit freeze-out. Both the Dodgers and the Yanks could "buy the pot" in their leagues, but only the Yanks did.

Steinbrenner saw the chance, at least in theory, to build an almost defeat-proof organization—a leakproof ship with a double hull. The Yanks not only amassed frontline stars, but collected more second-line stars than they could ever use. This compulsive duplication of talent was a system. George III understood that players got hurt, got old, got lazy or went sour. The solution was to have so many that only a catastrophe could keep you from winning, or at least being so close to the top that you remained where the stay-ahead cash was. That's the insurance policy nobody ever thought of—or was willing to pay the premiums on.

While other clubs built one team, then trusted to luck, the Yanks assembled a team-and-a-half and thus bought their luck.

In this system, an aged player, like fifteen-year Yankee Roy White, is only a liability if you feel loyalty toward him one day longer than the harshest realism dictates. And a rookie, like Jim Beattie or Dave Righetti, is only a danger if you consider him precious and are worried that shipping him back to Tacoma or Columbus at midnight and calling him gutless might endanger his development. The Yanks removed these sentimental bugs from the system by paying top dollar. The catch was that they owned you lock, stock and dignity. As resident dissident Graig Nettles, who wore a "Fido" T-shirt because he was always in the owner's doghouse, once said, "Some teams are under the gun. We're under the thumb."

Thus Steinbrenner has proved himself to be the perfect Yankee-owner. The man and his team have become, over the years, a standing ethical question about means and ends, even about American values and capitalist morality. The point that's often missed is that the Yankees have been at the heart of debates since our grandfathers' times. It's a baseball fan's birthright to maintain a lifelong ambivalence toward the Yankees, respecting their great players while condemning an ownership that pays cash for its Ruths and Jacksons, brazenly buys players for every stretch drive and regularly cashiers lovable old managers like Stengel and Lemon.

Contrary to the highbrow consensus, the Yankees' corporate bad manners and their poised athletic talent, their repetitious controversies and their ostentatious victories and, above all, their bickering, slapstick collapses, aren't "bad for baseball" but in fact may be the most compelling public theater the game offers.

What makes Steinbrenner and the Yankees so confounding is that to reject them is to reject something so basically American that it unnerves us. The Yankees represent free enterprise and long hours and justification by works, and being crafty enough and brave enough to make the system work for you by figuring the tilt of the wheel. To root for the Yankees is a delicious vice in a bourgeois society.

Also, Steinbrenner is the most transparent sort of paper villain.

Everybody sees through him, so nobody really fears or truly hates him. He believes in "competing" and "winning" and "hanging tough" and "weathering criticism" and "sticking by your guns" and "setting an example for America's youth" with such silly confidence that at times he seems charmingly quixotic. After Steinbrenner hires yet another "stand up guy," then invariably humiliates him at the earliest opportunity, he is always stricken with a fit of conscience and rehires the guy or renegotiates a bigger contract.

In one sense, Steinbrenner's place in baseball history is clear. His purpose was to devalue victory, prove its essential emptiness as an end in itself. No one in baseball will ever again find it quite so easy to countenance bad conduct or compromise of principles for the sake of winning. When, in April of '82, a Yankee Stadium crowd of 35,458 chanted "Steinbrenner sucks" for two minutes, it was a minor and refreshing emancipation for the nation's spirit; crude certainly, but so basically decent that many thought it was an all-cornball Great Moment in Sports.

However, that night may also have been a sorrowful watershed. What angered those fans may not have been Steinbrenner's callous firing of managers and exiling of stars but, rather, a sense that the whole fabric of Steinbrenner's Yankee project was in danger of disintegrating. In the early '80s, all of Steinbrenner's behavior patterns accelerated as he became progressively more isolated in his corporate attic, unable to attract anyone but the most abject yes-men to help him make his baseball decisions.

The firings, the emotional tirades, the damage to the farm system in the grab for veterans, the scattergun free-agent signing, the kaleidoscopic alterings of team style and personality, the manufactured controversies, all left a residual dizziness, like a bad soap opera that has finally exhausted its story line.

Centuries ago, Montaigne wrote, "So marvelous is the power of conscience that it makes us betray, accuse and fight ourselves, and, in the absence of an outward witness, it brings us forward against ourselves."

In Steinbrenner's case, we shall see.

Historically, trades have been a major factor in team building, especially the brave trade of a respected but limited veteran for a true prospect: Ernie Broglio for Lou Brock, Frank Duffy for George Foster. However, in this era of agents, no-trade clauses, right of veto and the like, trades are so tangled that their importance has diminished.

Nevertheless, a fellow who knows what he wants—and who also has the good fortune to want what nobody else treasures—can still pull it off. Already, in the '80s, general managers Whitey Herzog and Jack McKeon have proved that point. In '82 Herzog's Cards won a world title, and McKeon's Padres finally climbed above .500; both of these surprises were almost entirely the result of two winters' worth of adventurous trading, based on guiding ideas that nobody in baseball recognized until the White Rat and Trader Jack had finished their Winter Meeting larcenies.

Herzog's creation of the first truly modern turf team is a culmination of trends that have been building since the '60s. His final product—the Runnin' Red Birds of '82—provided the World Series with the most dramatic and perhaps most significant contrast of playing styles since the National League champions of the '20s, reared in dead-ball times, were forced to cope with Babe Ruth and the home runs of Murderers' Row.

What Milwaukee, a team built along entirely traditional lines, saw beneath the giant arch in St. Louis was a glimpse of the future. That Series showed the general public a trend that insiders had been watching with fascination and suspicion for a decade: the division of baseball into two sports, one played in cozy grass parks and another in spacious turf pinball arcades. Almost invariably, teams built for one surface seem disoriented and demoralized on the other. St. Louis' victory was one more sliver of evidence that turf teams may adapt to grass less miserably than slower slugging clubs do to turf.

When a team with 67 homers beats a club with 216—the biggest power gap in Series history by a huge margin—then even stodgy baseball minds take note.

And will, most likely, be quick to copy.

Herzog's first notion is that speed and raw athletic ability are to be preferred at every position over any other virtue, even if this pinches other facets of the game, such as power, consistency or sophisticated baseball intelligence. Herzog didn't invent the all-out running attack with six or seven thieves who steal whether they're ahead or behind. Chuck Tanner did that in Oakland in '76 (with 341 A's steals); Herzog just followed suit.

Next Herzog realizes that a team which hits the ball from middle to top, instead of from middle to bottom like a power team, has the advantage of turning current pitching theory on its head. The knee-high strike—a pitching *sine qua non* since the home-run age began—holds no fear for the Cards, who only hit homers by accident. The low strike just fuels their game.

As clearly as anyone, Herzog has understood how team speed in a big park can turn a mediocre pitching staff into a good one. Cardinal pitchers live by one commandment: Make 'em hit it, but not out of the park. Forget "stuff," forget strikeouts, forget everything except making decent pitches in good spots. Then let the speedsters chase the ball. Want proof? Only one Card pitcher struck out more than eighty-five men in '82. No world title was ever won so unprepossessingly.

All Herzog's pitching theories are thoroughly modern. He much prefers a great reliever with forty-five wins-and-saves to any mere twenty-game winner; to Herzog it's axiomatic that the contemporary Ace of Staff lives in the bullpen. Herzog starts with speedsters and relievers; *then,* as a kind of apologetic afterthought, he looks to see if any stray sluggers or starting pitchers— you know, the category of players who monopolize the Hall of Fame—happen to be left lying about. To Herzog, the most over-abundant commodity in baseball is a respectable starting pitcher who can give you a few presentable innings. John Stuper, Dave LaPoint, Steve Mura—sure, dime a dozen. Win it all with 'em.

Now perhaps we can see why Herzog could build his team so quickly. He could get the guys he wanted because nobody else thought much of them. He sought precisely the baseball commodities that were most undervalued. With this in mind, he had little trouble trading for the heart of his new team—Lonnie Smith, Ozzie Smith, Willie McGee and Bruce Sutter. These and other personnel moves, like signing free agent Darrell Porter, weren't uniformly brilliant, but they all had the thread of Herzog's guiding purpose. Each trade was greater than the sum of its parts, because each new Card complemented the others.

In the wake of his lightning transformation of a mediocre team, other clubs will study his model. Their luck may not be as blessed. The man who has a good idea first is the only one who gets to buy cheaply. Many a big-league executive is anxious to see how well Herzog's Cards, who contended but never jelled in '83, prosper in the next few years. Were they a trend or a fluke?

If Herzog's success was invigorating to watch, then McKeon's work in San Diego was nearly inspirational. He was bequeathed a bunch of overpaid, malingering lumps and in two years got them into a September pennant race.

McKeon inherited a Padre team of back-stabbing malcontents who responded to defeat with an extra helping of chili and a belch. Some players take the money and run; the Padres motto was, "Take the money and walk." For years, many fans thought the Padres were America's revenge on Ray Kroc for inventing McDonald's—cast Big Macs on the water, get back Oscar Gamble. Every year, as Kroc spent $11 million on free agents, it was predicted that the Padres were about ready to go somewhere. And every year it turned out to be the beach.

San Diego is the perfect place to retire after you've made your fortune. Unfortunately, that idea prematurely occurred to several Padres. This is the team that once fielded three born-again zealots at the same time. Unfortunately Willie Davis believed in Buddha, Mike Ivie in Christ and Tito Fuentes in witchcraft. The captain of the all-subversive team, edging out macho-man Guillermo Montanez, was grumpy Gaylord Perry, who walked out on the team and went home—with four weeks left in the season.

"They're even worse than I expected," McKeon told me a month after he took over the Padres, in '80. "The only solution is for me to bring a fire hose into the clubhouse and wash 'em all out."

When McKeon started his housecleaning, going through the clubhouse like a berserk Zamboni, the silk-suit front-office guys around both leagues all thought they'd slick this overmatched pigeon; they couldn't wait to beat the sawed-off former bush-league catcher in the back-room trades. The Smart Money listened to McKeon as he said "ain't," cussed a blue streak, chewed his cigars and acted just a little dense. They mistook him for a mark when he was the one running the game.

McKeon, who'd been in pro ball for thirty-three years, made a dozen deals so fast that nobody had time to figure out what he was doing. By '82, seventeen of the twenty-five Padres were his new bodies, and nasty Dick Williams—just the sort of grand inquisitor McKeon wanted—was the body in charge. All those amusing Padre deals in the fine print—goofy, trivial stuff like getting Salazar for Bevacqua, Bonilla for Lacey, DeLeon for Olmstead, Wiggins and Montefusco for nothing—proved to be the sounds of a franchise being rebuilt.

All these deals were Jack McKeon's reimbursement for a lifetime. They were his paycheck for all those lonesome years in hotel rooms away from his wife and kids, seeing—he figures—three hundred games a year in person and two hundred more on TV and cable. All those unknown players that this unknown man saw in all those unknown places were tucked away in the corners of his memory.

When the big-timers gathered 'round to take him to the cleaners, McKeon just let them keep talking until they began mentioning the raw diamonds they didn't even know they had. Then, one by one, he picked their rich pockets. "Always let the other guy be the first to mention the player you really want."

For thirty-three years McKeon got the dirty jobs: minor-league catcher, coach of every kind, itinerant scout, scouting director, farm director, assistant general manager, field manager in thirteen major- and minor-league cities. That doesn't count the six winters in Arecibo, Puerto Rico. They called him "the mayor of Arecibo" —kind of an inside joke, like being the governor of Siberia. The hot-prospect managers work the Condado strip in San Juan and wear the white dinner jackets in the casinos. Arecibo is poor, remote farming country. But McKeon liked it fine. Kept going back. These days, McKeon wears only one diamond ring, and it's not from a World Series; it's a huge thing with about twenty-five diamonds set in a square that looks like, when it grows up it'll be the first set of diamond brass knuckles. Worth a bundle.

"The people of Arecibo gave it to me when I left," McKeon says proudly.

In Arecibo—and in Lodi and Amarillo and Reading—McKeon learned that he was a man with one true gift: "What I do best is judge talent. But I can't explain it. It's just my guts tellin' me. I can see the talent inside, even when it hasn't come out."

This humble, hard-won knack puts McKeon squarely in the tradition of men who have been at the heart of winning teams. One of the sport's most basic appeals is the degree to which it rewards the creative, conceptualizing work of one guiding brain, or at any rate, a tradition of ingrained organizational intelligence.

In the past quarter century, the only franchises with winning percentages above .550 have been the Orioles (.570), Yankees (.559), Reds (.554) and Dodgers (.553). It's hardly accidental that all four have an organizational "book" on how every technique and fundamental of the sport should be executed; this links the lowest busher with the big leaguers. All except the recent Yankees have been characterized by great patience—never firing managers precipitously, seldom giving up on old stars too quickly and usually working prospects into their lineups in can't-lose situations that bolster confidence.

Countless factors go into a team's success. However, the most important may well be the person or small inner circle of people who nurture the central idea of what the final team on the field should look like. In baseball, any one of many proven approaches to winning will work. But only if the people running the ship have the courage of their convictions.

And that's even rarer than a good idea.

4

OF DICE AND MEN

From all over America—from Washington State to Washington, D.C.—they came to Falls Church, Virginia for the United Baseball League all-star game on Roger Duncan's kitchen table.

Some pitched tents in the backyard. Others slept under the banana tree in Duncan's living room. The brave owner of the Oshkosh Marauders even put his sleeping bag under the poisonous dieffenbachia plant in Duncan's dining room. The travel, cost, inconvenience and even the ridicule of friends were all worth it to be there when Jim Palmer, the thirty-one-game winner of the Nassau Bombers, faced Bert Blyleven, Cy Young winner of the Manhattan Blue Jays.

This was it, the showcase of the United Baseball League, perhaps the most complex, fascinating and obsessive parlor game ever devised. The UBL "sport" is played with two 10-sided dice, cards that rate individual players in every category from "gopherball factor" to frequency of hitting into double plays, and five play charts explaining what each roll of the dice means.

Before anyone snorts, "Ha, just another Monopoly game," one thing should be made clear. UBL is serious business and the UBL's sixteen members, each an owner of a franchise, are arguably the most sophisticated and fanatical baseball fans alive.

Last night, the National Conference manager decided to let

Pete Rose try to stretch a double into a triple because "the outfield grass was wet. We had had a rain delay." In the kitchen?

The first roll of the dice determines if the batter walks. The UBL system naturally takes into consideration the pitcher's control rating, the batter's walk frequency and the pitcher's durability factor at that stage of the game. Wild Nolan Ryan will walk selective Joe Morgan 30 percent of the time (dice numbers 1 to 30), while Mark Fidrych walks Mickey Rivers only 1 percent of the time.

Once in full swing, the UBLers can ask the dice to answer a dozen questions in rapid fashion: Where is the ball hit? How hard? Does the fielder have the range to reach it? Did the relay man bobble the throw? Did the baseman miss the tag?

Say there is an injury at the plate. Which man is hurt? Upper- or lower-body injury? How many days will he be out of league play? When he returns, how much will his efficiency increase with each additional day that he heals? Was it his power or his speed or both that were affected? On a single UBL play, the two ten-sided dice could conceivably be rolled as many as seventeen times, producing an incredible number of ramifications. However, five rolls are about average.

This is no game for kids, not even the most brilliant, but for adults who have at least a thousand hours a year to spend "owning" a team.

Each club, right down to the Creighton Cruisers, has a sixty-man roster, including a triple-A team. Teams draft minor leaguers so far in advance that when Garry Templeton of St. Louis broke onto the major-league all-star scene, the Louisville Chargers of the UBL already had him protected in their system for three years. The UBLers not only serve as owners, general managers and managers for their beloved teams but also act as statisticians, historians, sports reporters and creators of elaborate mythology.

For instance, Ted Simmons, owned by the Nassau Bombers in the UBL, not only batted .318 in 121 games one season but also grounded into fourteen double plays, was hit by four pitches, was caught stealing twice, had ten errors and five passed balls and walked twenty times. Oh yes, he had only one sacrifice bunt.

Such statistics, from balks to bunts to picked-off-first, are kept for 960 players. Every play in the eleven-year history of the UBL is on record. Want to know who led the New York Sultans in batting a decade ago? Carl Yastrzemski—.329.

But all this is just the tip of the iceberg. Every month, the UBL puts out a duplicate of *The Sporting News* which reports on every team, with feature stories and columns. The "owners" are, of course, the sports writers too, building up incredible "histories" that continue from year to year, and now decade to decade.

The gentle, affectionate parodies of *The Sporting News* style are masterpieces. Listen to Blyleven explaining how he lost the fourth game of last year's UBL World Series to the accursed Bombers: "My fast ball wasn't there, and my curve, well you saw what Jackson did with it. Now I've got to listen to all that crap about how I can't win the big one. If we win the next two, I'll show everybody that I don't choke."

Raise goose bumps? It should. The verisimilitude is frightening. The UBL's yearly guide and *Sporting News* imitations have pictures of the UBL players with their major-league uniform insignia erased and UBL insignia in their place. To read the thousands of words written about the Bomber-Blue Jay "fall spectacular," right down to the stirring dateline, "Oyster Bar, Nassau County, Oct. 10," is to believe that this thing happened.

"Don't expect me to say anything about champagne," said Bomber manager Gene Mauch after the fourth series game. "The Jays have stunned Windsor by winning every big game they had to. They could still win three in a row and make me look like a fool."

UBL teams also get into brawls, and players are ejected or suspended. Owners have been known to feud with each other for years over shady trades or questionable use of a relief pitcher. Duncan, host of this year's all-star game, made one rival owner take his sleeping bag to the basement. "Personality conflict, you'd say," he explained.

The feud arose in part because Duncan likes to play a recording of "The Star-Spangled Banner" before the game begins, set off fireworks after his team's homers, and bring in his relief pitcher's card in a tiny bullpen car painted in the Creighton Crusader colors. Duncan even has a toy mule—"Roger W."—modeled after

Charles Finley's "Charlie O," that sits next to him during play. "I just did it for fun," said Duncan, "but I think it got on this guy's nerves."

The UBLers are naturally wary of appearing foolish, since they are all convinced that the world will never quite be ready for them. After all, they have searched the country for years just to come up with sixteen souls with the phenomenal patience and punctuality needed to make a league that is run by mail operate smoothly.

"This is an utterly frivolous hobby," UBL commissioner Steve Lasley said proudly. "Our game is a hybrid . . . the final amalgamation of all the simulated baseball games that have been designed, plus eleven years of our refinements.

"We have fine-tuned our game to the point where it mirrors the major leagues down to the last percentages. That is to say, we've perfected it until it is completely useless and unmarketable."

In recent years, special UBL committees have been formed to investigate the higher mathematics of how they can correct minor flaws in their aggregate year-end league statistics: a few too many errors by third basemen, not quite enough wild pitches, and a real stumper: why big-leaguers hit so many sacrifice flies.

Never fear, it took five years for UBL math whiz Mike Baran to produce a formula relating a pitcher's ability to pitch, with and without men on base, to his ERA. If Baran and his buddies beat that, what chance does a sacrifice fly have?

More touchy are the lengthy meetings at which the defensive range of every player in the majors is discussed.

Since every player's "rating card" is based on the previous season's statistics, UBLers look at current box scores with next year in mind. As if worrying about both past and present were not enough, an owner must give his first priorities to the future: whom will he draft? Thus, every UBL owner actually lives three different games of baseball and is fanatical about each.

"The key to this game is studying the minor leagues," said Duncan. "Every one of us reads *The Sporting News* from back to front so we can study the A and AA leagues in the fine print first. You want to spot the next Willie Mays when he plays for Pulaski and draft him."

In such a world, it is not surprising that Duncan said, "We don't usually explain the game to our families, or to anybody, really . . . Have you ever tried to tell your boss that you're taking a week's vacation to drive a thousand miles to play a dozen face-to-face games against the Boise Barons?"

This weekend's combination all-star game and three-day "convention" is the highlight of the UBL year. "My mom once came to see the convention when it was held at our house," said the wife of the owner of the Cape Cod Hornets. "One guy lost three straight games to the [awful] Wallingford Cubs and he ran into the backyard and dove into a swimming pool with only six inches of water in it.

"Another owner shredded the playing card of Steve Renko and burned it. He said he was going to put the ashes in an envelope and send them to Egypt, back to the owner in Cairo who had talked him into making the trade to get Renko.

"That's when my mother left, saying 'I never saw so many crazy people in my whole life.' "

If the UBL sounds redolent of Kafkaesque fiction, it should. Years ago, novelist Robert Coover wrote a mordant comic fable, *The Universal Baseball Association, Inc., J. Henry Waugh, Prop.* Coover assumed that Waugh—who wavered between fantasy and reality while spending the deep hours of the night playing a game in which every baseball play could be duplicated by a roll of the dice—was a flight of his imagination. Little did Coover know that one Joe Sanchez, a political-science professor at Adelphi University, had fathered the actual UBL two years before, establishing in reality a league that made Coover's wildly fictional one-man UBA seem elementary.

Far from being eccentric, the UBL owners are, in Lasley's words, "addicted game players . . . very orderly and reliable . . . attentive to details, especially administrative details."

Nevertheless, the range of UBL professions stretches from college professor to high school football coach, from music teacher to inspector general of the New York City housing authority. Two owners in Rochester, Washington—Chris and Jeff Snell—are married. They played the famous "Bedroom World Series" of 1972. She won.

One owner devised a way to conduct last year's transcontinental minor-league draft, involving 160 long-distance telephone negotiations for a total bill of $19.60. Let it suffice to say that a typical phone call beginning, "Will you accept a collect call from Mr. Mark Fidrych of Oshkosh?" was a central ingredient.

But the whole day and night of the All-Star game, the phone was off the hook. No disturbances.

"I doubt if I'll sleep tonight," said Tim Janicki, his pup tent standing in the yard. "I've got about thirty-five games scheduled this weekend and they take about forty-five minutes each."

"We've been in the closet so long . . ." Lasley said and grinned. "We don't like to waste these days."

Janicki's daughter, Heather, her head barely as high as the game table, wandered through the room and watched the adults (average age 28.37) bent over their cards, calling out "sixty . . . seventy-two . . . thirty-nine. Possible hit. What's the fielder's range? Diving stab. Pitcher's durability rate going down. Don't I hear a phone ringing in the Hornet bullpen?"

Heather knitted her forehead, then said decisively, "Silly."

The owners of the United Baseball League fell silent and looked at her for a nervous instant. Then they began to laugh. She would have plenty of time to learn.

5.

FROM LITTLE
NAPOLEONS TO
TALL TACTICIANS

When he managed the San Jose Bees, in the Pacific Coast League, Rocky Bridges once said, "There are three things the average man thinks he can do better than anyone else: build a fire, run a hotel and manage a baseball team."

Sometimes it *is* hard to figure out exactly what a baseball manager does that's tougher than rubbing two sticks or handing out a room key. The general manager makes the trades. The scouts find the talent. The owner, or his money, buys the free agents. Coaches and minor-league instructors do the teaching. The pitching coach knows when to change pitchers. Thousands of fans at any game know all the sport's ancient strategies. And the players play. The manager's singular role often seems to be to trudge to the mound, glare at a wild pitcher and growl, "Babe Ruth's dead. *Throw strikes.*"

Sometimes it seems the manager's function is to make himself available to be second-guessed, then, ultimately, fired. He is the useful scapegoat for every loss and, in the end, the sacrificial lamb who pays for the sins of others when defeat becomes intolerable.

Despite this tempting view of the manager as ballast—a sort of human sandbag to be heaved over the side when more altitude is needed—the belief persists among baseball buffs that no job in sports is more likely to reveal a man's basic temperament, his leadership qualities and his judgment under stress than being a major-league manager. Similarly there's a steadfast conviction in big-league dugouts that the manager's style and personality almost always become a part of the team's makeup and performance.

When ballplayers talk about their managers, they're far more likely to discuss the man's soul and psyche than they are his preferences in tactics. A manager embodies qualities, not ideas. Anybody can call for the hit-and-run, but it's almost impossible to con twenty-five men into believing that you have great reserves of patience or determination or baseball judgment if you don't.

Because a manager's character is considered so central to his job, it shouldn't come as a surprise that certain archetypes recur in the sport. As extreme a proposition as it may seem, a strong case can be made that every vividly remembered manager in baseball history has fit into one of four distinct personality types. These four prototypes were locked in place long before the lively ball was ever born. Each generation since World War I has reverently duplicated the typecasting reincarnation.

In the embryonic years before that Great War, when baseball was deciding what to make of itself, three supremely successful and charismatic men defined what a manager ought to be. Even their nicknames were perfect, capturing their characters and giving birth to what have become classic types.

Profane and combustible John McGraw, of the scrappy New York Giants, was the antisocial "Little Napoleon."

Handsome and phlegmatic Frank Chance, of the mighty Chicago Cubs, was the popular Peerless Leader. At age twenty-nine, he won an all-time record of 116 games.

Icy and patrician Connie Mack, of the Philadelphia Athletics, was the forbidding Tall Tactician.

From 1901, when the American League was born, until 1914, McGraw won five pennants, while Chance and Mack each won four. In these early days the World Series was their personal showcase. Before they finished, the members of the trio had twenty-three pennants and were all in the Hall of Fame.

In time, Mack and McGraw finished first and second in career managerial victories; that speaks for itself. Chance's fame has diminished until now he seems just an afterthought, as in Tinker-to-Evers-to-Chance. But in his day he was glamour personified; in his first five full seasons as manager, his Cubs had a .695 winning percentage—the best five-year record ever. When he went to manage the New York Yankees, in '13, the Big Town gave him a Manhattan parade and a huge floral tribute. A Peerless Leader indeed.

One additional type of manager was of course necessary. After all, what did you do when one of these paragons had to be fired? Or when a reasonable facsimile wasn't available? The '02 Orioles solved that problem when they replaced McGraw with lovable and eccentric Wilbert Robinson—the jovial mediocrity known as Uncle Robbie.

Just as the game, over its formative decades, had developed certain narrow concepts of what made a good leadoff man or cleanup hitter, so the sport, perhaps without knowing it, got the notion into its head that Little Napoleons, Peerless Leaders, Tall Tacticians and Uncle Robbies made the best managers. An anthropologist studying an insular subculture would not be surprised if all the chieftains fell into a few set patterns. So why can't baseball have its own little collective unconscious when it comes to picking field bosses?

Let's take a quick time-machine trip and watch how the generations of Napoleons, Leaders, Tacticians and Uncles have succeeded each other.

First, however, since managers don't wear feathers or warpaint, we'll need to know their identifying markings.

Little Napoleons are easy to spot because they usually have their teeth imbedded in an umpire's ankle. Any skipper who is known by his single-digit number ("What does 'No. 1' say?"), who blusters his way out of fights or who sucker-pitches marshmallow salesmen is well on his way to Napoleonhood. This Mugsy McGraw school is usually composed of former infielders of modest talent. Napoleons, as a group, are students of the rule book and incessant talkers. Some actually develop traces of a Napoleonic complex and become hard drinkers.

If the Little Napoleons are the most emotionally complex, the most interesting, the best survivors and frequently the most successful, the Peerless Leader is the most one-dimensional and the most widespread of the breeds. Peerless Leaders can be identified by their profiles. Any manager who folds his arms, clenches his teeth, stares profoundly into the middle distance and looks like a recruiter on a Marine Corps poster is a purebred Peerless.

These imposing fellows, some of whom are unable to speak, are usually former first basemen or outfielders of statuesque batting stance. These men of stoic imperturbability all have reputations for volcanic but restrained tempers which erupt only a handful of times in their lives—usually to the spectacular detriment of proximate inanimate objects. Just as Napoleons, known for having real fistfights in their scrappy youths, learn the wisdom of bluff, so Peerless Leaders seldom have fights, because of their youthful reputations for one-round victories over watercoolers and walls.

Some baseball archivists think that Tacticians, because they are relatively rare, must be a subspecies of the Peerless. This is false.

It is true that the Tactician also folds his arms, clenches his teeth and stares. He, too, sometimes can't speak. Tacticians, however, have that ineffable something called "class." Class serves as a sort of camouflage in their native habitat and keeps them from getting fired, no matter what their record. Tacticians are known for strategic inventions: their five-man infields, their defensive shifts, their bunt-defense plays. Fortunately for them, they are judged more often by reputations than by records.

Uncle Robbies are a snap to spot. They usually have a rumpled, basset-hound look, and the people around them are usually laughing—either at them or with them. Uncle Robbies are almost never what they seem. If they come across as a trifle dumb, then they probably have hidden smarts. Uncle Robbies traditionally have unexpected longevity and success, because they live by the game's Zen-like credo of doing nothing: let 'em play.

Once upon a time, baseball had its originals—McGraw, Chance, Mack and Robinson—as its Napoleon, Leader, Tactician and Uncle. Even in those early, dead-ball days, disciples and duplicates began to appear. Crazy Hughie (Eeee-Yah) Jennings was a McGraw protégé. Fred (Cap) Clarke, as an upright player-manager, was a kind of poor man's Chance. Clark Griffith was cut from the same frugal, crafty cloth as Connie Mack. Only the Uncle Robbie model was slow to develop a clone.

After them there appeared, category by category, Bucky (the Boy Genius) Harris, "Marse Joe" McCarthy, Branch (the Mahatma) Rickey and Charlie (Jolly Cholly) Grimm. They were mirrored in their own day by another quartet: Miller (the Mighty Mite) Huggins, handsome Bill Terry, "Deacon" Bill McKechnie and Chuck Dressen.

Soon new incarnations of the types arrived. Frankie Frisch (the Fordham Flash) and Leo (the Lip) Durocher picked up the tough-guy role. The men's men were Lou Boudreau and Joe Cronin. Tacticians were a trifle scarce, but the ultimate dopey-smart Uncle turned out to be Casey Stengel.

By World War II, it got eerie. Everybody, bar none, fit so perfectly into the Types that it seems they must have had to pass a test.

By the '50s, the names rolled over again, but the Types remained eternal. We had those twin pests Eddie Stanky and Bobby Bragan, he-man Fred Hutchinson (who smashed all the light bulbs in his clubhouse bare-handed), severely intellectual Paul Richards and new Uncles like Billy Southworth, Birdie Tebbetts and Jimmy Dykes.

By now, any true screwball fan should be addicted to the search. "Who's next?" you say.

Try out Alvin (Blackie) Dark, from Comanche, Oklahoma, as your would-be Napoleon. Walter Alston arrives as the pluperfect Peerless Leader. Gene Mauch stakes his claim as the nonpareil, brilliant, win-nothing Tactician and Danny Murtaugh, in his rocking chair with a glass of milk, is the Uncle.

If you don't like that last quartet, how about: firebrand Solly Hemus, war hero "Major" Ralph Houk, sober professor-of-pitching "Señor" Al Lopez and (the Uncles never end) Sam Mele and Fred Haney.

As we get deep into the '60s, we find that old 1890s Oriole Mugsy McGraw has been replaced by his karmic double, Earl Weaver. What more Peerless Leader could we want than rugged Gil Hodges? Bill (Specs) Rigney gets his Tactician's stripes by retiring with a reputation for brains despite getting fired six times and finishing above third place only twice in eighteen seasons. For Unclehood, Mayo Smith, Herman Franks, and Red Schoendienst will do nicely.

Now we switch the projector to fast-forward for the past decade.

Of Little Napoleons we have no shortage: Billy (the Kid) Martin, Sparky Anderson, feisty Dick Howser and Dave Bristol.

In the strong-silent, occasionally intimidating Peerless Leader role, we find Chuck Tanner, Dick Williams, Dallas Green, Joe Torre and Darrell Johnson. You could remake *The Guns of Navarone* with these guys.

Even the sometimes sparse Tactician ranks are graced by dignified John McNamara, with his sub-.500 career record, and horn-rimmed Bill Virdon, both of whom are considered crack minds despite never reaching a Series.

For Uncles, we have a full family-reunion supply with lovable George Bamberger, corny-crafty Tommy Lasorda, tell-me-your-troubles Joe Altobelli, comatose Bob Lemon, folksy Harvey Kuenn, out-to-lunch Danny Ozark and the gerbil of record, Don Zimmer. They all come across as terminally dim; some are, a couple definitely aren't.

Even the newest faces find their places.

The day tough Tony LaRussa cursed Ron LeFlore in the clubhouse, then invited him into his office and locked the door behind them, he became an heir to the Peerless Chance, who was so adamant about *not* moving his head out of the way of fastballs that he was beaned repeatedly and died at the age of forty-five.

Steve Boros, of Oakland, with his degree in English literature from Michigan and his ever-present stopwatch, has a chance to become a Tactician. And Altobelli is a sweetheart of an Uncle.

The obvious question at this point is, How many important managers *don't* fit into these four types? In our double-time march through the game's history, how many major managerial figures have we had to finesse because they couldn't be positively identified as Napoleons, Leaders, Tacticians or Uncles?

Since 1900, forty-two skippers have managed to stay employed for ten full seasons (i.e., fifteen hundred games). These are the men who have defined the profession.

Of these forty-two well-known managers, *two* have not been listed above.

They're Lee Fohl and Steve O'Neill, gentlemen best lost in the mists of time.

At this point, it should be noted that the existence of a fifth discernible group of managers has been suppressed out of kindness: superstars.

Plenty of "stars" like Boudreau, Schoendienst, Lemon, Frisch, Hodges, Cronin or Terry have made the transition to long or respectable managerial careers.

But, of the "immortals"—the men who get three thousand hits or five hundred homers or three hundred wins, not one has left a significant mark as a manager. Ty Cobb, Tris Speaker, Ted Williams, Rogers Hornsby, Walter Johnson, Nap Lajoie, Eddie Mathews, Christy Mathewson, Frank Robinson and Mel Ott—to name ten such fellows—managed in the majors a total of sixty-one seasons (after zero years of minor-league experience); they won two pennants among them.

Now, as at a masked ball, it's time for these caricatures to take off their outward costumes and reveal their true natures. We have not really been talking about Little Napoleons, Peerless Leaders, Tall Tacticians, Uncle Robbies and immortals. Those are just masks. What lies behind them?

By a Little Napoleon, we mean a man of intensity, emotion and competitive drive. In a word, we mean a person of passion.

By a Peerless Leader, we mean a man of discipline, honesty, courage and dignity. In other words, we mean a person of character.

By a Tall Tactician, we mean a man of savvy, judgment and raw intelligence. We mean a person with brains.

By an Uncle Robbie, we mean a man with compassion, humor and a sympathetic understanding of others. In other words, we mean a person with wisdom.

By an immortal, we mean a man with physical genius plus, probably, abnormal ambition and, certainly, athletic arrogance. We mean a person with charisma.

What we have been sniffing at is a shopping list of idealized

human virtues. In fact, we've almost exhausted the whole highfa-
lutin catalog.

The question here is one of degree. When we call McGraw,
Durocher, Frisch, Martin, Weaver and their like "Little Napoleons," we mean that, in their time, the quality for which each was
best known was his inordinate passion. In some cases, of course, a
man's central virtue may also be his central flaw. The best managers, it might be argued, have been those who, while having one
conspicuous characterizing trait, were also strong in other managerial areas.

To be great, a manager certainly needs a trump suit—whether it
be passion, brains, character or wisdom. But to an almost equal
degree, a manager—or should we say a person—needs to achieve
a balance in his "off" suits. He must cultivate secondary strengths
while compensating for his weaknesses.

For illustration, let's look at four famous managers of recent
times, each of whom comes fairly close to embodying one of our
four prototypes: Napoleonic Billy Martin, Leader Whitey Herzog,
Tactician Gene Mauch and Uncle Tommy Lasorda.

Seldom has a man done so little with so much as Billy Martin,
the best manager God never made. This is a fellow who, if we
judge him by his depth of passion and breadth of baseball brains,
was meant to be a Hall of Fame manager.

No skipper of his era has approached his ability to bring competitive fire to dormant teams; no known collection of deadbeats
has been beyond Martin's powers of inspiration and intimidation.
In Minnesota, Detroit, Texas, New York and Oakland—so far—
he inherited mediocre-to-awful teams that needed a life-support
system to stand up for the National Anthem. All five clubs became carnivores under his hand. Players always draw upon their
manager's qualities in inverse proportion to their lack of them.

No manager has taught the techniques of "inside baseball" half
so well, or had such a visceral feeling for using the right tactic at
the psychologically proper moment. In the three areas of baseball
brains—judgment of talent, game strategy and analysis of statistics—Martin is a master of the first two and competent in the
third.

To Martin's credit, there is no such thing as Billy ball. There is only baseball. And Martin teaches whatever chapters in that total text serve him best. "Martin's teams don't have any particular style," says Weaver, looking at Martin's whole career. "That's why he's so good. The first thing you notice is that no two of his teams are alike."

It's said that the surest proof of sincerity is craftsmanship. The proof of Martin's sincere affection for baseball is his consummate knowledge of every aspect of the game. Where others saw mediocrity, Martin brought forth sluggers, twenty-five-game winners, relief monsters, Gold Gloves, .300 hitters and speedsters.

What makes Martin's life a continual tragedy-in-progress is the total imbalance in his complex nature. If he ranks first among managers in passion and brains, then he may rank last in his profession in character and wisdom. "Billy understands baseball, but he doesn't understand life," Weaver once said, commiserating rather than judging.

Billy the Kid's personality runs on iron rails. Once the track is chosen, there is no way to swerve or go back. An absolutist in almost everything, Martin treats his players, his bosses, his interviewers and his public just the way he treats a pitcher who must be relieved. "When I go to the mound," he says with relish, "we don't have a discussion. I tell 'em."

In all his offices, Martin hangs a sign that reads: "Company Rules—Rule 1: The boss is always right. Rule 2: If the boss is wrong, see Rule 1."

As a consequence of this intemperance, Martin has never made it to Year IV of any job. It is always a close race whether he'll collide with the owner, the front office, the press or a few key players.

The idea has taken shape seven different times that victory may not be worth the price if the price is Billy Martin. Victory is all that Martin promises, all that makes him tolerable. When he doesn't win, he's gone fast.

Why is Martin so hard to swallow? Because he lacks all the qualities of a leader or an uncle. Martin is grossly lacking in self-discipline. Often he's the last man to get to the park. He hasn't time to be a handler of men, because he has his hands full handling himself. Martin's reputation for dishonesty with his players is legendary; at every stop his exodus has been followed by player complaints that "Billy lied to me."

Also, Martin is close to compulsive about shifting blame; no loss is even partly his fault. After the last game of the '76 Series, in which his Yankees were swept in four games, Martin was at his most unappealing. He sat at his desk crying and blamed umpire Bill Deegan for calling a "brutal game," said Deegan was unqualified to work the Series, and even charged that Deegan had tossed three balls at him in the dugout, once hitting him in the chest. That's paranoia full-blown.

As Martin's situation gradually deteriorates, all his persecution symptoms repeat themselves. His pinched, fever-blistered lips clench tighter, his Durante nose juts defiantly and his eyes dart suspiciously. Victory has been bought at the cost of innocent pleasure. Progressively, his mood sinks toward an unrelieved caustic melancholy.

What makes Martin so poignant is his childlike chagrin. One day in 1982, Martin arrived at the park with a wooden splint on one finger and bandages on two others. The night before, he'd locked himself in for ninety minutes and gone ten rounds with his Oakland office. Don Quixote tilted at windmills; Martin fights rooms. The office won.

"I'm getting smarter as I get older," Martin said, almost plaintively. "I finally punched something that couldn't sue me."

Later, sitting in his office, Martin asked Oakland team president Roy Eisenhardt if he wanted a drink.

"Anything but wine," said Eisenhardt.

"You won't let me forget that, will you?" said Martin.

"It's not everybody whose lady orders a three-hundred-dollar bottle of wine," said Eisenhardt.

"She just has good taste," Martin said of his companion.

"Yes," said Eisenhardt, "but I didn't know she was going to order it for all ten tables. Take Billy Martin to dinner and you get a three-thousand-dollar wine bill."

Martin, now in a mood that makes him so charming you can't believe you ever shivered when you met him, says to his boss, "Roy, you know what [infielder] Dave McKay did before the game? He walks through the dugout with all ten fingers taped up in splints."

Martin started to laugh, his giggle building until he had to put his head on his desk. "Then," gasped Martin, looking at his own bandaged hands, "McKay says, 'Hey, skip, wanna go bowling tonight?' "

Eisenhardt laughed until they were both crying.

Three months later, Martin was fired for the sixth time.

Martin might well explain his plight as one of Turgenev's tragic characters did: "I could not simplify myself."

While Martin is the most imbalanced of recent managerial personalities, Whitey Herzog is exactly the opposite. The White Rat is the most well-rounded and hard-to-characterize of baseball's modern skippers.

At first glance, Herzog seems a prototypical Peerless Leader. He's a barrel-chested, two-hundred-pound former AL outfielder who has blow-dried haystack hair and rugged good looks that go well on magazine covers. Herzog is slow-talkin' and can do a good imitation of a smoldering volcano when it suits his purposes. Herzog demands team discipline and once dragged Garry Templeton into the dugout bodily after he made obscene gestures at the home St. Louis crowd. Herzog then fined, suspended, chastised and traded the spectacularly talented Templeton in an impressive show of authority and self-confidence. "Somebody in our society has to draw the line somewhere, and I'm drawing it here," said Herzog. The next season, Herzog won the world title with Ozzie Smith, not Templeton, at short. In an era when many managers are terrified of their rich players, it was an unprecedented vindication of a strong, principled leader.

Herzog is considered a blunt straight-talker by his players. Because he's been everything from a player to a farm director to a general manager, his respect within the game is large. He's perhaps the only manager in history who could eventually be mentioned as a serious candidate for commissioner. Unlike almost any other manager, Herzog isn't the least bit shy about voicing his opinions, some controversial. He suggests rule changes, takes stands on labor relations and revenue sharing. He's called George

Steinbrenner "completely without integrity." And he'll even blast the sport's unmentioned deity—the great money god of national TV—saying that scheduling playoff games in the twilight to suit TV makes a farce of the game.

If this guy isn't Peerless, who is? He even wins, compiling the best percentage in his division five times in seven years, from '76 through '82.

However, what makes Herzog special, and what in time may make him one of the game's great managers, is his ability to play the Napoleon, the Tactician and especially the Uncle, when it's necessary.

Almost every manager of recent times, even the best, has been a complete void in at least one of these areas. For instance, Earl Weaver has all the passion and brains you could ask; he was a Napoleon outside, an innovative stat-freak Tactician inside. In fact, Weaver's judicious baseball brains made him one of the few Napoleons who could resist overmanaging.

In the character department, Weaver was always dead honest, even though his occasionally childish temper and his after-hours penchant for drunk-driving citations sometimes eroded his respect among players. To his debit, Weaver was almost devoid of sympathetic Uncle qualities, delegating the duties of clubhouse compassion to his senior coaches. In a dugout, he found fire and friendship incompatible and thought any manager who tried to meld them was a soon-to-be-unemployed sap.

Herzog sometimes seems to be two people. The three-piece-suit public man is a wheeler-dealer, a celebrity and perhaps even something of an owner-pleasing, apple-polishing con artist. However, with a fishing rod or golf club in his hand, or with his stockinged feet up on his desk and a cigar in his mouth, Herzog is a tall-tale teller, a smart-ass, a needler. He has the rare ability to relax with the people he must boss. Herzog finds it natural to know every member of his team's family and, it seems, their state of health; they're convinced he cares.

By contrast, Weaver, like Dick Williams, knew nothing about his players' private lives. Once, Weaver used Sammy Stewart after Stewart had been up all night as his wife had their first child. In a World Series, Weaver used Mike Flanagan in pointless mop-up relief just hours after Flanagan's wife had had a miscarriage—something Flanagan's family never forgot, nor completely forgave.

With time, it will be interesting to see if Herzog's kaleidoscope personality wears well in one locale, or whether he will, as he has in the past, change job descriptions and organizations every few years . . . usually, it should be noted, to move up the game's totem pole to greater success.

Trim and hard as a man in his mid-fifties can be, and dressed in black from head to toe, Gene Mauch, with his steel-gray hair and his steel-blue eyes, looks like a figure from Zane Grey—the Rancho Mirage Kid in late middle age.

Then, in a twinkling, Mauch puts on a cheerful red plaid sports coat and suddenly he is transformed from a hawk-eyed man of menace into the most dapper and agreeable of grandfathers.

Being around Mauch is like being around a pearl-handled knife. The exterior is elegant and expensive—one of its kind and classy. But a sharpness, like the point of a knife, is always glinting in Mauch's eyes. His famous destroy-everything-in-sight temper is part of it. The larger force, however, is his blade edge of mental sharpness. To Mauch, baseball is high-speed chess with human pieces. A half hour after a game, his metabolism is still racing, his mind still at 1,000 rpm. He sucks cigarettes voraciously, his eyelids dance, he cannot stay still.

In chess, there are masters, like Paul Morphy in the middle of the nineteenth century, who, although of the first rank, showed their most brilliant efforts only when they were desperately outmanned. Playing a "handicap game" without their queen, or saving a supposedly lost tactical position, was their forte, their way into the chess anthologies.

Mauch is the baseball equivalent—a strategic purist so in love with the subtleties of his game that he might rather take a last-place team and finish fourth than waltz to a pennant with the '27 Yankees. For nearly forty years, man and boy and now silver eminence, Mauch has played and managed the game for the game itself. In a century, there's never been a case like Mauch's, where it's difficult to decide if a man is the best of managers or one of the worst.

Mauch seems to have every managerial strength. His passion is legendary. "Your worst day as a manager," he's said, "is when you realize *you* care more than *they* do." He also looks the leader. In a profession of job-hopping, tobacco-chewing, ungrammatical men whose dignity is continually ground down, Mauch can seem as out of place as a prince.

Above all, Mauch lives the game at a level of detail perhaps never before reached—some would say which never *needed* to be reached. He has pitch-by-pitch records, box scores and personal notes on every game he's managed back to 1961. And they are not kept in an attic. "Oh, I look back at those notebooks all the time," he says, "especially in the winter . . . You wake up at 4 A.M. and can't sleep. It's fun remembering and reliving."

A copious Mauch sheet on an old midseason Minnesota game: "As good as [pitcher Paul] Hartzell can do it—strike, strike, strike. Worked inside enuff to help him away. Breaking ball needs a little more tilt. Was in hurry to get game over in ninth. Just strikes—no particular location. All fast balls and up. Think down when edge goes from velocity."

With all this, how to explain Mauch's record? His .473 career percentage is an embarrassment. His teams have won a division flag once, finished second once, finished third once, and ended up fourth or lower twenty times. Ever since his '64 Phillies blew the pennant, losing ten straight, Mauch has lived in a self-imposed purgatory; he flares at any mention of the Fold, like a shamed captain who has ignobly survived a wreck in which all hands were lost.

Two explanations have been offered for Mauch's record.

Friends say he brought home mediocre-to-bad teams well ahead of predictions. To romantics who like outgunned generals with exotic battle plans, Mauch has made a career of being Robert E. Lee with his supply lines cut.

His detractors contend Mauch is the consummate overmanager. Weaver says tartly, "Play for one run, lose by one run . . . Over a season, three-run homers beat 'inside' baseball every time."

The Mauch melodrama had its denouement in 1982. Throughout that season, Mauch managed as he always had, though his Angel lineup had stars like Fred Lynn, Rod Carew and Reggie Jackson. True to his lights, Mauch endangered big innings with bunts; his Halos led the league in sacrifices. He juggled the lineup, cooking up seventy combos in one season; some called his lineups a Mauchery. And, as always, he was impatient with his pitching, sticking with hot hands at the risk of burning them out while forsaking slumpers quickly.

Finally, in the playoffs, Mauch was one win from the Series. "Pressure is the emotion I get when I think of the people who care about me and how they'll feel if I lose," said Mauch then. "I don't lead the world in friends, but I have enough so that I don't want them disappointed."

In the last three playoff games, he stuck with every Mauch MO, letting his personal history repeat itself as though a career's vindication were at stake. In '64, Mauch pitched Bunning and Short five times with one less day of rest than usual; Philly lost all five. In '82, Mauch used John and Kison with one less day of rest than usual. As the hard-eyed world knows, the Angels became the first team to blow a pennant playoff after leading two games to none. Before the Series was over, Mauch was fired.

Historians might have suspected as much. Cornelius McGillicuddy managed fifty-three years and was 249 games under .500. Clark Griffith won a pennant as a rookie, then never again in twenty years. Branch Rickey didn't get a whiff of first or second place as a manager. So it always goes with Tacticians.

Perhaps the moral of Mauch's career is that, of the basic managerial gifts—passion, character, brains and wisdom—the least valuable, at least as a guiding virtue, is intelligence. In baseball, as in the rest of life, brains make a good servant but a poor master.

Who says the unexamined life is not worth living? Not Tommy Lasorda, the man whose Dodger Blue monologues make *The Power of Positive Thinking* sound like a suicide note. Lasorda, baseball's best-loved hyperbolist, is a mint-quality specimen of the genial Uncle Robbie.

Come October, it's the success of managers like Lasorda (who's the complete inverse of Mauch) which makes fans wonder if we've really got a fix on the nature of a manager's job. If you came into Lasorda's office with the most elaborate statistical or theoretical tome, he'd grin at you, throw your theories in the trash can and howl, "What the fuck is this? Hey, relax and have some of this clam linguini. Say, have you met Don Rickles? Come here, Don. I want you to meet the greatest sports fan [or greatest sportscaster, greatest sportswriter or greatest gravedigger] who ever lived. I mean the fuckin' best ever . . ."

Lasorda raises a disturbing question: Is it possible that a manager is above all a glorified cruise director whose central function is to establish and maintain a ball club's day-to-day tone?

The portly pietist makes it seem that way. His gift is the ability to take a top-dollar, talent-soaked club and keep it relatively content for eight months. His appointed task is to make everyone in his vicinity smile at all times. Just as a test, walk around his clubhouse for a few minutes looking like your dog just died. The third time his eye catches yours, he'll track you down, then cheer you up. Lasorda thinks frowns are more contagious in a dugout than Legionnaires' disease. His solution to inheriting the most glum-looking player in baseball—perpetually morose Burt Hooton—was to rename him "Happy" Hooton.

Visit Dodgerland in Vero Beach in spring training (of '82) and there's Lasorda removing sawdust from his hair, eyes, nostrils and from deep inside his floppy ears. "You see what those fuckin' guys did to me?" he says plaintively, dropping his pants and exhuming enough sawdust for a lion's litter box. "I was showin' 'em how to slide in the pit [spit, spit] and they all jumped on me and covered me with this shit. [Sneeze.] Jesus H. Christ, I hate sawdust. [Cough, cough.]

"Is this any way for the champions of the whole fuckin' world to act?" he announces, feigning fury so well that unless you've seen his act dozens of times, it's hard to know if he's really mad.

"Here's Jay Johnstone, America's guest," continues Lasorda, spotting the various culprits with whom he must square accounts. "All winter long, you'd think this guy was Lou Gehrig. He was at every function. 'Our guest today is the man who hit that pinch home run in the 1981 World Series, the guy that helped the Dodgers to the pennant, Mr. Jay Johnstone.'

"The big dumb cocksucker got seventeen hits the whole year. Shit, Hooton had ten. Johnstone's the only guy who ever parlayed seventeen hits into a fortune . . .

"And here's Rick Monday, the man who hit the Home Run That Won the Pennant," Lasorda thunders as the team, half-listening, giggles. "If Monday meets three guys in the men's room, he thinks it's an interview. 'Well, it was a high fastball and at first I didn't know if I got it at all, but . . .' The poor guy's been washed up for *years*. We're carrying his ass out of the goodness of our hearts.

"So what does this motherfucker do?" bellows Lasorda. "He shoves *sawdust* in his manager's *ears.*"

Former Oriole Mark Belanger wanders past the scene, rolls his eyes, starts laughing like he's eight years old, not thirty-eight, and says, "It was never like this with Earl."

But it's always like this with Lasorda. In a rich, stuffy franchise like the Dodgers, rife with organization men, a borderline screwball like Lasorda can be a godsend. What the public sees and hears are Lasorda's bear hugs, his platitudes, his celebrity hobnobbing and his obliviousness to the niceties of technical baseball. With his calculated bonhomie, his practiced epigrams, his religious Dodger cheerleading, Lasorda has somehow made the most blatant insincerity palatable. It has something to do with his face. You can't practice a twinkle in the eye. Lasorda just has it.

He wants you to laugh. He wants you to have some more lasagna. And he wants you to go out tonight and play hardball. The unexamined life, it's wonderful.

Basically, that's how all the Uncle Robbies approach their task: as though a game, a pennant race, a World Series with eighty million people watching, a drama with a lifetime of wealth and fame hanging in the balance, weren't a task at all, but the greatest fun, the biggest circus imaginable.

It's a profound con that works more often than it seems it should. Year after year, we see Lasorda or Lemon or Kuenn or Murtaugh or Altobelli in the World Series, or a Bamberger, Ozark or Zimmer easy-riding his team to ninety-five or more wins. And every year we scratch our heads and wonder whom the joke is on.

The problem, you see, is that it's hard to tell the quality Uncle Robbies from the frauds. By comparison, it doesn't take long to weed out the lousy Napoleons—the Eddie Stankys, Frank Lucchesis and Maury Willses who act like Mickey Rooney on speed. And the poor-imitation Peerless Leaders, like Darrell Johnson, can't keep falling out of trees and landing on their feet. But a second-rate Uncle Robbie, once entrenched, can bring a Series-quality club home in second place year after year, as Ozark, Zimmer and Jim Fanning have recently proved.

Uncle Robbies survive by a sort of unconscious reverse psychology. They appear to be so blissfully dim, dribbling tobacco juice on their shoes, that everyone assumes they must really be closet wizards, since nobody as doltish as they appear to be could find the ballpark 162 consecutive times.

Uncles often specialize in goofy parables and tall tales of dubious profundity; such yarns set a campfire tone, as though they were the elders passing down the lore of the tribe. For instance, Danny Murtaugh loved to tell an anecdote about his mentor and manager Billy Southworth.

One spring training in his playing days, Murtaugh and roommate Ernie White spent an entire night finding ways to distribute seven hundred dollars that Murtaugh had won at the track. They reported unshaven to the ballpark next day without ever returning to their roadside motel room.

"Have a good night's sleep, fellows?" asked manager Southworth.

"Sure, skip," fibbed Murtaugh. "Like babies."

"That's good," said Southworth. "I was afraid you might have been disturbed by the tractor-trailer that crashed through your room in the middle of the night."

Murtaugh told this story with such conviction, sitting in his office rocking chair and sipping milk to pacify his ulcer, that no one seemed to want to know whether the tale might be apocryphal. Uncles are experts at glossing over such details when it serves them. Once, when Don Zimmer was discovered in his office *six hours* before game time, he double-talked his way around whether he might have mistaken a night game for a day game. "I just want to make sure nobody's in my uniform," retorted the always-about-to-be-fired Zimmer.

Many a fan has wished that he might sneak into such a uniform. After all, if a novice like Paul Owens can end up managing in the World Series, who's to say what manner of impostor might not pass undiscovered if he mumbles sagely?

What other job which is so coveted has such vague requirements and so few minimum requisites? And what other task in baseball, once undertaken, is so all-consuming and weathering, such a proven man-eater? Weaver retired at fifty-one. Martin should have. Bamberger quit, then came back, then quit again. Mauch, still the prime age for most jobs, can't face returning to the dugout.

Perhaps the White Rat should give a course in avoiding such burnout.

Among current managers, perhaps Herzog alone enjoys the job while also remaining its master. In his dugout, he's a man in his element. Thumbs in his belt, stomach confidently thrust forward, Herzog spits a little Red Man in the red clay before him. It's the spring of '83 and his team is the Cards, but it could be any season and any team as far as Herzog is concerned. He rarely lets winning or losing faze him; the game tastes too good to him, and the joy of battle is too sharp for anything to spoil his pleasure. Perhaps he has his own, private way of keeping score.

At this moment, pitcher Bob Forsch has just hit a home run. "You see why I let him hit," crows Herzog to his bench. "I had to talk that man into goin' up there." When Forsch returns to the dugout, Herzog ignores the celebration until, eventually, he catches Forsch's eye. "What was that," says the bored Herzog, "a home run?" The next time the pitcher is due to hit, Herzog sends up a pinch hitter, saying to Forsch, "Sit down. I can't stand to watch you hit another one. It's embarrassing to my other players."

Forsch exits and Bruce Sutter enters, throwing his split-finger fastball. One perfect pitch drops a foot, leaving a young Philadelphia hitter agape; the kid has just seen as unhittable a pitch as baseball has ever offered. Herzog can't resist. "Give him that good

one now," Herzog snaps at Sutter like a drill sergeant. The Cards
snicker behind their hands. The rookie, perhaps wondering what
in the world "the good one" might look like, takes strike three.
The Cardinals laugh out loud.

When Herzog's favorite part-timer, Dane Iorg, a .297 career
hitter, gets a seeing-eye hit, Herzog mutters affectionately, "Hit
the ball right, Dane Iorg. Damn eight-hoppers up the middle . . .
And you think we're not gettin' smarter."

When it's mentioned that his Cards always tag up at second
base on routine long flies, Herzog says for cryptic explanation,
"They don't drop too many flyballs in this league, do they?"

Herzog, who's dreamed about managing since he listened to
Babe Ruth's radio show on Saturday mornings as a kid, claims
they'll have to tear the uniform off him, that he relishes bad seasons almost as much as good ones. His '79 Royals once lost fourteen of fifteen, which got Herzog fired, but the Rat insists, "I
managed my ass off to keep us in the race until the last week. We
even set an attendance record, and I enjoyed it." Then as now a
typical Herzog summer day begins with a 6 A.M. wake-up, three
hours of fishing or a rapid round of dew-sweeping golf, a late
breakfast, then a good nap before heading to the ballpark in the
afternoon. "First things first," he says.

Once, asked how he could use an off-day before the sixth game
of the Series to fish in the morning, play golf in the afternoon and
give his team a complete day off, Herzog shrugged and said,
"Weatherman says it'll be a nice day."

If any quality unites the best managers, it is this breezy, inexplicable and almost unshakable self-confidence. For instance, Herzog
thought (and said) that it would be good for baseball if the American League, after losing nineteen times in twenty years, won the
Golden Anniversary All-Star game in 1983. So Herzog, managing
the NL team, did his best to make sure the other guys won.

With a yawn, Herzog left Steve Carlton, Nolan Ryan, Tom
Seaver and Sutter off his pitching staff, while sending nervous kids
Atlee Hammaker, Pascual Perez and Lee Smith to the mound,
where all were shelled. No one will ever prove Herzog tanked an
All-Star game, perhaps with the blessing of the game's brass, but

his sly postgame smile was a cheerful piece of incriminating evidence.

However the traces of Napoleon, Leader, Tactician and Uncle may be woven into a manager's personality, one trait is essential: that rare appetite for making difficult and public decisions with millions looking over your shoulder.

"Don't hold back. If you're going to do something, then do it. Don't apologize. Lose it your way or win it your way," says Herzog. Then instinctively Herzog thinks back to the worst moment of his career: the ninth inning of the fifth game of the '77 playoffs against the Yanks, when his Royals had a one-run lead until he played a hunch and lost a pennant.

"Damn," says Herzog, "I'd still bring in Dennis Leonard."

6.
LIVES OF
NOISY DESPERATION

Major-league umpires know that when the argument gets too hot, when the veins in the neck get too pronounced, they always have one last recourse to settle all disputes. "When in doubt," drawls American League umpire Durwood Merrill, "it's always Rule 9.01 (c). That's the one that says, 'Use common sense.'"

Words to live by.

Unfortunately, many an umpire, as his years of service mount, wonders if any man with common sense would ever become an umpire. Umpires lead lives of noisy desperation. Sometimes they wake up in the night screaming. "I roomed with an umpire in the minors who woke me up at four o'clock in the morning," says American League umpire Mike Reilly. "He was standing in the middle of his bed, yelling, 'You're out. You're out. And I don't want to hear any more about it.'"

Of all the men on a baseball field, umpires are the most watched and the least comprehended. Umpires are thus a breed known only to themselves. "I worked with an ump in the Northern League," says AL arbiter Ken Kaiser, grinning, "and I was the only one who knew that he had a glass eye."

An umpiring crew may be the closest fraternity on earth. "We're four men controlling forty thousand people, most of whom aren't so sure they want to be controlled," says the most famous of recent umps, clown prince Ron Luciano. "We're men with huge egos, huge wills. My ex-wife says we're all mindbenders. Many times, I've known I was dead wrong, but I convinced millions of people I was right in a split second."

Umpires are masters of bleak humor, sarcasm and repartee. Like the smart-aleck shamus versus the cynical cop in fiction, the ump and the ballplayer go around and around eternally, trying to one-up each other with barbed dialogue. Bill Haller, an ump for twenty-five years, recalls the night Baltimore first baseman Eddie Murray asked him, after a pickoff play, "Bill, would he have been out if I'd tagged him?" "Well," drawled Haller, "you'd have had a better chance."

Umpires do not expect any of this to change. Nightmares will always be an occupational hazard. Their eyesight will always be maligned as crowds demand their heads. They'll never be certain which night Billy Martin will start a bumping contest or Bill Madlock will decide to rub his glove in their faces. They know they have no protection. From that black day in '82 when Earl Weaver punched Terry Cooney in the face, then got off with a five-day suspension, no ump has doubted that he was fair game for almost any abuse.

Perhaps no man without a trace of masochism could become a big-league umpire. "We're always like the first cop at the scene of the crime," says Kaiser. "We see people when they're on their worst behavior. Don't ask us our opinion of human nature."

"Every night, we have to meet a challenge with a TV camera looking over our shoulders," another umpire says. "And believe me, when you've had two open dates in two months, you don't always feel like being challenged . . . The road can drive you crazy. Counting spring training, we may work two hundred games a year, AND EVERY ONE IS ON THE ROAD. An umpire never has a home stand."

"I once went four months—from March 3 to June 28—without seeing my wife one time. I remember the dates because, on June 29, we decided to get a divorce. This job is perfect for broken marriages and alcoholism," Luciano once said. A year later, not yet forty-five, Luciano "retired" from umpiring. He'd had the ruined marriage. He didn't want the rest.

"The first five years I was in the majors, my four sons never got to see me," says ump Lou DiMuro. "I'd try to catch a plane home for a few hours, then hop back out to the next town. The kids at school asked my oldest boy what I did for a living. He was real proud. He told 'em, 'My daddy works at the airport.' "

Few families approach the closeness of four umpires. "We're married to each other," Haller once said. They have to be. Otherwise, they'd have to endure seven months in itinerant solitary confinement—traveling thousands of miles amid millions of people, yet knowing nobody better than they know the next cab driver. Umpires are constantly in the presence of ballplayers, yet almost never speak to them off the field. Though they've known each other for years, they're strangers every time they meet. Even a coffee-shop breakfast between umps and players would be a scandal. "I had one beer in twelve years with one player: Rod Carew," says Luciano.

Of all the characters in the game, umpires are the most isolated. Search out the umpires' room in the bowels of a stadium—no identifying mark is on the door—and knock. The four faces inside will look at you with shock when you enter. In their netherworld, no one knows where they are, much less searches them out. And no one chooses to talk with them unless they've got a beef. The greeting, if they recognize you, is almost painfully warm, as though they can't believe anyone would ask them anything. Compared to the I'm-young-strong-and-rich hauteur of even mediocre players, the humility of umpires makes you want to cry.

If you walk into the umpires' cubbyhole and are on a first-name basis with one or two of them, the others look at you as though you're from Mars. The plain fact is that a major-league umpire is unsettled when he's treated with common courtesy. The camaraderie among arbiters exists because no one outside their fraternity begins to understand why they do what they do. Sometimes when they lose hold of the "why" they have to remind each other.

"I was in the minors for thirteen years," Ken Kaiser told me while he, Luciano and Reilly had a postmidnight crab-and-beer fest in Baltimore. "I thought about quitting fifty thousand times, like we all do. In my last year in the minors ('76), I was making six hundred and fifty dollars—a MONTH, not a week. That's for five months a year. Just try to get an off-season job. It's murder. I was everything from a pro wrestler, to a used-car salesman, to a bouncer in a bar. I tried to get an American Express card and they laughed at me. They told me I could make more money on welfare."

"You tolerate the minors because you dream of the majors," says former National League ump Steve Fields, who spent eleven years in the bushes. "In my first year, in the Midwestern League, I made five hundred dollars a month. In Cedar Rapids, the other ump and I would share a four-dollar-a-night room by the railroad tracks next to the Ralston Purina factory. No bathroom, no fan . . . so hot at night you had to keep the window open. The stink and smoke and whistles were unbelievable.

"Even in '78, when I was the *highest-paid* ump in the minors, I was only making about ten thousand dollars a year, plus whatever you get in the off-season in winter ball. What kind of salary is that for a thirty-seven-year-old man with eleven years' experience in his profession?"

Those extra dollars from South American winter ball come hard: ever think what happens when a gringo ump blows a call in Caracas? "In Mayagüez, in Puerto Rico, Terry Cooney and I opened our dressing-room door after a game and two guys with machine guns said, 'Come with us.' One look at that crowd and we didn't even ask where we were going. We just went . . . We got an escort halfway around the island [to dodge the crowd]."

Ballplayers dress quickly, their aggressions and frustrations washed away by the daily balm of sweat. Umpires dress slowly, culling the day's decisions, exonerating each other, since no one else will. "You develop an aggressive sort of defensiveness," says Kaiser. "An umpire will only take criticism from another umpire . . . In the off-season, my family teases me and tells me, 'Okay, calm down now. You don't have to tell us all what to do. You don't have to yell. You're not on the ball field.' "

Often the most important part of an umpire's day comes after the game, even after midnight. Those are the hours of forgetting. "You can't 'leave the game in the clubhouse' when you go, like they say," says Reilly. "When you come back the next day and open the door, it'll be right in there waiting for you." So umpires are great talkers, exorcising pain through storytelling and heated debate. That is the antidote for being constantly misunderstood.

"If we didn't have each other to talk to, we'd go crazy," says Kaiser. "Most people just have no conception of what you do. You say, 'I'm a major-league umpire.' So they say, 'Oh, how nice. With which team?' That's when you know it's hopeless."

"You get used to people saying, 'We've got a softball game a week from Tuesday. Can you work it?' " says Reilly. "But you never get used to the stuff they yell from the stands."

One Detroit fan told Kaiser, "You've cost the Tigers more games this year than they've lost," which the ump thought was amusing. But when the fan asked the ump, "Did your mother have any children that lived?" Kaiser saw red and broke new ground in baseball. "I ejected the fan," said Kaiser. "Had him thrown out of the park."

Nonetheless, umpires don't dream about fans. They dream about players and managers. Especially managers. Many fans assume mistakenly that baseball arguments are largely tongue-in-cheek, a mandatory show of anger to please the crowd. "Sometimes they're funny afterwards, but never at the time," says Reilly. "You can always see it getting out of hand and ending in a fight."

Few umpires can bear the thought of a mass brawl; it's the ultimate symbol of their failure as mediators. "You take a man like Billy Martin, who is a violent person to begin with . . . he's punched many people," says one veteran ump. "When he starts screaming in your face, frankly, you have no idea what to expect."

Kaiser, the 270-pound former bouncer and pro wrestler, is an exception. "I kinda enjoy breakin' 'em up," he says, not specifying whether he means fights or the players involved. "In fact, I've gotten a directive from the league to stop doing it. Seems they think I enjoy it a little bit too much. I would never want to accidentally hurt one of these fine gentlemen."

Because of the long careers and the large number of games, no sport has the long-term official–player relationships that baseball offers, with the consequent potential for bitter feelings. Barroom baseball debate has always asked the question, "How much revenge is there in an umpire's heart?"

The sensible answer is probably "Same as anybody else." Which is to say, for a few umps, plenty. Certainly it's tough to find a player who doesn't think ancient history bears on current events. Between the lines, retribution or the threat of it is not only the umpire's strongest weapon but, in a sense, his only effective one.

Watch the fate of any rookie who shows up a home-plate umpire more than once. His own teammates cover their eyes in horror; his manager chews him out with a lecture on common sense; and the veterans on the other team prepare to pick his bones in the knowledge that many a close call during the rest of that series will go against the youth. Umpires break rookies to balls and strikes the way cowboys break horses to the bit and bridle. It's essential; otherwise, chaos.

"Son," the umpire says, "you're up here to learn, not to teach."

More to the point, what happens when the same umps, players and managers keep chewing on each other for years? In recent seasons, the ultimate example of such feudin' and fussin' surrounded Earl Weaver and his Orioles. Never were so many umpires elated to see one man retire. Every spring for the rest of this century, they'll pray that Weaver, who won't be seventy until the year 2000, stays happy with his golf and tomato plants.

Weaver's special dimension was his grasp of the language. He would begin his encounters with profoundly elevated sarcasm, then conclude his stomping exodus with multisyllabic profanities. Weaver began one of his encounters with Luciano, whom he was convinced was beyond human help, by saying, "Well, you put your right hand up three times. With some umpires that means 'strike three' and the batter heads back to the dugout. But I notice this guy's still here."

Toward the end of Weaver's career, umpires didn't even bother to hide their active hatred for him. Even before games—their shoes off and their blood pressures low—umpires would talk themselves into a tirade at the mention of his name.

"Weaver is a militant midget," said Steve Palermo. "He just uses us umpires as props in his circus act . . . But baseball is not a circus and the game is not Earl's show. It's not 1892 anymore, where umpires are wooden Indians for the fans to boo . . . It's a different world, as Earl may be finding out."

"Once you've run Weaver, he's like a recalcitrant child that can't accept authority . . . He goes through the whole logbook of everything you've ever done to him," said Larry Barnett. "I've never seen him do anything funny. No, I take that back. I once saw him slip and fall coming out of the dugout. That was funny."

"Weaver just goes goofy, like a raving lunatic . . . he's like a nightmare that just keeps coming back . . . raspy voice, four foot two . . . to me, he's like the real ayatollah of the '80s," said Nick Bremigan. "I think his bad relations with umpires hurt his club. Human nature tells you that. You're more of a man not to take it out on his players and I try extra hard not to. But human beings can be vindictive and umpires are human beings . . . His players think so too. They've said to me, 'Oh, no, here he goes again. This isn't going to help us.' The question is, Does he intimidate umpires or alienate umpires? How could you live with yourself if you let him intimidate you?"

Among all the protagonists in baseball's play, umpires are the most ambiguously tragicomic. At times, their lives seem to be the unsullied playing out of boyhood fantasies. Almost without exception, they are men who dreamed about athletic heroism as children; becoming umpires was their compromise with their own lack of talent.

Umpires are the ultimate fans, sitting in the ultimate seat; they're part spectator, part participant. They feed on the daily excitement of the arena and enjoy their proximity to heroes. For instance, when Ted Williams managed Washington, he constantly picked the umpires' brains, saying, "You guys see more baseball closer up than anybody. Nobody should know more about it than you do." Then he'd ask, sincerely or cunningly no one knows, "Tell me if you think this Rodriguez can hit the inside fastball . . . See if my right-hander isn't overthrowing a little."

In a sense, umpires are fortunate. What other class of fellows who have, by and large, only a high school diploma, earn a twenty-five-to-forty-thousand-dollar annual wage while working just eight months a year? They do their labor outdoors, yet lift nothing heavier than a whisk broom. They travel the country in modest expense-account style, and their toil lasts only three hours a day. All have a kind of notoriety, while some, with time, actually become famous.

Many a man thinks he would trade places.

Yet, in disturbing ways, umpires, as a class, are baseball's victims. Baseball has a callous record in its treatment of those who give the sport their lives but never strike it rich—i.e., the game's career minor-leaguers, its lifelong coaches and its umpires. Perhaps baseball's most consistently ugly trait is its cynical certainty that the game's bit players should be thankful just to be along for the ride. For every man who leaves baseball rich, famous or proud, there are many who question whether they should ever have touched the game at all.

"Umpires have kept this game honest for one hundred years," Luciano once stormed while he was still an active ump. "We must have integrity, because we sure don't have a normal family life. We certainly aren't properly paid. We have no health care, no job security, no tenure. Our pension plan is a joke. If you ask for a day off, they try to make you feel three inches tall."

Adds Bob Engel, past president of the umpires' union, "The league presidents have let us know that they think, with our lack of education, we're lucky to have the jobs we have and be making the money we're making."

That is baseball's vicious scissors play. The sport grabs hundreds of young men in its minor-league umpiring net and encourages the best, promising them promotion, while stringing the rest along. Even for the elect it's chancy. One day, the cream of that young crop wakes up in middle age with twenty years of professional umpiring experience. These men are untrained for any other job. And baseball says, "Take what we decide to give you and shut up, or we'll fire you and hire some guy from a bar who can yell, "Out" and "Safe."

If this description sounds too severe, consider the brief case history of Steve Fields, who was hired as a replacement when big-league umps went on strike in '79.

In the '60s, Fields was a young man with a steady railroad job. He earned extra cash by umping high school games on the same Alexandria (Virginia) fields where he'd played and dreamed of the majors. Then, one day, a couple of Washington Senators, Moose Skowron and Ed Brinkman, told the big, husky guy that he worked a nice game and maybe ought to aim a little higher.

Fourteen years later, after eleven seasons in the minors and three traumatic ones in the National League, Fields wondered if taking their advice wasn't the biggest mistake of his life. At forty-one, Fields found himself back working those same Alexandria schoolboy games, not as a youngster on a lark but as a fellow facing middle age who needed the thirty-three dollars a game to make ends meet.

"I've given the game fourteen years of my life. Now I'm wiped out," said Fields one winter day in 1982 after he got his NL pink slip. For months, Fields tried to find work. He came up with a part-time job driving an oil truck on snowy days. "I feel like I've been ten thousand places for jobs. All I know is baseball. I ain't got nothing. I'm just the scab ump who got fired."

The day Fields got the boot, he not only found himself without a job but with no vesting in a pension fund, no hospitalization or life insurance, no education beyond high school and no practical work experience. When he went to the post office and the railroad yard, hoping to resume one of the modest careers he'd left behind, they looked at him as if he were crazy.

"Baseball used me when they needed me," says Fields. "Now they're discarding me. They told me I was fired for incompetence, but I know better. They're afraid of another umpires' strike, so they've decided to throw a bone to the union to appease them. I'm the bone . . . Maybe I was lucky to be fired and get out of it with my sanity . . . I don't know if the seven other nonunion umpires [still in the majors] can exist like this indefinitely. They'll all go crazy."

From 1979 to 1981, Fields endured three seasons in hell, feeling the full burden of one of the ugliest episodes in baseball history: the ostracism and harassment of nonunion umpires by their indignant union brethren. This chapter is so bleak that even Blake Cullen, the NL official who told Fields he was fired, and Paul Runge, president of the umps' union, pitied him.

"I feel terrible for Steve," said the NL's Cullen. "He's got a great temperament for the game, like a big cop on the beat. I couldn't sleep the night I learned he'd been hit in the face [by a foul] and bled the whole game, 'cause nobody would go and help him.''

"The leagues put the hammer to those guys' heads," said union president Runge, who is also the son of former umpire Ed Runge. "It was made clear they either broke our picket line, or else they'd never make the majors. Guys making eight thousand dollars a year in the minors were offered two-year contracts in the majors at eighteen thousand dollars. It doesn't surprise me that eight guys crossed our line. What amazes me is that four guys in the minors refused to come up. And all four of 'em are still in the minors . . . I don't blame Fields. I blame the league presidents."

In a job where four-man camaraderie is almost a prerequisite for survival, what was Fields' life like?

"I only had one civil sentence spoken to me by another umpire in three years," said Fields. "I met up with a new crew in Atlanta and I was in the toilet. The crew chief snuck in, opened the door a crack and whispered, 'You're working second base tonight.'

"All I heard was sarcasm and silence. They roomed in different hotels, took different airplanes. Once, when I was stepping on a plane in Houston, the rest of my crew saw me, turned and took another flight . . . In Cincinnati, I was hit in the chin with a foul that required seven stitches after the game. But none of the other umps would take my place. They just let me stand out there for three hours and bleed. Every inning, I'd go into the Reds dugout and their trainer would put on butterfly stitches and patches. But every inning, from the sweat and moving your jaw yelling out pitches, it would all bust open and I'd bleed like a stuck pig."

Gradually Fields went into a shell. "In the minors, I never took crap off anybody and I always tried to have fun," he says. "In the majors, I had to hide, because once you did anything, both teams would eat your ass alive."

Said Pittsburgh catcher Steve Nicosia, "No human being should be treated like Steve Fields was. In triple A, Fields was the best umpire I ever had . . . always had a smile on his face and some crazy joke. In the majors, you'd say, 'Hi, Steve,' and he didn't do anything, like he didn't even want to acknowledge that he was there."

"I've known Steve Fields since I broke in with Durham in '69," said Bob Boone, veteran catcher who was NL player spokesman during the '81 strike. "He's a good guy and a decent ump. What happened to him sickens me."

Finally, Fields was simply too demoralized to function normally. The sadness in this is that none of the umpires, union or nonunion, who still are involved in this ongoing feud are truly to be blamed. The fault belongs to baseball's heirarchy. Baseball has always used its arbiters as though they were beasts of burden. It is widely believed that the sport's brass took a hard line against the umpires' union in '79 so it could precipitate a strike and thus show the *players'* union how tough the bosses could be when it came time for player/owner negotiations the following year: make an example of the umps. Baseball's pooh-bahs could have met *all* the umpires' demands in '79 for less than Pete Rose's annual eight hundred thousand dollar salary; but they took a strike instead. And created a legacy of ostracism.

Throughout its history, baseball has entrusted its crown jewel— its integrity—to the care of its umpires. Now, by its niggardly treatment of those umpires, baseball has ensured that it will attract a group of men who are tied to the game by bonds of love but who, over the years, will run an increasing risk of growing bitter toward the sport.

That baseball has not had one crooked-ump scandal in a century may be an unmerited divine dispensation.

"A few years ago, they assigned former FBI agents to check our off-the-field connections," says Luciano. "You'd see the same guy sitting in the same back corner of bars from Seattle to Baltimore. Maybe we're too dumb to cheat and maybe we're too honest. But nobody's dumb enough not to spot those FBI guys."

It's a baseball axiom that a good umpire, like a good FBI agent, is never noticed if he is doing his job. That, in its way, is why umpires have been overlooked and neglected for so long. In a sense, they've done their job too well.

If, in a fable, the poorest and most abused yet most honest member of a great enterprise were left to protect the largest pot of gold, we might say that the situation was artificial; one would assume that, in reality, the distance between irony and tragedy would never be allowed to grow so dangerously narrow.

Yet baseball lives that strained fable every day. The old and lucky game had better pray that life never imitates the final act which would appeal to art.

7

HOW TO CONTROL
THE ARMS RACE

Baseball is, above all, pitching, and pitching is, above all, rotation. Sluggers and speedsters are nice; fancy fielders and smart strategists, helpful. But, out of twenty-five men, the four or five starters are the backbone of the team.

The value of pitching is unquestioned; to win a pennant race it is usually necessary to control the arms race. Just ask the 1950 Red Sox, the last team to score a thousand runs in a season; despite a team batting average of .302 and a manager named Joe McCarthy, they finished third. Their starting rotation featured Joe "Burrhead" Dobson, Chuck Stobbs and Mickey McDermott. The 1950 Yankees had Vic Raschi, Allie Reynolds, Eddie Lopat, Tommy Byrne and Whitey Ford. Many of the most fundamental questions about the rotation are seldom asked outside major league dugouts. Inside them, no topic gets more attention.

Why do the same teams so often have the best rotations, as though they could grow starting pitchers like prize melons? What is the proper midseason care and feeding of a rotation? What rotation tricks can a savvy manager use to squeeze out a few extra victories? How do you take over a bad team and suddenly create a rotation out of whole cloth? If you've got a lousy makeshift rotation, how do you fake your way through September, as a few blessed teams have done?

To find the answers to all these questions, just examine the Seven Commandments of Pitching.

I. Thou shalt juggle thy rotation.

Earl Weaver had a calendar in front of him; his pitching coach, Ray Miller, looked over his shoulder. Beside each date for the next month was penciled the name of a pitcher. When one name was moved, others shifted position. The rotation is the Rubik's Cube of baseball.

"When is Flanagan's wife due?" asks Weaver.

"The eleventh, when we're in Oakland," says Miller. "And Mike's scheduled to pitch that day."

"He won't be worth a damn," says Weaver, Mr. Sensitivity. The juggling of names and dates begins until, suddenly, Weaver's eyes light up. "If we move Flanagan ahead a day while we're still home, then he can work July 4 in Detroit and the eighth in Seattle and fly back home before the team, if he wants."

"He'll appreciate that," Miller says.

"Look up Flanagan's record against Oakland," says Weaver.

Miller discovers that while the southpaw owned the A's for years, he has been mediocre against them the last two years.

Weaver, assured that his sympathy isn't costing his team a dream matchup, says, "Okay, tell him it's all right to leave the Coast early, as long as he flies back at his own expense."

Then Weaver adds to himself, "Besides, if we do that, Mc-Gregor will get an extra turn against California, and he's beaten the Angels eleven straight times."

For years whenever Weaver looked at his big calendar, he always tried to keep Jim Palmer from pitching in the Kingdome and McGregor from hurling in Fenway Park, while at the same time trying to arrange the future so that Dennis Martinez never missed his Toronto cousins and Flanagan always got to pick on Minnesota.

"During the season, a manager doesn't do much that's brilliant. Mostly, it's your job to make sure that you don't lose games unnecessarily. Sometimes I think about the only way I might win a couple of extra ones for us is right here," Weaver once said, tapping his pencil on his rotation calendar.

II. Remember thy daily routine and keep it wholly.

The George Bamberger art of arm maintenance is one of the game's cult phenomena. Pitchers who worked with him in Baltimore, Milwaukee and New York have sworn by his cantankerously old-fashioned notions.

"I learned the program from [Manager] Charlie Metro in the minors," says Bamberger. "I'd had a bad arm for five years and after this program, it came back. It's been bringing back arms and keeping them strong ever since." And what is his mystery cure that brings soup bones back to life and allows a four-man rotation to work more than a thousand innings? Acupuncture? Aerobic dance? Brain scan? Arthroscopic surgery? Laser transmutation of genes?

"You've got to play catch every day for fifteen minutes," says Bamberger. "I'm not kidding. You don't know how tough it is to convince these guys they got to play soft toss continuously for fifteen minutes. It's boring. Your arm gets tired because, in that time, you make a couple hundred throws.

"I tell 'em, 'If you don't renege, it'll do the same for you that it did for me, Dave McNally, Dick Hall, Mike Caldwell and a lot of others.' "

But, George, what about all the scientific exercises that other teams adore?

"They do more fancy exercises now than ever in history and there are more injuries, more sore arms, more pulled leg muscles than ever. The more they exercise, the more they think that two hundred innings is a lot of work. All you need to do is throw and run. All these new exercises are like tits on a bull—useless."

Bamberger's conditioning program is, compared to more exotic teams like the (strength-training) Phillies and the (aerobic-dancing) Mariners, simplicity itself. First, pitchers do ten minutes of running: sprint seventy-five yards, walk briskly back, then sprint again; in all, maybe twenty-five sprints. Then they play soft toss for fifteen minutes. Finally, they do ten longish, foul-line-to-foul-line runs along the outfield warning track. For an Olympic decathlete, this wouldn't even constitute a warm-up, much less a workout. But then, nobody said pitchers are athletes.

III. Honor thy pitcher's sensitivity.

Dave Stewart, who wanted desperately to pitch his way into the rotation of the world champion Los Angeles Dodgers, tried to make himself invisible as he walked into the manager's office. Tommy Lasorda, as usual, was telling stories about his career as an itinerant bush-league southpaw. The topic of the moment was how to find a starter when everybody in the rotation says he's too tired.

"Once, in Havana, our [winter ball] club was being managed by Adolfo Luque, who was the meanest son of a bitch God ever made. Luque said to one of our pitchers, 'You're starting tonight.' The pitcher said, 'The hell I am. I've only got one day's rest.' Luque left and came back with a revolver as long as your arm and stuck it right in the guy's neck. The pitcher reached above his head for his traveling bag, and Luque said, 'What are you reaching for?'

" 'My uniform, Skip,' he says, 'You know, I got to pitch tonight.'

"And," concluded Lasorda the moralist, "the guy pitched a three-hitter."

When the chuckling stops, young Stewart approached Lasorda and, in a voice not much above a whisper, said, "I'm sorry."

"Sorry?" boomed Lasorda. "Hell, you won the game tonight!"

"Yeah, but they gave me a big lead and I didn't finish," murmured the right-hander, who, with a 6–1 lead after six innings, had faltered. "Sorry."

"That's the attitude I want," said Lasorda. "Christ, this game's full of too many guys who can't wait to get help from the bullpen. They're always looking over their shoulder.

"When I was pitching in the minors, they couldn't get the ball away from me. I'd walk all around the mound when the manager came out. One day, he said, 'Lasorda, you can walk around all you want, but sooner or later you're going to have to come up here.'

"I remember one day I came out to get Pedro Borbon," Lasorda told Stewart, "and when I reached for the ball, he threw it over the light tower.

"After the game Borbon said, 'Tommy, I apologize for showing you up. I was just mad at myself.'

"I said, 'Pedro, is that the first time you've ever done that?'

"He said, 'Yes.'

"So I told him, 'Then, you got to do it twice more to tie me.' "

Stewart grinned and left.

IV. Be at thy best in September even if thou must fake it.

Each September, the story seems to be the same. The contenders come to the head of the stretch in a bunch, hanging in the pennant race with thirty games to play. During that month, we linger by the radio, listening for partial scores. Slowly we recognize a familiar pattern. The same teams seem to have the same score almost every night: "And the Dodgers lead 1–0 at the end of four." Or it might be the Phillies, Yankees, Royals, Orioles or Expos.

This lucky team never seems to have anything bad happen to it for at least four or five innings. Even though the club must be tight and feeling pressure, the opposition allows it to make the first move, take the early lead, establish the tenor of the game.

Then the final score arrives. Another victory. In September some teams seem immune to misfortune. The reason is the pitching rotation. A team in a tight pennant battle can have no greater advantage, no more basic psychological crutch, than dependable starting pitchers.

"The pennant race comes down to September and September usually comes down to one thing: your pitching rotation," says Bamberger. "The good pitchers get better when the thing gets tough, and the not-so-good ones are worn out and show it."

Then there are notable exceptions. In 1967 in Boston, Dick Williams had a rotation with no balance (all right-handers), only one true quality starter (Jim Lonborg) and essentially a one-man bullpen (Fat John Wyatt).

For two months, Williams juggled like a madman. His only constant was Lonborg's never missing a turn and, toward the end, working on two days' rest. As for the other folks in a weird, five-man rotation—Gary Bell, Lee Stange, Darrell Brandon and Jose Santiago—they seldom knew whether they'd be starting or coming out of the bullpen. Bell saved three games, while starter Stange was called out of the pen eleven times. Brandon (nineteen starts, twenty relief games) and Santiago (eleven starts, thirty-nine relief) were schizophrenics, appearing more times in relief, even though most of their innings were as starters. If any club ever faked its way through a pennant race, that was the one.

Now Williams just laughs at those closing weeks of madness. "All our starters would go to the bullpen on their 'throw day,' says Williams, meaning the second day after a start. "We'd wait to see if we needed them for an inning or two. If we didn't, then they'd do their off-day throwing."

It's one thing to ask for an inning on a throw day. It's another to ask for a complete game with two days' rest. What Williams did not do was commit the cardinal sin of wearing out half a rotation while losing confidence in the other half. That had already been done in textbook fashion by Gene Mauch in September of '64, when he brought back Jim Bunning three times and Chris Short twice on two days' rest and the Phils lost every time. That helped them blow a six-and-a-half-game lead as they lost ten in a row. "I wish I could have done as good a job as the players," said the young Mauch manfully.

"Actually the best part of our rotation that last month in '67 might have been Carl Yastrzemski," says Williams. "Don't think any hitter ever had a month like that. Every time he came up, we had two more runs, and that makes the pitching look a lot better."

At his next stop, in Oakland, Williams had a nucleus of starters —Catfish Hunter, Vida Blue and Ken Holtzman—which lacked only one member of the firm to rank as a great rotation along with the early-fifties quartet of Early Wynn, Bob Feller, Bob Lemon and "Big Bear" Mike Garcia or the Baltimore crews of 1969–71.

As September arrives, those teams with proven quality starters have a history—if they're still in the race—of reassembling their rotations and making a rush. On the other hand, clubs that have been patching and bailing all season find their makeshift heroes wearing out.

Once a club reaches the stretch, it can often, with the help of September off days, trim its rotation to three men. In addition, a club should almost always cut down to three starters once it reaches postseason play. The 1981 Dodgers did this, riding three men—Fernando Valenzuela, Jerry Reuss and Burt Hooton—all the way to a World Series victory.

V. Thou shalt covet a great rotation with a makeshift bullpen over a great bullpen with a mediocre rotation. But not by much.

"I think baseball's reached the point where, for most clubs, relief pitching may be the most important part of the pitching staff," says Sparky Anderson. "And I'm saying that as one of the managers who goes the longest with his four starters. Right now, on this team, my starter will be beat before I take him out. Why? Because . . . ," says Anderson, nodding toward the bullpen that had betrayed his Detroit team all season.

What Anderson wishes is that he were back as Captain Hook with the Cincinnati Reds, the world champs of '75 and '76. "Pitching and defense is the key to winning, always has been. But it doesn't matter where the pitching comes from," says Anderson. "In Cincinnati, I'd start anybody, any warm body that we could get four or five innings from, and then I'd get the bullpen going. We had Rawly Eastwick, Will McEnaney, Pedro Borbon and Clay Carroll. You wouldn't believe all the one-, two- and three-run games we played in which we used four or five different pitchers."

In '75, for instance, no Red hurler worked more than 211 innings or won more than 15 games; the four most used starters averaged only 192 innings. The whole team had a pathetic 22 complete games. Yet those Reds won 108 games, the most in the National League since 1909. And thanks to four excellent short relievers and two decent spot starters and long men, plus fifty saves, only three teams in baseball allowed fewer runs than those Reds, who were known as a slugging machine.

"Ralph Houk [did] the same thing in Boston with Mark Clear, Bob Stanley, Luis Aponte and Tom Burgmeier," said Anderson.

"I remember," says Bamberger, "when Dave McNally, Mike Cuellar, Jim Palmer and Pat Dobson all won twenty games for us in Baltimore in '71 . . . greatest rotation I ever saw. From the seventh inning on, if they had a one-run lead, they smelled victory and wiped 'em out. When they didn't hold the lead, that's when you were surprised. They'd all reach back for that little extra desire. Why can't you be your own relief? Now it's changing. I hate to see all these pitchers, leading 2–1, 3–2, in the sixth or seventh, start slowing down and looking out at the bullpen. They just want to be taken out in a situation where they can only win; they're protecting their record."

The era of the partial-game pitcher is so securely with us that well-known hurlers who would once have taken umbrage at being called "seven-inning pitchers" are now willing to call themselves "six-inning pitchers." New York's Ron Guidry freely cited the strong Yankee bullpen and the way he was seldom asked to work more than six or seven innings as major reasons he signed a new contract with New York. One reason Billy Martin was fired before the 1984 season was that Guidry and other Yankee starters complained that Martin made them pitch too many complete games in 1983.

Baltimore's Jim Palmer is, as usual, a more complex example. From '79 to '81, he thought he was still a great six-inning pitcher, in the Guidry mold. However, his stubborn manager, Weaver, still thought he was the old, nine-inning Palmer. In September of '80, Palmer was shown a statistic that said that, for the entire season, his ERA for the first six innings was under 2.00; from the first batter of the seventh onward, it was over 9.00. Instead of being insulted by this stat, Palmer's instant reaction was "Show that to Earl, please. I've been trying to get him to understand that for two years."

"When you start ducking the hard part of the game," says Bamberger, "that seems to take some of the personality out of the sport . . . "Four starters who have a proper conditioning program can all go 275 to 300 innings. The record books prove it. You need a fifth starter in spots."

In recent years, Chuck Tanner in Pittsburgh and Whitey Herzog in St. Louis have also had success with teams whose starting staffs were, without question, in the league's bottom half. What's happening?

"Nothing's much harder than building an excellent rotation," says Anderson, who has had trouble doing just that in Detroit.

"Baseball people aren't stupid. Nobody gives up good pitching for good hitting [in a trade]. You only get pitching by giving pitching. You have to develop your own through the farm system. And that's tough, because there will never be more trial-and-error mistakes than in pitching."

Anderson has reached the conclusion that, for most teams, it is easier to find four guys who can provide one or two good innings of relief every other day than it is to find four pitchers so talented that they can give nine good innings every fourth or fifth day.

Nonetheless, even Anderson admits, "You got to have one guy, at least, who can go out and just slam the door to stop a losing streak. That overpowering stopper gives your club such a lift. And nothing drains a team mentally like a long losing streak."

VI. Trust in thy fourth starter.

The essence of a rotation is having four or occasionally five reliable starters. Over 162 games, three solid men just aren't enough. The year 1982 was the perfect example.

When the ace goes sour or is injured, it actually has a double impact on the staff. The secondary curse is that, in effect, a club's fourth- and fifth-best starters suddenly assume the importance of the third and fourth starters. That sounds trivial, but in practice it can be very debilitating. For instance, when the Dodgers suddenly lost Hooton and the Yankees lost Dave Righetti, strange and unqualified folks began getting the ball for starting assignments. In Los Angeles, Stewart went from a solid spot starter and long reliever to an unproven rotation regular; the world champs' spot starter became (shudder) Vicente Romo. In New York, Righetti's departure for the minors created an ugly rotation that, at times, included promising but unprepared Mike Morgan and career loser Roger Erickson.

Before the 1982 season, the best rotations in baseball, based on past performance, figured to be in Los Angeles, Montreal, Houston, Cincinnati, Baltimore, Oakland and New York.

But that was before:

• Hooton got injured and won only one game through late July;

• Ray Burris, an Expo mainstay in '81, began the year 3-11;

• Houston's Bob Knepper, No. 2 in the NL in ERA in '81, went 3-10 before the All-Star break;

• Tom Seaver, the top-percentage pitcher in baseball in '81 (.875), began the year 4-10 with a 5.46 ERA;

• Palmer either pitched poorly, begged out in the late innings or pulled himself out of the rotation with mysterious injuries so often that Baltimore's shallow bullpen was shredded trying to compensate for him;

• Almost the whole Oakland rotation finally got the sore arms predicted for it after bringing Martin glory with ninety-four complete games in '80;

• Righetti's delivery and control were so messed up he was back in the minors for three weeks.

As a consequence, none of these seven teams found '82 as pleasant as expected. Conversely, several teams thought to have mediocre rotations stayed in pennant races far longer than expected, because they managed to find third and fourth starters who held together much better than anticipated. Seattle unearthed universal cast-off Gaylord Perry and stole Gene Nelson from the Yankees. The Phillies made a sharp trade for Mike Krukow and got help from the annually exasperating Larry Christensen. The Padres got John Montefusco for next to nothing and discovered two hot pitchers in Tim Lollar and Chris Welsh, both compliments of the Yankees. California got unbelievable mileage out of a pair of thirty-five-year-olds, Geoff Zahn and Ken Forsch, plus thirty-seven-year-old Steve Renko.

One basic reason why baseball seasons are so hard to predict is that just such rotation shake-ups happen every year and their consequences are as important as they are impossible to foresee.

Bamberger explains best why four decent gents can often do better than two stars and a couple of major disappointments: "When you've got a solid rotation, you always feel that sometime during the season you're going to have a winning streak of at least eight games in a row, 'cause sooner or later all four of those guys are going to have good outings back-to-back. And you know you're probably never going to have a long losing streak, because who's going to beat all four of those guys in a row?

"On the other hand, great hitting teams with a weak starter or two are always getting their winning streaks broken up before they get momentum."

VII. Thou shalt always seek new solutions.

A good pitching staff needs a secret weapon: a great trainer. "He's the extra man in the rotation," says Bamberger.

"He's got to be a doctor and a counselor and, to tell the truth, an all-around medicine man who's slinging the bull and pumping guys up.

"A few years ago we had a starter who was raving about this special new stuff that the trainer was rubbing into his shoulder before he pitched. He said the stuff kind of fizzed and stung when you put it on, and then it got sticky and warm. Said it was helping him a lot.

"So I asked, 'What are you using on him? Maybe the other pitchers ought to try it.'

"The trainer told me, 'This guy kept asking if I had anything new or special. So I figured he thought he needed something. I looked around to see what I had. I rubbed the only thing on him that I could find: Coca-Cola.'"

8

SEASONS OF THE HILL

Sometimes, under the spell of a gray day, it seems that every professional athlete lives out the same life as every other career athlete.

The early promise of exceptional talent often changes the malleable banks of the personality like a riverbed at spring flood. Soon the young man is tempted to believe that his temporary skill is a form of personal luck or destiny which can be trusted like a hard currency that he can mint at will. Soon enough, a sobering realism is introduced, often through injury, but just as easily through divorce, alcoholism, drug addiction, chronic narcissism, sudden illness or accident, financial folly, isolation by fame, inexplicable loss of form or some traumatic failure on a large stage. What percentage have escaped?

Perhaps man is the creature who, once struck down, defines himself by his ability to rise. A mid-career accommodation to adulthood begins as the flawed body and tempered soul learn the arts of athletic and personal compromise. Then begins the long strain of hanging on, of enduring in a profession where deterioration is not only inevitable, but abnormally accelerated.

Much of writing about a sport is chronicling the way that an endless variety of people cope with, or are crushed by, these familiar yet riveting variations on the Ages of Man. In baseball, this is particularly true of pitchers, who face a more precarious existence than almost any species of athlete. The pitcher's mound offers us its Seasons of the Hill. Each year, we are given new illustrations of: the Phenom, the Fallen Star, the Comeback, the Gracefully Aging Veteran, the Hall of Famer's Last Stand and the Aftermath. In a passion play, perhaps these characters would be identical each season. In reality, there are no stock characters, and each of our protagonists, no matter how familiar his situation, has a human face.

THE CHIEF, BEGINNING, SPOTS IN TIME

Spring 1981—The rookie is taking his licks in batting practice. Since he can't speak or understand much English, he doesn't know what his teammates are saying. His eyes twinkle with pleasure as he tries to pick up their tone of voice. His grinning, swarthy, twenty-year-old face looks enthusiastic and open, but somehow it also looks tough and maybe just a trace mean.

On the mound, the Los Angeles Dodger manager, Tommy Lasorda, is pitching batting practice. The first pitch is what remains of Lasorda's best fastball. It goes exactly where Lasorda aims it: at the rookie's head.

He hits the dirt.

The Dodger veterans around the cage laugh at the brushback pitch. "Hey, Tommy, be careful. That kid's your ticket back onto the talk shows," says Ron Cey, the third baseman.

"We thought Tommy'd lost his little black book with the phone numbers of all the talk-show hosts . . . you know . . . David Hartman, Johnny Carson," needles Dave Lopes, the second baseman.

"I been on 'Good Morning America' seven times," yells back Lasorda. "I don't need to call anybody. All the biggies call me."

Lasorda throws his next pitch.

The rookie, who looks like a pudgy kid—maybe five foot eleven, 190 pounds and some of it in the wrong places—takes an easy, flicking swing. Since he's a pitcher himself, it's just a make-shift hack, not a polished, big-league swing.

The ball takes off like a rocket and sails over the fence.

"Hey, Tommy, you can burn that black book," yells Lopes.

The Dodgers laugh again. The little fat kid is going to take all of these once-famous, recently scorned Dodgers back to the big time. And they know it.

"Protect him?" asks Reggie Smith incredulously. "You're damn right we're going to protect him. "He's the Natural—the one in a million. It's like the Man Upstairs reached down, put his hand on the kid's shoulder and said, 'You're the one.' "

Once, Reggie Smith was a natural, the switch-hitter they compared to Mickey Mantle. Before the injuries—to knees, shoulders—he knew the feeling of that hand on his shoulder. Nobody in baseball had the tools he had, once upon a time.

"People say his 'body form' isn't right, because he doesn't look like a weight lifter," says Smith, spitting a curse. "Watch him dribbling that ball," says Smith, pointing to the Natural, standing alone in the outfield playing with a baseball as though it were a soccer ball; the kid bounces it from thigh to thigh, knee to knee, off his chest, off his head, playing an effortless, casual game of hot potato.

"Pure coordination," says Smith. "He doesn't think about what he does. He just does it. They said that Willie Mays always had a lot of little boy in him. Well, this kid really is just a boy. When you play baseball only for enjoyment—not money or fame or all the other things—it's one fun game. That's this guy. He likes to do two things: eat and play baseball. I hope people leave him alone and let him enjoy it. To tell the truth, I hope he never learns to speak English. Sometimes, especially in this game, ignorance is bliss."

So far, the kid only has one hobby, if you don't count an addiction to Space Invaders, which is a generational disease. He collects hotel room keys. It started two years ago in the California League. At each new glamour town, like Lodi and Visalia, he would send the room key back as a souvenir to his mother in his home town of Etchohuaquila, Mexico (population 150).

"He's so innocent you can't believe it," says Lopes. "What I want to know is, Where has he been all these years to get so old on the mound?"

Fernando Valenzuela, the man whose name sounds like a mailing address in the lower Andes, isn't the hottest young player since Mark Fidrych or Willie Mays or since anybody. He, at this moment, is the hottest rookie in the history of the game.

Baseball is the sport of statistics. They explain everything. And nothing. That's their charm. And it is statistics that have given the chubby Valenzuela his current, gigantic stature.

At one glorious point, as Valenzuela won his sixth straight game of the season, these were some of his numbers:

—36 consecutive shutout innings.

—70 innings in the majors, one earned run, driving his career ERA at one fabulously lucky moment down to 13. That's 0.13.

—34 hits allowed (a .140 batting average against him), 11 walks and 66 strikeouts.

Last September he proved that he could win in a pennant race as he made ten consecutive shutout relief appearances, earning a save and winning two games (one in extra innings against Houston on the last, vital weekend of the season).

He won in the cold (in Candlestick Park), he won in the rain (in San Diego), he won indoors (in Houston), he won in another country (Canada). In lovely Chavez Ravine, where he is a full-blown folk hero, Angelenos there wear T-shirts that read, "I live in the Fernando Valley."

He beat Don Sutton, Vida Blue and Bill Gullickson, twice driving in the winning run. He won, 1–0, on the road against the champions of the West Division (Houston), and he gave up only one run in winning in extra innings against the favorites in the East Division (Montreal).

Despite all this, little is known about Fernando Valenzuela.

He is the ultimate baseball mystery.

What does he think about on the mound? How did he get so savvy at the age of twenty? What will the arm-wrecking screwball, which he learned only eighteen months ago and which catapulted him from a good minor leaguer to a great major leaguer, do to his arm? Does he have season-long stamina? How will he react to the pressures of being a megacelebrity, especially in Southern California, where Spanish-speaking media abound?

In almost any other sport, such a start to a pro career probably would carry with it the certainty of long-term stardom. But baseball is more subtle. What you see isn't necessarily what you get.

Many young pitchers have blown the doors off the league their first time through the loop. Dave (Boo) Ferriss, of the 1945 Red Sox, won his first eight starts, including four shutouts in his first six games, the same shutout ratio as Valenzuela. The next year, when the World War II vets were back, Ferriss won twenty-five games. But he hurt his arm, retired after six seasons, and now is the coach at Delta State College, in Mississippi. Few remember him.

This seventh son and youngest of twelve children, raised on a truck farm smaller than an infield, is surrounded by constant Dodger concern. The scout who discovered him in an obscure Mexican league four years ago—Mike Brito, a Cuban who was once a Washington Senator farmhand—travels with the team, ostensibly doing such things as catching batting practice and clocking runners going first to third, but really keeping a paternal eye on Valenzuela. Proud as a peacock, GM Al Campanis, who tightfistedly believes that Latin players are "hungrier," also is along on this trip to make sure nothing happens to his prize.

"Everyone knows he would be easy to exploit," says Steve Garvey. "This will be a real test for our front office and public relations people. He's definitely lucky he doesn't speak English. There are times when a lot of us wish we didn't."

"The kid's lucky he can't understand all the people yapping at him. Nobody can mess up his mind," says Houston's Don Sutton, adding devilishly, "of course, Lasorda speaks fluent Spanish." To this proposition, Valenzuela responds (through a translator), "Maybe he's right. I just go pitch how I know best."

"You have to look out for him, because you can tell everything is new to him. He's wide-eyed and always smiling," says Lopes. "But you can't lead him by the hand and tell him when to blow his nose. You can't turn him back into a baby and have him lose his manhood. It's a fine line."

"What's all the excitement about?" protests rightfielder Jay

Johnstone. "He's a twenty-year-old left-hander with control, poise, brains and stuff. Just 'cause there hasn't been one in a century, everybody gets worked up. For example, my agent calls and says he wants to replace me in my Pillsbury Doughboy commercial with Valenzuela. I told him, 'Calm down, man. The kid can't even laugh in English.' "

More seriously, Johnstone is asked of whom Valenzuela reminds him. "Just so he never reminds me of Bo Belinsky. I was with the Angels when Bo came up, pitched a no-hitter and got the same star treatment. It ruined him."

All those potential problems are mercifully in the future. For now, Valenzuela is happy with his forty-two thousand five hundred dollar salary; just last week he and Lasorda went on a shopping excursion and Hollywood Tommy picked out the kid's first expensive suit: a $450 pinstripe job. The irony was not lost on the Dodgers; they knew that the other team in the bidding skirmish to buy Valenzuela's contract from Puebla, of the Mexican League, in July 1979, was the New York Yankees, the pinstripers. The Dodgers won with a $120,000 bid, $20,000 of it going to Valenzuela, the rest to his sticky-fingered native team.

For now, Valenzuela also is protected by the genuine affection his teammates have for him. "He hates to see a relief pitcher get up, and he's never been hooked," said Smith. "None of us wants to be the first one to pinch-hit for him. We've set up an executive committee of older guys, over thirty-five (Smith, Johnstone and Rick Monday), to appoint the first pinch hitter for Fernando. It's definitely not going to be me. We think we'll probably sacrifice Pepe Frias."

No matter what happens to Valenzuela, whether he wins twenty-five games every year until he's forty, or whether he proves to be merely another mortal pitcher given to gopher balls, elbow miseries and stretches of lost control, these will be the most vividly remembered glories of his career.

Nothing is more fascinating than the unknown commodity. For now, he is the embodiment of the nickname his bush-league buddies gave him last season: the Amazing Chief. At first, they called him the Chief, because he was silent, inscrutable, strong, yet secretly mischievous and intelligent like the character of the Chief in *One Flew over the Cuckoo's Nest.* That Chief, after two hours of stoic, apparently moronic silence, proved, in the last reel, to be articulate, cynical and funny beneath his cigar-store Indian façade. However, after seeing Valenzuela pitch, his San Antonio mates started calling him the Amazing Chief.

"You feel yourself drawn to him," says Smith. "When I'm on the bench, I feel like I'm throwing every pitch with him. In this game, you judge a player over ten years, not ten starts. But I think he'll stand the test of time."

"Webster doesn't have words to define him," says Lopes.

To all of this, Valenzuela begins every response to a question with the reflexive word *"Bueno* [good]." Whatever he is asked, his first contented thought is *"bueno."*

"I've been reading a book that reminds me of Fernando," says Garvey. "It's a study on sports psychology that talks about all the factors that go into ideal performance . . . you know . . . try-ing to figure out what happens those rare times when you do it all perfectly, whether it's a home run in the Series or a touchdown pass or a last-second basket or, I guess, a slap shot into the upper right-hand corner."

Garvey gives a little smile. He likes this book title. "It's called *The Sweet Spot in Time,"* he says.

That sweet spot in time is where Fernando Valenzuela lives right now. No one knows for how long.

COMEBACKS AND ROLLER COASTERS

Spring 1979—Mark Fidrych still looks the same as he did when he inhabited that sweet spot in time, in 1976. His face is boyish, handsome and intense one moment, comic, coarse and dopey the next.

His blue jeans and denim jacket are old and stained by motor oil, his sandals well made and well worn. His hair still is a wild mop of blond rock-star curls that looks greasy even when clean.

Fidrych looks like a relaxed, young, gum-chomping gas-station mechanic who can't keep from boogying along with the disco on his transistor radio. The $125,000-a-season pitcher lives frugally here in Lakeland, Florida, in an efficiency apartment, barbecuing chicken and cooking vegetables, then gobbling them straight from the pot.

In the Detroit Tiger locker room, Fidrych is the same, hopping from stool to stool. In ten minutes he can start a dozen conversations or tell a dozen jokes. Yet he never seems to be in a hurry, just more full of energy, good spirits and himself than anyone else.

"I count these hairs on my chest every day," he says to a teammate. "It's up to nine. Come on, you hairs. Get growin'.

"Hey," Fidrych says to a clubhouse flunky, "the only way I autograph four dozen of these balls is if I get a dozen of 'em to sell for myself. Nobody does nothin' for nothin' in this world."

Then he laughs, signs all four dozen, squeezing his signature between those of the others, returns the balls, keeping none.

"John Wockenfuss," says Fidrych, inspecting his catcher's signature on one ball. "Still misspelling your name, I see."

A radio interviewer sticks a microphone in Fidrych's face as he sits autographing. "Here I am today in sunny Florida with the Bird," intones Golden Throat, proceeding to read a melodramatic recitation of a question.

Fidrych eyes the microphone, seemingly as resigned as a wise owl on a perch. Then, in a moment of radio silence, he very loudly clears every sinus passage in his head and spits into a tobacco-juice receptacle.

The interview is short.

Radioman blanches. Fidrych looks at him with blank, Gee-ain't-I-stupid innocence. That'll sound great on the old Wolverine sports network. Back to you, WQRK.

After his shower, Fidrych sits outside the Tiger clubhouse in the sun in the rightfield corner with a towel around him. Several late-staying fans, including two middle-aged women with binoculars, are Bird-watching from fifty yards away. Fidrych nonchalantly drops the towel and makes a couple of naked turns before stepping back into the clubhouse, with no change of expression. Towel, no towel; it makes as much difference to him as to an eight-year-old.

The world is always scrutinizing the Bird, poking him with

microphones, watching him with binoculars. He stopped watching back long ago. He gives them what they want, but in a way they never expected. And don't quite know how to take.

When Fidrych steps on the Tiger mound to throw batting practice, everything about him looks the same too. The delivery is smooth and free, the control pinpoint.

"I'm back on the mound, where I belong," he says. "Man, I get out there and I'm so happy that I just start singing along while I'm pitching, ya know what I mean?

"I'm not throwing hard yet. I'm takin' my time. But it feels great."

The sight of Fidrych, baseball's pop idol in exile, is enough to send the four hundred fans here into a standing ovation. He must step off the mound and tip his cap to quiet them. The thought of the Bird back where he belongs makes many people, even those who couldn't care less about the Tigers, want to sing and cheer.

"Bird looks super," says Ron LeFlore. "Wouldn't surprise me to see him start the season." Fidrych, in unrestrained moments, has said the same. It would, however, surprise a great many other people.

No one wants to say it here, not even in a whisper that the exuberant Fidrych might overhear, but the Bird may be washed up. Not shelved for another season or two, or even permanently reduced in pitching effectiveness, but flat-out finished forever, at age twenty-four. The question after two years of mysterious shoulder miseries is no longer whether the Bird can come back and be a twenty-game winner. It is whether he can win twenty games the rest of his career. When the Tigers talk about the future, they do not mention the gate sensation of '76 who attracted 901,239 people to his twenty-nine starts.

"We're not counting on Mark this season" is the official line, from new manager Les Moss on up. "Anything he gives us is a bonus. He must rehabilitate himself slowly." That was not the Tigers' policy the last two seasons, when, impatiently, they did not discourage Fidrych's natural tendency to rush everything. Three times, he came back too soon with Tiger blessings and ended up again on the disabled list.

"The way young pitchers are treated is practically a scandal,"

Philadelphia's Jim Lonborg said. "Give him a little rest and get him back out there" is the common theory.

"I can see it happening with Fidrych," said Lonborg. "He's done it twice . . . now he's doing it a third time."

Less than a month later, Lonborg's words were born out as the Tigers sent Fidrych to Lakeland to work out, then ballyhooed his return date, selling tickets in advance. Fidrych's shoulder broke before he ever got back to Detroit.

Every pitcher expects arm trouble. But what Fidrych has had for almost two years, limiting him to eighty-one and twenty-two innings in '77 and '78 after pitching twenty-four complete games in a 19-9 '76 season, is not mere arm trouble. It's called "broken arm."

"Is anybody going to interview us today?" Milt Wilcox (13-12) says to Dave Rozema (9-12) in a clubhouse stage whisper that Fidrych can hear as he is being interviewed.

"Nah," answers Rozema. "We don't have broken arms."

Actually, Fidrych's teammates are almost as fond of him as the fans, and they keep their jealousy on simmer. It is a mark of the Mark of '79 that he can now joke, and be teased, about his psychic and physical pains. That's a breakthrough, since the Bird's ills have always been treated like a Detroit state secret. No one with the Tigers will confirm or deny the scuttlebutt about Fidrych's initial injury: that he ripped knee cartilage while horsing around in the outfield here in Lakeland two years ago.

Fidrych returned from knee surgery in just seven weeks. He went on a six-game winning streak, but apparently changed his delivery unconsciously. On July 12, 1977, a date that may yet live in Tiger infamy, Fidrych first felt the pain and stiffness in his shoulder that has plagued him ever since. He pitched only twenty-two innings in the next 250 Tiger games.

"A year ago at this time Mark was exactly where he is today," says Hiller. "Looking good throwing BP [batting practice]. In high spirits."

Again, Fidrych and the Tigers couldn't wait.

The Bird opened the season with two powerful, complete-game victories, bringing his three-year career statistics to an efficiency level reached only by the Walter Johnsons of the sport: 33 complete games in 43 starts, a 27-13 record and a 2.47 earned-run average with an undistinguished, poor-fielding team. In 353 innings, he had just 70 walks.

"You don't lose your control," says Fidrych, "and that's all pitching is: gettin' 'em to hit those sliders at the knees to the infield."

Fidrych has gone from "a beanpole kid" to a strapping 190-pound athlete whose bony chest is starting to fill out.

"He's just become a man," says pitcher Jack Billingham.

"I don't know what all the muscles will do," says Fidrych, grinning like a kid who has traded in his '56 Chevy for a new Maserati. "Carryin' that extra fifteen to twenty pounds could make you stronger, or you could tire easier, I guess. We'll have to see.

"But nobody can ever say that I didn't work to get my arm back. I was in that hospital every day doin' those exercises."

Then Fidrych got the shock of his life. A group of orthopedists from all over the country came to a symposium on Fidrych in Orlando after last season. Fidrych returned to Detroit, never hearing the group's conclusion. Minnesota team orthopedist Dr. Harvey O'Phelan compared Fidrych's chronic problems to those of Luis Tiant from 1970 to 1972, when el Tiante was pink-slipped twice and considered finished.

It was O'Phelan who first said Fidrych needed to totally rehabilitate the atrophied pitching muscles in his arm—a long-term process—and that if he rushed back as soon as he felt healthy, he would just destroy himself again.

"That really woke Mark up," says one source close to the Tigers. "He realized he may have to do his exercises religiously for years to get his arm as healthy on the inside as it looks on the outside. He's finally buckled down."

Fidrych's greatest enemy is the very competitive temperament that made him a pitching phenomenon. Fidrych had a fire inside his head. All his antics—talking to the ball, landscaping the mound—were part of a manic intensity, a pitching trance, in which he blocked out the world of distractions, fed off the energy of the crowd and reached back for a sustained effort.

In that trance, Fidrych was incapable of taking it easy. When he went to the mound, he stopped being Mark Fidrych, the Massachusetts man-child, malnourished on TV and rock 'n' roll, and became that primal athletic animal the Bird, who called up resources that go back to the cavemen.

"We all worry about Bird 'cause he's such a great guy," says the veteran Billingham. "He's the naturally loosest, most uninhibited, most in-touch-with-his-deep-feelings athlete that I've ever seen."

Fidrych contains many delightful contradictions and considerable intuitive wisdom. After his great year, he signed a three-year, three hundred thousand dollar contract, saying, "I could have gotten more if I had wanted to sign for one year, but I want to make sure I get my [four-year] pension if something happens to me."

"Just like that crazy Bird," joked the wise guys, laughing at the toast of baseball who would talk of pensions. Now Fidrych will get his pension. It may be the smartest thing he ever did.

Fidrych has not grown dumb with the years.

Is this a make-it-or-break-it year? he is asked.

"I've already made it," he says.

In the end, Fidrych has survived adversity and acclaim by remaining defiantly simple. All those laid-back flower-child lyrics of the Grateful Dead proved to be the perfect philosophy, the ideal psychological armor for the first rock 'n' roll pitcher.

Most important, Fidrych has stayed rooted in his Worcester, Massachusetts, family. He has bought his schoolteacher father a forty-three-acre apple orchard.

What does Fidrych plan to do with the land?

"It's my dad's land," he answers.

But you bought it, he is reminded.

Fidrych looks genuinely puzzled.

"Man," he says, "what's mine is his and what's his is mine. We're a family."

His mother's parting words to him when he signed a pro contract were "You make sure you come home the same nut you've always been." Everyone in Worcester knows he got his flakiness from his mother. But don't mention it to Fidrych.

"Makin' fun of my mom?" he says, in a tone of voice that indicates it would be extremely unwise.

Fidrych has been buffeted by a world of changes in just three years. Yet a roller-coaster ride that might have unbalanced others seems to have excited him.

Fidrych reported to spring training a day early this year, only to discover that the Tigers' hotel had no reservation for him. Two years ago, he was given Lakeland's key to the city. This spring, he couldn't get a room key. Was the Bird bitter or driven to thinking deep, ugly thoughts about the fickle world?

"No big deal," says Fidrych. "I just called LeFlore and asked him if I could sleep on his floor."

THE UNEASY GHOST OF J. R. RICHARD

Spring 1981—Today is J. R. Richard's birthday. He is thirty-one. Baseball has a statistic for everything, and according to the studies, thirty-one is the best of all possible ages to be if you're a ballplayer. That's the peak. The skills of youth and the knowledge of experience meet here.

That's good, because Richard needs every edge he can get.

Contrary to popular belief, the most vital part of the J. R. Richard story is finished. His comeback is already complete. His comeback to life, that is. "The most important thing is, I'm here," he says with his big smile and tiny teeth.

Let us, in the interests of both accuracy and decency, decree right now that Richard's recovery from his massive stroke last July is already a success. "I can see, I can talk, and I can think," he says, "even though maybe I'm not the best at any of them."

Few things are more disturbing to a stroke victim than being watched. Everybody, morbidly but inescapably, looks for the signs of loss. Is the face the same? Does an eye or lip droop? Perhaps we are fascinated because we feel that we are seeing the visage of death lurking in a living face.

If the six-foot-eight, 250-pound Richard were a Martian, he could not be watched any more closely than he is here. And he can guess the first thought of almost every baseball observer who sees him for the first time: "No way."

Richard has his private field at the back of the Houston Astros' rather bleak and remote facility here in Cocoa Beach, Florida. He looks like a giant child playing with two lonely friends. One is Astro exercise specialist Gene Coleman, the other a ball boy. Gently, Coleman taps harmless grounders toward Richard as a father might hit a ball to his eight-year-old for the first time. The grounders start soft and stay that way. For good reason.

One time, Coleman accidentally swung a bit harder, caught the bottom half of the ball and hit a respectable line drive back at Richard.

Nothing happened. Nothing.

Richard never saw it, never moved his glove hand, never defended himself as the ball went past his head.

If the baseball isn't where Richard expects it to be, if his eyes have to roam to pick it up, then judge its speed and direction, he's in trouble. It's a problem of depth perception, especially on the left side. Some doctors say it will improve and that Richard will see normally. Some don't think so. "Right now, it's like trying to find a ghost," says Richard. "I don't see the ball right away yet. It's hard to find."

Until Richard can unerringly pick up the flight of a rifle-shot liner, there is no way his career will ever get beyond this little field. Even the greatest of pitchers, and that's what he was when he struck out more than three hundred men in '78 and '79, has dozens of rockets hit back through the box every year.

Even when Richard sees the hopping ball perfectly, he's not a pretty sight for the squeamish. A national TV newsclip of Richard's first day of practice showed him bobbling or missing the first couple of balls nudged back to him. It was reported that by the end of his workout he was fielding normally and throwing hard to all bases. Never let the facts get in the way of a "good news" story. Who wants to know that Richard can't field as well as a Little Leaguer?

Sometimes Richard grabs the ball cleanly, and sometimes he whirls and throws it accurately to the ball-boy baseman. And plenty of times, he doesn't.

When Richard began leaving his solitary diamond to participate in some Astro drills, he stood in the outfield and watched other people shag flies. "The wind was bad. It was tough to get a good jump," said Richard, who didn't catch one fly. And he put on a batting helmet to try to take bunting practice against a pitching machine. Then that metaphysical wind came up again. "Wind's pretty strong," said Coach Bunny Mick, referring to an imperceptible breeze. "Let's skip it today."

Asked later whether Richard has been able to bunt a ball against the machine, Mick answered with a standard team joke: "You'll have to ask [general manager] Al Rosen." All the Astros have been given a gag rule regarding Richard.

Nuances of coordination and shades of eyesight are almost as hard to detect as a blood clot. While at this stage Richard can perform some everyday physical acts, he can't do much more. For daily life, he's normal. For an athlete, he's not even close. "The Comeback Begins," blared a *Sports Illustrated* cover this week. Our national obsession with soap opera may be a major problem for Richard.

Another inescapable difficulty is Richard himself. He has been told by his neurologist, Dr. William Fields, that "the biggest key to complete recovery from a stroke is motivation, attitude, point of view."

If you'd been told that, how would you talk? You'd talk just like Richard: unrealistically, with blind optimism and refusal to entertain hypothetical questions about failure. But the truth, the real odds against him, are not Richard's friends. So he's not inviting them into his brain. His conversation sounds like fantasy, but it is really just self-hypnosis.

In midwinter, Richard was telling folks over the phone that he hadn't ruled out pitching on opening day. He raised expectations then and he continues to constantly. He insists, "I don't think I have any problems." His eyesight, his coordination? "I don't consider those problems." Has he made improvement here? "I improve every day in every way." Could he be specific? "I can tell the difference." What about all those who go away from here shaking their heads sadly? "They don't know how far I've come already. They haven't seen yet what I'm capable of doing . . . Everybody's on my side, I know, but they don't believe. When they see me pitch again, they'll be shocked off their feet." When will he throw hard? "Soon." When will he throw his first slider? "Soon . . . it'll be like seeing an old friend again." How soon is soon? "How soon do you think it is? Time will tell me. When it's autumn, the leaves fall. When the time comes, I'll know it."

But Richard knows the state of affairs. It sneaks in the back door. "I know people are rooting for me," he says. "I thank them, especially for the prayers. I need 'em." When you say, "Good luck," to him, he gives a soft smile and says, "Thanks, I need it." Do his teammates tease him yet—the sure sign they think he's really going to make it back? "No, it's still too serious for that."

Sometimes it seems that half the teams in baseball have some once-great pitcher trying his umpteenth comeback, but none is trying to overcome as much as Richard. Nevertheless, Richard has an enormous advantage. Somewhere, he has found a sense of identity that shines in a way it never did before his tribulations.

"I see things differently than I used to," he says. "I used to drive fast all the time. I'd come in the gate here at Cocoa and make doughnuts in the dirt doing wheelies by spinning my car.

"But, you know, as fast as I always went, I was always late. I'd start late, hurry, then get there late. Now I go slower. I start early, go slow, and get there early."

Is there some philosophy buried in there?

"Somewhere," says Richard with the smile he uses far more than he once did.

Richard's two trademark expressions now are "That's history" and "I have no timetable." By the first, he means that he has tried to wash away all the sins of the past, including his own. By forgiving others, he can forgive himself.

When he says he's torn up the calendar, he means it. "I'm not on baseball time," he says. "I'm on J. R. Richard time. I think I've always been on my own time. But I'm sure of it now." Then he lights up the grin that changes his face from dull to delightful. "Maybe all us fishermen are on our own time."

It's said two things help a person take control of his life, make him self-reliant and independent: great wealth and a brush with death. Richard has had both. The year before his stroke, he signed a four-year, $3.2-million contract, which was guaranteed even if he never pitched again.

That contract, plus his stroke, made Richard an inviolable, fiercely separate island. The breach between Richard and Astro management is total; if he were in good health, they might well be in open warfare. Richard and his agent, Tom Reich, considered a lawsuit against the Astro doctors. The mere mention of agent Reich, who has criticized the Astros from pillar to post for what he considers their neglect and disrespect toward Richard, is like uttering a four-letter word in the Astro offices.

Richard's two best Astro friends, those who stood up for him in the clubhouse when he was openly doubted—Enos Cabell and Joe Morgan (both Reich clients)—have been traded or let go. "They are going to be greatly missed around here," says Richard, sounding ominous. "The locker room is real quiet now. This team is basically a different club now." At another time, he says out of the blue, "We only have three blacks left in the club now."

Richard's a sort of uneasy ghost lurking around the edges of the Astro banquet. He has his own field and his own coach to hit him dribblers. He has his own press conference every Wednesday. He sets his own schedule. His best friends on the team are gone. His agent has the good sense to stay clear of the people here who loathe him. Richard collects an $800,000-a-year salary.

His place in the starting rotation has been given to Sutton, who is making $900,000 a year. The Astros call Sutton "insurance in case J. R. doesn't come back." Everybody here knows better.

Despite all this, Richard is more pleasant, more outgoing, more generous with other people than ever before in his life. Once, he was the most forbidding Astro. Now he may be the least, signing interminable autographs and seeking out chitchat. After a lifetime as the Goliath overdog, he is now everybody's underdog, and he enjoys it. Richard may even have become the symbol of a decent, long-out-of-fashion idea: mutual tolerance.

The talk of Cocoa is Richard's incredible, bone-crunching handshake. Somehow, for ten years, nobody noticed it. "I think," says one Astro regular, "it's because he never shook hands with anybody before."

"I've found it's not hard to get along with people," Richard says. His conversation is sprinkled with spontaneous bits of harmless laconic wit. "I don't know how fast I'm throwing, 'cause I haven't run alongside one of my fastballs yet."

Where another athlete might see enormous, probably insurmountable problems, Richard only knows the sweet pleasures of being, now and forever, on his own, slow, Lou'siana fisherman's time. Why does he seem so contented when, of all the players in baseball, he undoubtedly has the most against him?

"A smile," he says in his low, deep, molasses voice, "is just a frown turned upside down."

TOM TERRIFIC COMES HOME

Spring 1983—Pitchers have a fraternal empathy that often outweighs any other consideration. They alone know how capricious their jobs can be, how performance hangs by the twin slender threads of injury and mechanics. One twinge in a muscle, one unconscious change in form, and the skill that seemed like second nature can become difficult or impossible. One small ill can beget another, and that leads on to the next until, finally, those complaints, each minor in itself, conspire like assassins. Gradually they infect the psyche, confuse the muscle memory and throw the body's coordination out of kilter, until, in the end, they make such a wreck of a great pitcher that he retreats and asks, "How do you throw a baseball?"

Even Tom Seaver understands this pitcher's nightmare. For fifteen seasons, the future Hall of Famer, who has returned to the Mets this spring, knew about health and fame. Then, last season he learned about the dark side of pitching.

As Seaver stood in the batter's box in Al Lang Field, in St. Petersburg, Florida, today he looked out toward the mound and saw this pitching disease, this occupational equivalent of delirium tremens, in its most virulent form. Seaver saw Mark (the Bird) Fidrych in the terminal stages of career disintegration. Fidrych, the child who once could hit the buckle on his catcher's shin guards with every pitch, couldn't even find the plate. Half his pitches were six feet high; his strikes were slaughtered.

By the time Seaver arrived at the plate, three runs were in, three men on and only one out. The previous spring, in '82, Seaver had been in Fidrych's shoes. In his first spring game, with an injured thigh and awkward delivery, Seaver allowed ten runs in one inning; the debacle ended with a homer by fellow pitcher Rick Rhoden.

That ugly omen spawned an awful season. As soon as the thigh improved, Seaver caught a mysterious flu that weakened him for months. His legs wobbled, and he pulled a muscle near the buttock. That, in turn, gave him shoulder and back miseries. Trying to compensate for aches and age, Seaver became a parody of Tom Terrific. By mid-August, he'd given up for the year. After going 14-2 in 1981, the Seaver of '82 was 5-13 with a 5.50 ERA and all the other statistical earmarks of a washed-up pitcher.

Cincinnati, knowing Seaver's market value was almost nil, granted his wish that he go home to expire. "The Reds had a horrible year [101 losses] . . . and I contributed more than anybody to that," said Seaver. The Mets got Seaver cheap.

So, as Seaver watched Fidrych, he saw a fellow in the same distress he had borne. And he had pity. Seaver turned to Boston catcher Rich Gedman and said, "Just tell him to throw it out there and I'll hit into a double play."

Seaver grounded to short for a double play to end the inning. True to baseball's hard reality, that act of mercy only saved Fidrych for another inning and another shelling. "I wish I could have gone out and told him to quit moving his shoulders horizontally," muttered Seaver as he recounted the story. "That's why he was wild and couldn't get any power. You have to work that front shoulder downward at a 45-degree angle."

A month previous, the chances of either Seaver or Fidrych making an inspirational comeback seemed slim. Fidrych, who loved the game as much as he is loved by those in the game, seemed further away than ever. Seaver, however, was raising eyebrows and hopes.

In his first two spring-training games, Seaver was battered. Then he turned a corner; against formidable Red Sox hitters like Dwight Evans, Jim Rice and Tony Armas, he was comfortably in command. "I did something right. I progressed. I had decent

control, mixed my pitches well, popped a couple of fastballs early
. . . the way I've been throwing down here, I didn't think I'd be
able to throw it by anyone . . . I'm very pleased. It's a step for
me," said a sober Seaver. "I'd be happy with fifteen wins this
season. If I pitch like I did today, I might make it."

Asked by the New York *Times* if he threw as hard as he once
did, Seaver said, "Today, I threw as hard as ever."

"Really," said the reporter, scribbling.

"But the ball just didn't get to the plate as fast," finished
Seaver.

"Did I get that hook in deep," said Seaver. "I wish I could take
you bass fishing with me."

These days, Seaver is trying to make the transition from a
power pitcher to a finesse pitcher. "From the first three or four
pitches, the first few hitters, you tell by their reactions what
you've got going for you that day," says Seaver. "I can't trust
myself warming up . . . or trust my eye. The hitters tell me
what's working and what isn't."

What if a reasonable facsimile of the old Seaver heater isn't
available? "You pitch, you pitch . . . the game is more interesting [now] because it's more complex."

Seaver has only one personal goal left: three hundred victories,
a quest that has consumed many a pitching mind. Few have completed the task.

THE K-Y KID

Summer 1982—Gaylord Perry, self-proclaimed spitballer and one
of the game's fiercest and most perceptive competitors, is approaching his three hundredth career victory in proper style.

Big-league hitters from coast to coast once again are cursing the
Great Expectorator to the heavens. Even though the ancient Seattle Mariner is forty-three, bald and fat, batsmen still insist that
they don't have a square chance against him.

During spring training, Perry was seriously worried that no
major-league team would give him a chance to go after his three

hundredth win, even at a bargain-basement price. "Every year, it's harder to talk 'em into givin' you a chance," said Perry, who, two weeks into spring training, was completely unwanted. "Peanut vendors are making as much as I was askin' for."

After swallowing his considerable pride and signing what he called "a day-to-day contract," Perry once again found himself the ace of a pitching staff. He was throwing so consistently well, was so beloved by the young Mariners and felt so confident that he was already looking past his three hundredth win to the day when he'd pass Walter Johnson in strikeouts. Some folks, of course, think that what Johnson had were "Ks," while Perry's strikeouts are often called "K-Ys," after the jelly he uses to doctor the baseball.

"They oughta put a tube of that stuff next to his plaque in the Hall of Fame," says California manager Gene Mauch.

With a Mariner catcher who calls him "Sir" and "Grandpa" and young teammates who ask him to get them dates with his nineteen-year-old daughter, Perry is so content that he says he intends to continue "until I can't find anybody who'll let me play . . . I love my job. Another thing is there's 10 million people out there unemployed and I don't want to be one of 'em."

When asked point-blank this week how many games he'd have won without the spitball, Perry, author of the autobiography *Me and the Spitter,* said, "I'd probably been farmin' about ten years ago."

Minutes after Perry walked off the Yankee Stadium mound with his 299th career victory, on Friday night, his right hand was a sight to see. Every finger and the entire palm was stained the deep, dirty, reddish-orange color that's often seen on the index finger of heavy smokers. What was really on Perry's hand only he knew for sure. It looked as if he'd been digging all day in the red clay of the North Carolina farm where he's raised peanuts, corn and soybeans for years.

If there was any vaseline, grease or jelly on the pitcher's person as he beat the Yankees, 6–3, then nobody caught it. As Mickey Vernon, the Yankee batting coach, said, "Gaylord mixed in the spitter well."

The only time anybody catches Perry is when he wants 'em to.

"I put the thought in their heads. You don't have to tell Graig Nettles, Oscar Gamble or Dave Winfield but just a little bit and they'll believe it. If I go over and shake hands with 'em and I got grease in my hand, they think I'm gonna have it there in the seventh inning," said Perry, his face incredulous that opponents would make such a tainted leap of logic. "I don't throw any illegal pitches. I just tend to leave a lotta evidence lyin' around."

On Friday, Perry even went so far as to grease up the palm of a mutual friend of his and Bobby Murcer's, then dispatch the fellow to the Yankee clubhouse with instructions to shake Murcer's hand and tell him, "Gaylord says hello."

"The only absolutely unhittable pitch I've seen in my whole career was Gaylord Perry's hard spitter when he was in his prime," said Murcer, who once sent Perry a gallon of lard as a gift. "I'd rather face a five-hundred-mile-per-hour fastball than that eighty-five-mph spitter Perry used to have. At least then I'd have a chance."

"Bobby Murcer is not all sugar and spice," said Perry. "Ya know, a few of those hitters have cork in that bat. They can't squeal too much, you see, 'cause I've played with 'em. I know what they're doin'."

"When he struck out thirteen of us a few days ago, he was loading up at least half the pitches," said California Angel Bobby Grich. "Oh, you expect it from him. But I'll admit he's still got a good 'mystery ball.'"

"I only saw two pitches all night that were legal," moaned Fred Lynn. "I have it on tape. He calls that thing a forkball. There ain't a forkball alive that does what that pitch does."

"I don't take one thing away from him for winning three hundred with the spitter," said former California MVP Don Baylor. "There are loopholes in the rules and you get away with what you can."

In a less than completely appetizing way, Perry is one of baseball's few genuinely symbolic players. He's sweat and spit and dirt on the knees of his uniform. He's cunning, intimidation and stubble-bearded meanness. He's practical knowledge, untutored wisdom.

Few men in the sport have such a self-evident, unadorned character. Perry was born in Williamsport, North Carolina, and grew up working hard and long on his daddy, Evan's, sharecropping farm. Gaylord and brother Jim (214 major-league wins) had one outlet from labor: baseball.

Today, Perry lives within spitting distance of the farm where he grew up, but now he owns four hundred acres of land that he works himself five months a year. Working the combine, staying outside in all weather, bending and twisting a thousand times a day, that's the reason, Perry thinks, he has lasted so long, still has the high leg kick and the full body turn. He still throws like a young man, because he still works like one.

Because Perry grew up tough, aggressive and straightforward, he's always approached others that way. Not always with success. Perry has been traded five times, released outright once, played for seven teams and left more than one of them with hard feelings in his wake. Even he admits that "I'm hard on my teammates. I need a lot out of them to win and I drive 'em." Perry's interminable on-field glares at teammates and his cutting remarks about poor fielding support are the standard by which dugout sarcasm is measured. At Cleveland in the early seventies, Perry and manager Frank Robinson had a legendary hate relationship. Perry, for instance, insisted that his contract call for one dollar more than the manager's. Robinson has always insisted Perry was the clubhouse mind-poisoner who got him fired.

In '79, one year after winning the National League's Cy Young Award at the age of forty, Perry got so mad at San Diego owner Ray Kroc over contract disagreements that he jumped the club with several weeks left in the season, went home and never came back. Since then, Perry has been with five clubs in less than three calendar years. In 1981, he actually led all Atlanta Braves starters in victories (with an 8-9 record and 3.91 ERA in the shortened season), yet was given a pink slip.

Perry's traditional prickliness—submerged these days as he does a little image-polishing—is, however, merely an inevitable side effect of a fiercely competitive personality.

At the age of twenty-six, after a 1-6 season in San Francisco, Perry's future looked nonexistent. "I needed another pitch and I needed to learn it fast. It was the spitter," said Perry.

Most pitchers are headed down the hill once they pass age thirty. Perry has won over two hundred games since that birthday. The reason: continuing education. "I just try to take the good parts of a lot of pitchers I saw when I was comin' up," said Perry in his drawl. "I got the high leg kick from Juan Marichal, determination from [Bob] Gibson. I watched [Don] Drysdale pull at his belt so much that I was sure it wasn't just habit. So I picked up goin' to the hat," said Perry, going through his famous series of cap touches and tugs that he uses when he wants batters to think he's getting his grease.

That education never stops. In preparation for his shot at #300, Perry came to Yankee Stadium for a press conference a day before the Mariners. He then left the ballpark so he could go back to his hotel room and watch the game on TV. Perry likes the centerfield camera angle, because it's better for watching hitters' stances—the better to read their minds. Also, he always likes to listen to the hometown radio announcers so he can find out who's particularly hot or cold.

It's hardly a surprise that, with such an omnivorous baseball mind, Perry wants to stay in the game after he retires, perhaps as a manager. "I think I could do better than some I've seen," he offers.

Perry seldom forgets anything—neither the day Pete Rose went five for five off him in long-ago-demolished Crosley Field nor how Richie Allen, after striking out four times, learned to hit Perry to right center and went four for four next time. He admires the hitters who adjust. Always, Perry makes his adjustments before he has to, working a year or two on new pitches before using them. "I threw my first screwball to Willie Stargell. He hit it over the centerfield fence. I never threw another one," said Perry. "I learned that you always try out a new pitch to a little guy."

In February 1982, Perry-the-student even telephoned Early Wynn, the last three-hundred-game winner, in '63, to talk about the old righthander's miserable experiences when he had 299 wins. Wynn tried to hook on with any club, failed to sign until May, then staggered until June before he could get that last, homely win. Not long after that conversation, perhaps coincidentally, Perry decided to drop his demands for a "good guaranteed contract" and take the humble Seattle offer, even though Perry says owner George Argyros "is so tight he doesn't want us to eat the peanuts on the airplanes."

Despite his skinflint deal with an expansion franchise (which has only won 301 games to Perry's 299), the old righthander, after twenty-five professional seasons, is finally getting his short hour in the sunlight of national attention.

"I'm forty-three years old and proud of every one," he said. "Out of uniform, I look quite a bit different than people might expect, so I can get by a great deal out in the streets or on airplanes. People think a guy who plays baseball has a full head of hair and doesn't need to lose ten pounds. Or should be wearin' a three-piece suit. So, most of the time, I'm kinda in disguise."

Because he has never pitched in a World Series, and in only one playoff (with the '71 Giants), because he has lost a larger percentage of his games than any other three-hundred-game winner (241 defeats), and because of the twin stigmas of his spitball and his clubhouse-lawyer reputation, Perry has perhaps been baseball's most anonymous great pitcher. After all, since World War II, only Warren Spahn has won more games than Perry, but how many would recognize his face?

Now, looking grizzled and acting mellowed, Perry seems due for a bit of the fan affection that has eluded him. "I think I'm known nationally for certain pitches," he said wryly, "but I think the three hundred wins will kind of override that [in time] . . . I think I'll have the credentials to be there [in the Hall of Fame] someday. I'm looking forward to it."

When the Perry plaque is put up in Cooperstown, it should not, as Mauch needles, have a tube of grease next to it, nor should Perry's record have a spitball asterisk beside it. However, it might be a good idea to place Perry in a wing of the Hall near those nineteenth-century old-timers who won three hundred, like Kid Nichols, Pud Galvin, Tim Keefe, John Clarkson, Mickey Welch, Eddie Plank and Old Hoss Radbourne.

Many of them came off the farm, doctored the ball as they wished, glared at any manager who dared to take them out of a game, chewed out their teammates and knocked down hitters who got too comfortable at the plate. The game was hard then, short on manners and long on sweat. And so were they.

Gaylord Perry, who has always looked as though he should be pitching in dungarees, not double knits, would grace their company.

THE TWO LIVES AND THE SIXTH SENSE

Summer 1981—With his legendary schnoz and his deep-set blue eyes that seem both merry and sad, Warren Spahn looks like a cross between Max Patkin, the clown prince of baseball, and Abe Vigoda, the character actor of television's Fish.

"Yup," says Warren Spahn, the honorary captain of the National League All-Star Team, "nobody's got a face just like this one."

The man who was one of the greatest pitchers in the history of a pitcher's game sat in the NL dugout, shoehorned into a modern double-knit replica of the old Milwaukee Braves uniform and, unnoticed by most, bemusedly watched the show.

One by one, old friends or old admirers wandered past to ask a question.

Watcha doin', Spahnie?

"Minor-league pitching instructor for the Angels."

How's the family?

"My wife died three years ago."

What do you think of the strike?

Spahn pauses. "I haven't been a part of the major-league scene for sixteen years," says the man who, after winning 367 big-league games, has spent those years everywhere from the Mexican League to various parts of the bushes. "So why the hell should anybody care what I think?"

Baseball men have two lives. Spahn calls them the young life and the old life. Rarely do the two bear any resemblance to each other. "Some get their just deserts early, some get them late," said Spahn. "Just so you get 'em sometime."

Around him Spahn saw strange things: Who was managing the AL All-Star Team, and being interviewed on national TV, but Jimmy Frey, who spent fourteen years in the minors with never a major-league game? And who was doing the interviewing but major-league nonentity Joe Garagiola?

"I always loved to see Garagiola comin' to bat," said Spahn as the announcer approached. "I owned him."

"Yeah," said Garagiola, "it used to embarrass me when you sent your limousine to the hotel for me and the guy would announce, 'Warren Spahn's car is here for Mr. Garagiola.' "

In his first life, Spahn won twenty games thirteen times. Nobody whose career was played entirely in lively-ball times since 1920 has come within fifty wins of his total. In his second life, Spahn is exactly the sort of moderately content, but invisible, minor-league laborer that men like Frey, or Earl Weaver, were in their youth. Perhaps this has a sort of symmetrical justice about it. But it's tougher when the hard life comes second.

"I get in uniform every day," said Spahn, now sixty. "There's a hell of a lot of travel in the minors. I get about five days off a month, and this is one of 'em . . .

"We always play at night, which is good, so I can play golf the next day. I had to have two operations [on knees] so I could walk, but now it's okay."

Spahn slaps his paunch affectionately. "I'm fat," he says matter-of-factly. "Don't get enough work."

The worst time for Spahn came when his wife of thirty-two years died after a stroke. "She lived a year and five days," says Spahn numbly. "She didn't suffer per se, but there were lots of related problems. It was a tough year. Maybe it was a blessing [when she died].

"It hit me hard. I was drinking too much. I didn't give a damn about anything," said Spahn. "Then this job with the Angels came along. Best thing that ever happened to me—working with young people."

In a way, Spahn is lucky that he played in the era before big bucks; for instance, Marvin Miller took over the players' union the year after Spahn retired. The marvelous southpaw never acquired the high-living tastes that are harder to lose than acquire. The minors suit him as comfortably now as they might have a Weaver or Frey twenty-five years ago. As long as it's baseball, Spahnie's home.

Spahn isn't a prime candidate for a big-league pitching-coach job, because he's had a tag for years: strongly opinionated, one of those superstars who could do better than he could teach.

"I hate that word 'superstar,' " says Spahn. "You're just a human being who accomplished something. With young kids, it's a cop-out. They say, 'You were great, but I can't do it that way.' They just don't want to set goals and then live up to them.

"If I have strong opinions, I don't give a damn. I have the truth of my convictions."

When Spahn speaks on pitching, there's an economy of expression that bespeaks volumes of experience condensed to a phrase. "Every hitter has a comfortable zone," says Spahn, holding his hands a yard apart. "You must pitch 'here' or 'here,' " continued Spahn, showing a foot-long area at either end of that dangerous yard.

"You have to remember that every good hitter is an egoist. If you can throw the fastball past them once, they'll make any adjustment to prevent it happening again," grinned Spahn. "That makes the best of them gullible for a change-up. Always remember: the best pitch is the one that looks like a strike, but isn't.

"When you're pitching, you have to watch the hitters more than your own pitches. The hitters tell you a true story. If they hit your fastball, then it's just not moving enough, no matter what you think or the speedgun says. You have to go to something else."

Spahn sits in the dugout, gazing onto the field. He can't even remember any longer how many All-Star games he was in. What does he think of today's pitchers? "Couldn't say," he says. "I don't watch 'em."

How is that possible? "I can't watch baseball on TV. You can't see it right, not on any camera angle," says Spahn. "You can't tell the ball's true speed or how it's really moving.

"There's a sixth sense you develop," says Spahn. "But it only works from down here on the field."

Whether he is in his young life, or his old one, Warren Spahn will never forsake that sixth sense, nor leave the one place where it works best.

9

HALF GURU, HALF BEAST OF BURDEN

"There must be some reason we're the only ones facing the other way."

—JEFF TORBORG, FORMER CATCHER

Catchers are different. No position in any pro sport is so out of sync with its game. All that baseball seems to be, catching would deny, like Caliban giving the lie to a cheerful world. Baseball is play and pleasure; catching is labor and pain.

Yet the professional backstop, with his gnarled fingers, his flat feet, his loose knees, his dray-horse thighs, is also the sport's most respected player. It is the position of last resort and first import.

"We're a rare breed," says the Yankees' Rick Cerone. "You've got to be crazy and have no regard for your body. You got to love to get dirty. But it's also the thinking man's position . . . I don't know how I got here."

"You're the leader of the squad, the quarterback," says Gary Carter, the $15 million Expo catcher and perhaps the game's best tool of ignorance. "It also helps to be a little goofy."

Catchers aren't like the other guys. Every other player shows his face; baseball is full of candid expression. Only the catcher hides behind a mask that you could rob a bank in. Other players' physiques have their own line and form. The catcher is encased, strapped and, in some cases, actually corseted—his movements a perpetual compromise with his armor. Behind the plate, he looks like a beached crustacean; at bat, he seems denuded as a molting lobster, shorn of authority without his equipment.

Others players are essentially reactors. The ball is hit, or pitched, and they react. Only the catcher creates and conceptualizes and shapes. Fittingly, he doesn't even position himself in fair territory. The pitcher of the day is his instrument. The first order of business is a chain of reasoning, leading to the decision: "slider down and in to set up the fastball tailing away." In the wake of his reasoning, which the large majority of pitchers gladly accept, everything subsequent is a chain reaction.

"A catcher needs the most concentration," says Yankee pitcher Rudy May, "especially if he's got a guy out there like me, who can't call his own game. I've never been able to evaluate my own stuff. I have to ask the catcher what's working best. Sometimes I think pitchers are stupid."

Above the locker of Chicago's Carlton Fisk is a one-word sign: THINK.

From his first day in the irons, the catcher learns that perhaps only his manager and mates really appreciate just how needed he is.

"Even for a good-hitting catcher, it's fifty-fifty whether your offense or defense contributes more," says Carter, who has won Gold Gloves the past two seasons.

"You'll always save more runs than you can drive in," says Cerone. "You squat for two and a half hours, then you're expected to drive in the winning run in the ninth inning.

"A catcher's hitting is almost an afterthought," says Jeff Torborg, now a Yankee coach. "In spring training, you'll see catchers taking batting practice with their shin guards still on, because they know they're expected to be somewhere else the next minute to catch."

Baltimore's Rick Dempsey couldn't agree more. "I didn't even know what a batting average was until I got to the major leagues."

In this game, in which the ego and the good of the team can usually coexist, the catcher must be the exception—the one true team player. Only the catcher is largely beyond the reach of baseball's ubiquitous stats, existing in that shadowy world of intangibles, like some NFL strong safety of whom only a dozen souls in Christendom have a truly informed opinion.

The catcher must scrounge for every edge. He'll tap an opposing player's bat on the plate after he's dropped it to hear if it might be corked. Once, Jim Essian, then with the White Sox, took to wearing a sponge in his glove, ostensibly because his poor, bruised hand was so sore. The first time an opponent had men on first and third and tried the double steal, Essian cocked his arm and fired the sponge toward second base. The runner on third, seeing the white blur, broke toward home and, of course, Essian, the ball still in his glove, picked him off by yards.

Thurman Munson would distract hitters with inane cordiality. For years Munson asked Mark Belanger, "How's the family?" just before the first pitch. Finally, Belanger threatened to hit Munson with the bat if he spoke to him again. "Gee, Blade, I didn't know you felt that way," said Munson. His silence lasted until the next at-bat, when the high-pitched "How's the family?" was back.

The strong, silent types—like Fisk—have their little tricks too. "Fisk controls the tempo of the game more than anybody," says pitcher Mike Flanagan of the Orioles. "He's by far the slowest catcher. It takes a hell of a long time to have a big inning against Fisk. He can kill your momentum just like a coach calling time-out in basketball."

At other positions, leadership is strictly optional. At catcher, it's part of the job description. Fair or not, the courage of a team is often measured by the grit of its catcher. When Darrell Porter tiptoed into home plate in the 1980 World Series, never even smudging his britches as he was tagged standing up, both he and his Royals were chastised coast to coast. "You reflect the whole team," says Cerone. "And you affect the whole team."

"Lack of confidence radiates out from behind the plate," says Dempsey. "Confidence can too. Before the 1979 World Series, I told Pirate manager Chuck Tanner, 'Go ahead, get them running. Let's go.' " The Pirates didn't steal a base in the Series.

At the other positions, personality type has little to do with success. Every sort of chap has succeeded as a pitcher or a shortstop. But all good catchers must be catchers at heart—responsible, inured to drudgery and dull pain, observant. Half guru, half beast of burden.

"The worst catchers are converted catchers," says Torborg. "They never seem to grasp the whole idea of the position."

Perhaps that speaks well for their survival instincts, because of all the differences between catchers and other players, the most fundamental is the ability to endure pain.

Baseball is the civilized game—shagging flies, loping to backhand a grounder. That is, until they hand you the mask. There's a message in paraphernalia: shin guards, chest protector, steel-barred mask, helmet, a glove as big as a bear trap: the proof of ignorance.

That first day behind the plate is a revelation. Henceforth, the hiss of pitches has a new malevolence, each a potential foul tip aimed at throat, biceps, fingers, groin. To this, add the joy of the crouch. Of all the positions man assumes in his games, none is so lost to dignity, so bereft of grace, so demeaning by its very name and nature, as the catcher's *squat*. What catchers do is in every sense work. They must approve a proletarian tradition that labels a broken finger a sign of virtue.

"A catcher and his body are like the outlaw and his horse," says Johnny Bench. "He's got to ride that nag till it drops."

In one 10-year span, Bench played 1,487 games—1,367 at catcher. That's why the best catcher in history became a third baseman before retiring at thirty-five. On one hospital visit, his sore foot was X-rayed. It wasn't broken. But three old, now-healed breaks that Bench had never noticed were.

Fisk calls the job the Dorian Gray position. "On the outside, you look young, but on the inside, you're aging fast. You're afraid one day you'll take off the equipment and discover you've turned to dust."

No other diamond position has a fraction of the self-destructive code that catchers feel they must obey. Like the NFL's battered lineman, their motto, especially in pennant races, is: "I can strap it on one more day." But in football, that day comes once a week. In baseball, it's every day.

"The amount of pain, the sharpness of it, and the mental strain of thinking about it, well, you can endure more each year," says Fisk, whose weight dropped from 218 pounds to 184 after catching a near-record 154 games in 1978. (The American League record is 155 games, by Jim Sundberg; the major-league record is 160, by Randy Hundley.) "Each injury immunizes your mind. You lose your ability to discriminate between degrees of discomfort. You don't think about the blood in the joints or the squished ligaments or the floating bone chips. So what if you're bleeding like a pig inside? It's almost a relief when you're so badly hurt it's impossible to play and you don't have to decide."

Thus, catching becomes an invitation to extinction. Only the catcher deliberately accelerates his own decay. As Bench once confided to Carter, "One game at catcher has as much wear and tear as five at any other position."

Tough, thankless jobs are such second nature to true receivers that sometimes they put their hand in the fire before they've thought. In 1981, when George Steinbrenner was berating his Yankees after a loss in the playoffs against Milwaukee, one voice broke the silence with a brief rebuttal: "Go screw yourself, George." Catcher Rick Cerone, naturally.

"You have to be strong-willed, battle your pitcher," says Cerone. "Yeah, maybe battle the owner once in a while."

Need a volunteer to go over the top? Look for a catcher. When the Players Association wanted to take the union's message to national TV during the strike, who stepped forward but catcher Bob Boone. When it's time to take the blame—for anything—the catcher knows his place: front and center. On the final day of the NL playoffs in 1981, L.A. won 2–1 over Montreal on Rick Monday's homer in the ninth off Steve Rogers. And who took credit for losing the pennant? Why, Carter. Maybe he should have called for a different pitch, or set his target differently, he speculated. Overhearing these mea culpas, Rogers said, "Maybe I should have thrown it different." Said with the character of a catcher.

Catchers are disabused of their illusions early. Many became catchers in the first place because they were told they were too slow for the glamour positions. Or because they bought the old chestnut about catching being the shortest road to the big leagues. "A lot are like me, guys who were high school offensive guards, but always wanted to be the quarterback," says Johnny Oates, a catcher with five teams and now the manager of the Yankee double-A team in Nashville. "Catching was our way of getting a chance to run the ballclub."

From the days of Bill Dickey and Mickey Cochrane through the more recent times of Yogi Berra and Roy Campanella, there always seemed to be just one or two famous star catchers at a time and many nonentities. Frankly, catchers were by far the game's worst athletes.

Now, however, the word is out that smaller, more nimble athletes are in. "With all the emphasis on base stealing in the game now, you're seeing better athletes become catchers," says Torborg. "Smaller, quicker guys who can deliver the ball to second faster." Gun arms like those of Dempsey, Alex Trevino and Cerone are showing up attached to bodies that are no more than six feet and 185 pounds.

Between the knuckleballs on the fingertips, the broken bones blocking the plate and the multitude of embarrassments inflicted by thieves, it's not an accident that the game's best dark humor seems to come from catchers. Why, for instance, don't you ever see two old catchers shaking hands? Because you'd need a surgeon to pry their fingers apart. Reformed catchers turned TV slickers, like Bob Uecker and Joe Garagiola, just show the tip of an iceberg of bleak self-insight.

"Catchers fall prey to a lot of strange mind games," says Torborg. "At some point, almost every catcher goes through a phase during which he can throw perfectly to second base but, with men on base, he can't throw the ball back to the pitcher."

"Happens to almost all of us, even the best," interjects Jim Hegan, once one of the best, as he and Torborg rattle off names of sufferers like Clint Courtney, Johnny Edwards, Fran Healy, Clay Dalrymple and Ray Fosse. "Sometimes it gets so bad that, like Fosse, they'll walk three steps toward the mound, go through a little windup and still not throw it. I went through it for a year and a half. It started in my first big-league camp when I was trying to make every throw to the mound perfect. Suddenly, I was making them jump everywhere for the ball. By the time I finished, they didn't need calisthenics."

Pitchers are harsh judges of their catchers. "They'll get on you about anything," says Torborg. "Johnny Podres used to holler at me for not making my glove pop loudly enough on his fastball: 'Get a new glove or make that one make some noise.' "

As if he doesn't have enough problems, a catcher has to do his best work in a three's-a-crowd tangle with an umpire and a hitter. Other players, by contrast, are unencumbered. There's space around them—and silence. The pitcher on his hill is like a monologist. The image of DiMaggio alone in centerfield is part of his mystique.

Catchers, on the other hand, make bridges between, say, an annoyed pitcher and the plate umpire, or an angry manager and a faltering pitcher. It's just another thankless task, this one requiring a sense of decorum and the skills of a mediator.

A little psychiatric training can't hurt either. Others may prosper by being mere behaviorists, noting which act gets what result. But only a catcher, Thurman Munson, would go to the mound in the last game of the 1978 World Series and prick the pride of an aging Catfish Hunter. "Cat, you better hit my glove exactly where I put it, 'cause you ain't got diddly tonight."

Ultimately, the catcher's role constitutes a unique metaphysic. What he feels, contributes and endures in his labors seems to be of a different world from the unfettered, adventurous, often joyously creative play of those at other positions. Each day, he must face the irony that he is the *second* most important man on the field, never the first. But pitchers change. Only he remains.

"My idea is really to play the game of baseball. Not many people know what that can mean," says Fisk, speaking of the way he has his hand on every pulsebeat of the game: calling each pitch, fielding bunts, intimidating runners, diving into the seats for foul balls, laying his body across the plate. "You don't give the other team a single extra out or base or at-bat. You don't even give them one extra swing.

"You have to know the game to understand why a catcher feels so special about his work. You have every part of the game running through your fingers."

To weigh such satisfaction against such pains—then call it all a square deal—requires a fine fortitude. Someone can always be found to catch. In its small way, that speaks well for man.

10

THE IMPORTANCE
OF BEING THIRD

COSTELLO: I'm asking you what's the name of the first baseman.

ABBOTT (rapidly): What's the name of the second baseman?

COSTELLO (more rapidly): I don't know.

BOTH (most rapidly): Third base!!

When Abbott and Costello named their baseball team, they picked the perfect moniker for the third baseman: I-Don't-Know.

For generations, it was said that the third baseman should have to pay his way into the ballpark. Now, increasingly, it's the third baseman whom we pay our money to get into the stadium to see. The hot corner has gone from a century of disregard, and almost disrepute, to a decade of glamour and demand.

It took baseball from the 1860s until the 1960s to get the picture in focus. Fewer third basemen are in the Hall of Fame than any other position: only six in 115 years. But now the idea has grown to ripeness that third base might really be hot stuff. Instead of the job being filled by afterthought and default, third is the place where the gap between an excellent and a mediocre player makes the most dramatic difference.

If you want to be around in October, then you had better understand the importance of being third. Consider the exploits of Robinson, Rose, Nettles, Schmidt. No position is so prone to hot streaks and given to the marriage of reflexes and confidence. No other position asks the player to do the unbelievable with such regularity. And in late-season pressure games, no section of the field seems to be the scene of so many game-shifting plays.

In the era of Mike Schmidt and George Brett, Buddy Bell and Graig Nettles, Carney Lansford and Ron Cey, Paul Molitor and Bill Madlock, Bob Horner and Doug DeCinces, Ray Knight and John Castino, it is hard to believe that for generations third base was the position that received the leftovers, the guys with not enough speed, not enough arm, not enough power, not enough anything.

Like tight end in football, third base is the last position in its sport to be defined and discovered. Even the value of the bullpen was understood before the virtues of third were fully appreciated. And just as with the NFL tight end, the revolutionary notion is that the proper man for third base is not the marginal major leaguer with a few odd and somewhat disconnected skills but, rather, the best all-around power athlete in the organization.

The Dallas Cowboys, for instance, look for their fastest big man —the one who can block down on a middle linebacker, obliterate a safety, snag a pass in traffic, shake-and-bake to get open deep and (indefinable gift) make the telling play—to be their tight end.

In baseball, a similar mission-impossible project is the vogue. Find the 6-2, 200-pound super jock, put him at third and you've got the game changer. The in-their-prime prototypes are Schmidt (6-2, 203), Brett (6-0, 200) and Bell (6-1, 185). They occupy the idealized place in the game that was reserved for fleet power-hitting centerfielders twenty-five years ago, when debate raged over the merits of Mantle, Mays and Snider.

Like the tight end, this new third-base creature is not necessarily the biggest, fastest, strongest, toughest, most sure-handed, rangiest or quickest man on the team. He's just the best athlete.

The job description for the exemplary third baseman—and both Schmidt and Bell fill it, while several others come close—is perhaps the most winnowing of any position, including baseball's traditional big three: centerfield, shortstop and catcher.

This baseball decathlete with the filthy uniform and the head-to-toe bruises must meet these ten simple requirements. He must have:

- the reflexes to dive for blurred smashes to either side;
- the range to cut off hits headed for the hole at shortstop;
- the agility to charge a swinging bunt or leap and twist for a liner;
- the dexterity to field balls bare-handed on the full run;
- the composure to recover balls that ricochet off his body;
- the arm to throw hard 125-foot pegs underhand, sidearm or from the knees;
- the courage to face bad-hop rockets approaching at more than 100 miles per hour from less than 100 feet away;
- the self-confidence to accept the worst fielding percentage on the team and be undressed most often;
- the knack, the position's *raison d'être,* of making the spectacular play routinely;
- the durability to survive all this every day for six months.

And, oh yes, he must be a great hitter and run-producer.

The days of the leather specialist at third are past. Few contenders can afford the luxury of a spaghetti-bat like Aurelio Rodriguez or, a generation ago, Clete Boyer, at third. Too many of their rivals have third basemen who rate from good to great both at bat and in the field.

For a phenomenon so young, it's surprising that our memories of third-base excellence seem so old. After all, this whole business started only a few years ago. To be exact, the era of the third baseman began on the weekend of October 10–11, 1970, in Cincinnati, when Brooks Robinson changed the understanding of an entire area of the field.

Okay, okay, so we all remember the highlight film with Robinson visiting the third-base coaching box to throw out Lee May. And we also recall the other robberies he perpetrated: on Tony Perez' hot hopper and Tommy Helms' roller. However, for Robinson, it was Sunday's play on Johnny Bench that, in a way, changed the public's conception of third base.

"For years, people have kept asking me, 'How could you catch

a line drive that was going to go foul? Isn't that impossible?' "
recalls Robinson. "I've never known what to tell them except
maybe that at third base you've got to learn how to be in motion
toward where the ball's going before it hits the bat." That magical
Robinson Series taught the public that something new was happening at third base.

The lightning hit the rod in the mid-1950s when Eddie Mathews and Harmon Killebrew showed that a five hundred-homer
man could survive at third without nightly humiliation. Previous
gentlemen of this sort, like Jimmie Foxx, had been driven quickly
to safer habitats. Then Clete Boyer, of the Yankees, showed that,
if you wanted something spicy for the eleven o'clock news, your
best chance was to put the camera at third base.

Finally, Robinson and Ken Boyer, of St. Louis, made the con-
ceptual breakthrough: One man could combine all the essential
gifts at third with the batting punch to lead the league in RBIs. In
1964 they were MVPs simultaneously.

"The history of third base," says Shirley Povich, who covered
his first World Series for the Washington *Post* in 1924, "is that
there were always a few good ones—like Pie Traynor and Ossie
Bluege—but a lot of poor ones. Until recent times, it was considered peasant's duty, a kind of thankless, painful blacksmith's position for a player who couldn't keep a job any other way."

After years of seeing nonentities with "3B" after their names
in the boxscores—forgettable chaps named Wert, Alvis, As-
promonte, Kasko, Jablonski, Zimmer and the like—there began
to appear uplifting folk with one sort of panache or another, like
Ron Santo and Richie Allen.

The revolution had begun and, with each succeeding year, it
was reinforced. Turn on the television in October and there, suddenly, was a succession of protagonist third basemen. It seemed
you couldn't be world champ without one.

From 1969 to 1971, Robinson epitomized the best damn team
in baseball.

From 1972 to 1974, who was the captain and barrel-chested
symbol of the feudin' Oakland A's but Sal Bando, a team leader in
RBIs.

In 1975 to 1976, Pete Rose was in his third-base incarnation and captaining the Reds to world titles. He was Series MVP in 1975.

Next came the champion Bronx Bickerers of 1977–78. By the end of the 1978 Series, Yankee third baseman Graig Nettles had gone from nonentity (Craig or Greg?) to mythic character (Puff the Magic Dragon).

Who was the final piece in the puzzle of "the family" in 1979 but two-time batting champ Bill Madlock.

By 1980, the hot-corner extravaganza had reached its peak. Schmidt and Brett seemed to have half the stage to themselves.

Now that the spotlight finally rests on third base, we discover another surprise. No consensus exists on how the position should be played. Third, as well as being the last position to be appreciated, is also the last spot to evolve a theory of proper play.

Traditional wisdom has been summed up in two dicta: "Hug the line, especially in the late innings," and, in the words of Bluege, "Play as close to the hitter as possible so that you 'narrow the cone.' "

"Protecting the line," one of the game's seldom-questioned gospels, is based entirely on one simple observation: If the ball goes by you to your left, it's a single. If it goes by to your right, it's a double. So, dummy, don't let it get by to your right.

"Narrowing the cone" is a slightly more sophisticated geometrical concept, analogous to a hockey goalie attacking a shooter "to cut down the angle." It means that the closer a hot-corner man crept in toward the hitter, the more balls he could—in theory—reach, even though they would be moving faster.

Unfortunately for these precepts, the man who has, in the past ten years, broken almost every significant fielding record for third basemen is a fellow who violently disagrees with both these laws. In fact, he thinks the reason he has set those records and, potentially, revolutionized the theory of his position is that he has turned those two notions on their heads.

Before opening the envelope, let us say that while most fielding stats mean almost nothing, one means almost everything: assists for a third baseman. Since a third baseman's job is to get every ground ball he can reach, and since no one ever cuts him off, it is fair to deduce that a third baseman's assist total is an excellent barometer of his range.

By this standard, there's no question which third baseman in his prime has done the most grounder-gobbling. It's not the aesthetician's dream, Robinson, but the savvy, iconoclastic Nettles, who has dared to defy every conventional notion on how to play third base.

"I play farther off the line than any other third baseman. Sometimes I'm as much as twenty feet to the left of where you're supposed to be," says the radical Nettles. "I also believe in playing deeper than 'normal.'"

Is that why you hold the all-time record for most assists in a season (412 in 1971 for Cleveland), as well as the mark for most assists per game for a career (2.2)?

"Probably," says Nettles, who, from 1970 to 1976, averaged 383 assists a year—a seven-year pace that no one has equaled. By contrast, during the same seven years, in the same number of games, Bando averaged 293. (For quibblers, it might be noted that during his last three seasons in Cleveland he averaged 376 assists, while in his first four in New York the figure was 388. So much for any drastic dependence of third-base assists on pitching staff, quality of team or ballpark.)

Why play far off the line? Isn't that suicide?

"Look at stats on which fielders make the most plays. They prove that far more balls are hit up the middle than down the lines," says Nettles. "For every ball that gets past me over the bag, I'll take ten hits from them in the hole.

"Also, because I get off the line, the shortstop on my team can shade toward second, and every hitter knows that by far the biggest hole on the field is up middle. That's why the hitting coaches are always screaming, 'Hit it back up the middle.' Also, the shortstop who moves toward second can make more of the tough plays behind second than he can the tough plays in the hole, because the throw is shorter and easier.

"So we close up two holes on the hitter and tease him with trying to hit a shot exactly down the line. That's hard to do deliberately.

"In a crucial game situation, sometimes I'll move closer to the line, but I hate it. Baseball's a percentage game, and I'm just convinced that's the wrong percentage. Late in games, I'm fifteen feet farther off the line than the other third basemen. A lot of them are afraid to get into the play. They'd just as soon guard the line, stay in the shadows and avoid the heat."

As if all that isn't sacrilegious enough, Nettles believes that a third baseman playing deep has a better chance than one "narrowing the cone," because he won't be overpowered as often by smashes, won't get caught by as many tough, in-between hops. "I even don't think you're improving any angles by crowding the hitter," adds Nettles, who believes his feet cover ground faster than the trigonometry of angle and velocity eats it up.

Next, this heartless destroyer of illusions will say you should break the holiest of ground rules by backing up on a grounder and letting it play you.

"Oh, yeah," says Nettles, "lots of times you should back up on the ball and gamble on getting a better hop. I believe in that more every year."

This callow geek probably thinks a third baseman shouldn't get in front of every ball.

"You have better perspective if you play the ball to the side," says Nettles. "I often try to get a little to the side of balls hit right at me."

What we have here is the sort of outside agitator who'd lead children astray by hinting that the key to turning the DP isn't giving a good chest-high throw to the second baseman so he can make a smooth pivot.

"I could care less about the second baseman," says Nettles. "The key to starting the around-the-horn double play is rushing the throw. Get it there as fast as you can, even if it's lousy. All those slow, accurate throws to second are why there are so many pretty force-outs that don't become double plays."

And no doubt that's why you hold the all-time single-season record for starting double plays (fifty-four).

"Sure."

While Nettles may have the most novel notions about third, there is little about the position that had the authority of doctrine until Professor Brooks—the Dr. Bad-Body of Baltimore—arrived in the late 1950s to show everybody what had been missing. Until Robinson, the rule at third was a decent arm, a cast-iron chin and a broad chest.

"When I was coming up, they'd stick anybody over at third," says Robinson. "It was the nowhere position after you flunked at short and second. They told me, 'Brooks, you sure can't make it at second. Go to third and catch everything that comes at you.' "

Instead, Robinson, perhaps hard of hearing, decided to catch everything.

"The two biggest things are probably concentration and anticipation," says Robinson. "Everything happens so fast at third, you have to take so many tough hops as they come, that if your mind wanders just a little, you're helpless.

"I remember one day in Kansas City, I looked down and realized I was wearing two different kinds of baseball shoes. Well, the next batter hit me a ball I should have had easy, but I got all tangled up and booted it. I said to myself, 'Brooks, you were thinking about those shoes.'

"You've got to keep concentrating even after you've missed a ball. I had a knack I couldn't explain for playing balls off the upper part of my body. Wherever it hit me, it'd just drop—'thug' —dead right in front of me and I'd throw the guy out. You try to engulf the bad hop, almost shrug and go limp as it hits you.

"I kid Doug DeCinces because whenever the ball hits him, it seems to bounce just far enough away so he can't get the guy. I tell Doug his body's too hard, that he ought to have a soft one, like mine.

"Anticipating is even more important. The pitch comes into your peripheral vision and you can see the batter start his swing. You can tell by his feet, hips and hands whether he'll get the bat head out quick enough to pull it to your right, or whether it'll be to your left.

"I'd have to say that by the time the ball hit the bat, I was on the way," says Robinson, who has the highest fielding percentage in history (.971), as well as sixteen Gold Gloves voted by managers and coaches.

"Before the pitch, I always anticipated to the left, because that's where most balls go. I thought to myself, 'Left, it's going to your left.' In my mind it was like I was already moving, even though I was still."

So perhaps the difference between Robinson, the position's instinctual genius, and Nettles, its current intellectual, is not so great.

It is odd that the primary necessity of every third sacker today is the same as that in the days of John McGraw, Home Run Baker, Pepper Martin and Jumping Joe Dugan. "You're going to get hit by an awful lot of balls," says Nettles. "You just have to tell yourself it's not going to hurt for very long."

Yet every third baseman has the same nightmare: the ball he never sees. "Sunday . . . lots of shirt-sleeves in the crowd . . . Frank Howard's up," says Robinson, recalling the 6-7, 225-pound capital punisher. "He crushed it. I jumped. I lost it. My hat flew off. My neck snapped back so hard I heard it crack. A blur went right over my face. By the time my glove was up to the level of my face, I swear I heard the ball hit the wall in the leftfield corner.

"When I got back to the dugout, I broke out in a cold sweat. Thank God that ball was two feet too high."

Vogues may come and go. The fickle affection of the baseball fates may rotate the glamour stars to some other point on the game's compass. But, now and always, cold sweats and the hot corner will go together.

11.
MYTHS

"The Americans have a genius for taking a thing, examining its every part, and developing each part to its utmost. This they have done with the [English] game of rounders, and, from a clumsy, primitive pastime, have so tightened its joints and put such a fine finish on its points that it stands forth a complicated machine of infinite exactitude."
—ANGUS EVANS, English commentator, on baseball in the early 1900s.

When hawking his novel notions, like the orange baseball or double-knit uniforms, Charlie O. Finley used to say, "The day Custer lost at the Little Bighorn, the Chicago White Sox beat the Cincinnati Red Legs, 3–2. Both teams wore knickers. And they're still wearin' 'em today."

Of all our sports, none is so tied to habits. That's why baseball has more myths than any of our games.

Once Americans completed that nineteenth-century job of tightening the joints and finishing the points of England's rounders, it became widely assumed that baseball was a polished, and thoroughly understood, product. If John McGraw ordained, "Take two and hit to right," then so it was. If Babe Ruth described batting as "Pickin' a good one and sockin' it," then what more science was needed?

The answer in the 1980s is "A lot."

Baseball, a national institution for fifty years before the lively ball ever arrived, has always had a hard time catching up with itself. While the NFL is already twenty years into its computer age, baseball is fighting to get out of its era of pad-and-pencil arithmetic. In every corner of the game, entrenched beliefs, which are really no more than venerated superstitions, are stacked up like totems to long-dead ancestors.

"Sometimes it seems like every other thing you hear is backwards," says veteran Oriole John Lowenstein. "They tell a hitter that he should 'swing down.' That would be great if the object of the game were to hit the ball between people's legs. But they've got fences out there and they let you run around the bases for free if you hit it over the wall. So, obviously, you should be swinging slightly up.

"They tell you all your life never to lift weights; then you find out it's just what you should have been doing all along," adds Lowenstein. "They tell you always to catch a flyball with two hands, but if you think about it, you should almost always catch it one-handed off to the side so your arms don't block your own vision.

"It goes on and on. You see guys stumbling running the bases because they're so determined to 'hit every base with the left foot.' You should question everything."

Ask almost any big leaguer what "myth" he would like to shatter and, like Lowenstein, he almost gets tongue-tied trying to pick his favorite target.

One of baseball's appeals in recent years is the way that the whole game has been on a demythologizing kick. How to hit, pitch, run the bases, bunt, devise a lineup, concoct game strategy, position defenders, evaluate statistics, handle a pitching staff, even how to think at the plate or on the mound—it's all up for grabs.

"Baseball defies an orderly process," says Oakland owner Ray Eisenhardt. "There are no wind tunnels where you can put a baseball idea and test it out."

In the absence of those wind tunnels—or, for that matter, any significant history of empiricism in the sport—baseball's wisdom is a patchwork thing.

"I'd like to find the guy who invented the sacrifice bunt and shove it in his ear . . . In the early and middle innings, it's the most overused strategy in baseball," says Weaver, a lover of big-inning home-run baseball who believes the sacrifice was a creation of low-scoring dead-ball days and that it should have expired back then.

Computer studies have been done—outside baseball—which claim to show that not only the sacrifice bunt, but the intentional walk as well, are so consistently counterproductive that the first team to completely scrap both strategies would have a clear advantage over a full season.

"All those old adages have to be qualified," says Weaver. "For instance, 'Play to tie at home but to win on the road.' You hear that a million times. Hell, I'll play to tie on the road, depending on who's up that inning in my order. If your weak hitters are up, then you better try to get one run then and take your chances later.

"Another one of my pet peeves is 'Always hit behind the runner with a man on second base and none out,' " says Weaver. "Good Lord, I never asked Lee May to hit behind no runner. 'Advancing the runner' is overrated. It's a lot like the sacrifice bunt. Why give up the out? Let your hitters hit."

Weaver even doubts all of baseball's blather about the supposed advantages of 'aggressiveness.' The former O's manager never ordered a knockdown pitch, never cared if a player ran into a wall to make a catch (unless the game was on the line), and almost never wanted to see a player run the bases aggressively. To his mind, the gamble or the potential injury involved just wasn't worth it.

"Most of the time, you don't have to be aggressive in baseball," Weaver says flatly. "Do the sure things, play within yourself and you'll win . . .

"What about 'guarding the lines in the late innings?' " continues Weaver. "That shouldn't be a hard-and-fast rule. That's why we have charts on where every ball is hit against us. Now you have percentages to go by, not rules of thumb."

"The one [myth] that drove me crazy," says former Brewer and Mets manager George Bamberger, "was 'You can't throw a change-up to a left-handed hitter with a runner on first base.' I'd ask why and they'd say, 'Because he'll hit a ground ball through the [first-base] hole.'

"Well, there are guys, like Dusty Rhodes in the old days, that the only way to pitch was with sixteen off-speed pitches in a row. If the seventeenth pitch is a fastball, they'll hit it out of the park. Are you going to pitch the guy wrong just because a hole's there?

"Also, who says you can't throw two or three change-ups in a row to a hitter?" asks Bamberger, demolishing another sacred pitching precept. "Ask a hitter, 'If they throw you a change-up, what's the next pitch?' and everyone will say, 'Fastball.' When you're the pitcher and they're thinkin' exactly what you're thinkin', that ain't good."

By the same reasoning, Bamberger is infuriated by the notion that an 0–2 pitch should be a waste pitch. "It should be anything *but* a waste pitch," says Bamberger. "[Former manager] Mel Ott used to fine a pitcher five hundred dollars if anybody got a hit off an 0–2 pitch. That's dumb. Why not get 'em out on three pitches? Have an idea and try to polish 'em off. Say, 'I'm going to make a perfect pitch [on a corner or just off it].'" If he gets a hit, give it to him. You've got two free chances to throw a perfect pitch, so why 'waste' one of 'em?"

The converse of this notion is equally fascinating: that just as a 0–2 pitch should always be a ball, a 2–0 pitch should always be a strike.

Tommy John, for one, believes that this is the pernicious Myth of the Cripple. "The same pitch that the hitters take for ball one and ball two, they'll swing at and ground to short on 2–0, because they think you're supposed to throw a strike," says John. "I've pitched plenty of games where I was *best* when I was behind in the count."

This, of course, is akin to Whitey Ford's sage saying: "You would be amazed how many important outs you can get by working the count down to where the hitter is sure you're going to throw to his weakness and then throw to his power instead."

Slaying another myth, John adds, "You should *never* give in to the batter, not even if the bases are loaded and there are three balls on the hitter. They say, 'There's no place to put the hitter.' Well, there's *always* an open base, even if it's home plate. It's better to walk home one run than give up two or three on a hit, or four on a grand slam."

As for the complex issue of pitch selections, Oriole coach Ray Miller has researched one riveting statistic from fifteen years' worth of pitching charts: none of the Orioles twenty-game winners has ever thrown less than 60 percent fastballs over the course of a season, and plenty have thrown close to 70 percent.

"We want our starting pitchers to have at least three, or preferably four, pitches," says Miller, "but sometimes we get carried away with all the breaking pitches and forget that the fastball is the best pitch in baseball. It's what got most of these guys here. Fear of the fastball sets up the other pitches and makes them more effective, not the other way around. If you can get a guy out with fastballs and maybe one other pitch, don't keep running through your repertoire until you find the one that he *can* hit."

So much for Stay Ahead of the Hitter, Pitch to a Batter's Weakness, Always Mix Up Your Pitches and Never Walk a Run Home.

Next someone will say that pitching high is a virtue, not a sin.

Actually, Miller does: "Most of the best power hitters in baseball are low-ball hitters," says Miller. "It must be like survival of the fittest. Everybody in the majors wants their pitchers to keep the ball down. So, naturally, a lot of the great hitters turn out to be low-ball hitters, because the others get weeded out [by a kind of natural selection].

"Reggie Jackson, Dave Winfield, Graig Nettles and on down the line—all low-ball home-run hitters. Get 'em out with high fastballs and even high curves," says Miller. "We have to constantly preach to our younger pitchers to work high in the strike zone, because they've never heard it before. To some hitters, like Greg Luzinski, a belt-high fastball is a weakness, but a knee-high fastball will get killed."

No hitter, Miller believes, has equal power in all four quadrants of the strike zone; for instance, in the 1983 postseason the Birds discovered that Mike Schmidt and Carlton Fisk could be thrown fastballs up but not down, while Tom Paciorek could be worked away but never in.

"When you throw Schmidt a *low* fastball," Miller told his staff, "never let it be the same speed as the high fastball he just saw. Take something off. Throw a batting-practice fastball." So according to Baltimore's radar guns in the '83 Series, Schmidt got a diet of letter-high fastballs in the high eighties or low nineties, while the fastballs at the knees were in the low eighties, usually tailing away or down. Schmidt was mystified, never figured out how a team of "soft throwers" could get him out with fastballs ("I was sure they'd throw me curves. I never see fastballs in the National League") and ended the Series one for twenty.

Obviously, nothing inspires heated baseball debate like pitching theory. And nothing has inspired more half-baked ideas.

"When I was growing up," says Baltimore's Mike Flanagan, "a pitcher was told never to lift a weight. It would make you muscle-bound. Don't tamper with success. Now half the pitchers on this team are on one kind of weight program or another. It's rehabilitated my shoulder and put three or four miles an hour back on my fastball.

"You may only be lifting five-pound weights, but if you're exercising the proper muscles, it's enough to show big improvement," says Flanagan. "Steve Carlton has a big can of sand and, every day, he works his hand all the way down to the bottom. Do that a few times and it takes all your strength to get down to the bottom."

Some, of course, take this with a grain of sand. Even O's coach Miller says, "I guess it can't hurt them, if the weight is that small, but sometimes I'm tempted to think that the only muscles they're exercising are in their heads."

A decade ago, weights and nautilus machines were unknown in big-league clubhouses. Now almost every team has them. "Guys like Brian Downing [of California] and I have probably *made* ourselves into major leaguers by lifting," says Baltimore's Lenn Sakata, a 170-pounder who can bench-press more than twice his own weight. "Contrary to what was always taught, weight lifting

not only increases your strength but also your range of motion
. . . College coaches have known that for years, and now it's
worked its way into pro ball, too."

For instance, Lowenstein, who had twenty-four homers in '82
after never having had more than twelve before, says that two
winters of a weight program have made him a power hitter after
the age of thirty-five. Chicago's Paciorek, who never became a
big-league regular until he was thirty-three, is also convinced that
weight-training methods from other sports are lengthening careers
and helping players make breakthroughs in quality of performance at later ages.

"Once, they said that if you hadn't made it in baseball by [age]
thirty, it was hopeless. I'm proof that that's not true," grins Paciorek, who at thirty-one was back in triple A but now has a king's-
ransom free-agent contract.

"In my day we didn't touch a weight, didn't really do any
exercise in the off-season," says Larry Doby. "We [older players]
would have been better off if we'd worked out year round. We
probably wasted a lot of years off our careers."

Perhaps this era's most successful myth breaker has been batting coach Charley Lau. He has stood the conventional notion of
the baseball swing on its head. In fact, the baseball swing that he
teaches is really the golf swing, only shifted into a slightly different plane.

In 1980, Lau's star pupil, George Brett, hit .390 with a swing
which might seem like heresy to a century of Hall of Famers but
which would make sweet common sense to Jack Nicklaus. Lau's
theories and Brett's success constitute the culmination of a technical revolution in baseball.

Lau's ideas about hitting fly in the face of half a century of
baseball gospel. Actually, Hank Aaron started the revolution
nearly thirty years ago. But Aaron was going strictly on instinct.
It took a student of the game like Lau to codify the message.

If it sometimes seems to pitchers that Brett and other Lau-
prototype swatters like Pete Rose, Reggie Jackson, Keith Her-
nandez and Mike Schmidt are hitting their best pitches as though
from a tee, perhaps it's not an illusion.

Decades of golf study with sequence photography, slow-motion

movies and sophisticated physics have finally been used to illumi-
nate baseball, a sport which, until now, has resisted scientific scrutiny. The Teachings of Chairman Lau could come directly from
any basic modern golf textbook. The chatter around a batting
cage sounds like an impromptu seminar on a practice range on the
PGA tour. Here is a sampler of Lau Laws—mantras Brett chants
to himself constantly—which should cause a tingle of recognition
along the spine of any addicted golfer:

• Discipline your head. Keep it down.

• Find a rhythmic movement before the pitch—a "waggle"—to
break tension.

• Keep your hands relaxed. Don't strangle the bat. Let the bat
do the work.

• As the pitcher winds, shift your weight over your back foot.
Only pause at the top of the swing.

• Don't wrap the bat behind your head; that is, don't go past
parallel to the ground.

• Shift your weight onto a firm front side. That's the key to
hitting the ball hard.

• Think "fluidity, grace, extension." Don't think "muscle."

• Lead the swing with your front arm.

• Pivot with your hips and let your arms follow in whip action.
Delay the hit.

• Swing through the ball, not at it. Visualize a liner through the
box.

Ironically, Lau did not consciously borrow his ideas from golf.
He simply developed a set of precepts from his own observations.
Only recently has Lau, who is a casual golfer, learned that he has
been walking in the footsteps of Hogan and Snead.

Yankee pitcher Tommy John, who's an avid golf student, "was
the first person who ever pointed out all the similarities to me,"
says Lau. "I've come to believe that the baseball swing is almost
exactly like the golf swing, except in a different plane. I just wish
I'd realized it ten years ago. Then I wouldn't have had to learn it
all, bit by bit, for myself."

After initial frostiness, Lau has warmed to the extended golf analogy so much that he has even borrowed from the language of golf to instruct hitters.

"The hardest thing in sports is not *making* a motion, but *starting* it, especially from a dead stop," says Lau. "Golfers use the 'forward press' and the waggle. I tell hitters, 'Get the stiffness out of there. The only thing tension is good for is a heart attack. Get an interior rhythm before the pitch.' Using a sort of propeller movement of whirling the bat seems to be good.

"Then, as the pitcher winds up, you take the bat back to the 'launch position,' much like a golfer coiling on his backswing. Golfers try to stay 'inside' their back foot. We say it's okay to take the weight over the foot, because our 'pause at the top' is a little longer and we don't lose balance.

"At that last instant of truth before the swing, both golfers and hitters have to overcome the 'hero complex': the desire to hit the ball too hard. Just like a golfer who takes the club back too far, or 'casts' the club from the top, the hitter has to be told to lead with his lower body, not his hands.

"We want to delay the hit and whip the hands at the last instant, then extend the bat toward the target. A small difference is that some golfers like to roll the wrists very strongly, because it gives them a draw-type shot that rolls a lot. Well, a baseball hitter doesn't get credit for roll. We want the ball to have backspin, so it will rise and carry, like a 'fade' in golf. Too much 'top' hand tends to give overspin and smother the ball, make it drive.

"If every golfer had to play his drive from where it landed, rather than where it stopped rolling, then you'd see nothing but fades. Our type of baseball swing would be more like Nicklaus', who talks more about 'extension' and a high finish [follow-through], than Palmer's."

Since Lau's notions seem so simple and logical, and since the results for so many previously undistinguished hitters have been so good, the first logical question is, How much of this is new to baseball?

The answer is, Almost all of it. To understand this, we need historical perspective. Perhaps it's because a golf ball is stationary, while a baseball is moving ninety miles an hour, that the golf swing has been thought of as primarily technical, while the baseball swing has been viewed as largely instinctual.

In golf, form and theory have been preeminent since the first days, as students struggled to find the unifying principles of the perfect swing. In baseball, the swing, like the stance, has always been thought to be idiosyncratic, a personal signature not to be tampered with. What could be more natural? No overlocking grip. No "tempo." Just grab the darn bat and whomp the ball with it.

This kind of attitude has so implanted itself in golfers that the phrase "baseball grip" suggests some poor fellow who has given up the search for aesthetic purity on the links and settled for brute force.

Historically, baseball has had only two schools of hitting. In the dead-ball era, before 1920, the crucial skills were bunting and place hitting. The paradigms of the age were Ty Cobb and Honus Wagner, both of whom were so concerned with making contact and guiding the ball, at the expense of power, that they batted with hands-apart (split) grips.

Babe Ruth had the power and the swing that created the necessity for a lively ball. Ruth, in his prime a strapping 6-2, 250 pounds, gripped the bat down at the knob, swung with an uppercut stroke for maximum distance and, though this is still debated, appeared to rock back a mite on his left foot as he lashed the bat at impact with a snap of the wrists. When he swung and missed, his body would be corkscrewed with the effort.

If you want to hit a baseball six hundred feet, as Ruth once did, this is the only way. For fifty years, the Ruthian blast ruled the game. Grunting sluggers like Harmon Killebrew were expected to have plenty of weight on their back leg as they launched their long flies, while artful power-and-average hitters like Ted Williams and Joe DiMaggio exemplified balance, showing no favor to either foot at the finish of their swing.

Perhaps the only universally agreed-upon doctrines were that anyone who successfully hit off his front foot was a freak, and that snapping the wrists at or immediately after impact was the ideal. Obviously, that made the golf swing verboten. No baseball genius wanted to hear about "hitting off a firm front leg" or "extending the lead arm" to prevent "breaking down." Those were the flaws, not the goals.

It has taken thirty years to change this way of thinking—and now the change has become the vogue. Lau is the last link in the chain. Since World War II, the conditions for hitting have changed. The proliferation of the slider (as well as a greater variety of pitches) has made it more important for hitters to wait until the last instant to commit themselves. The long, looping power swing must start early and is hard to stop or adjust.

Also, in the past fifteen years the trend has been away from home-run heavens, as old bandbox parks have been destroyed and symmetrical AstroTurf playing fields have replaced them. These fields naturally favor all-field, line-drive hitters who can scoot ground balls through concrete infields, scald liners up the gaps to the walls and still hit home runs according to the natural limits of their power.

The first player to force baseball people to reassess their theories was Hank Aaron, the Hammerin' Paradox. Photos of Aaron hitting homers baffled coaches. As the ball left his bat, his back foot was completely off the ground, all his weight was far forward, and sometimes—horror of horrors—his right hand flew off the bat an instant after contact, creating the illusion that he was swinging at the ball one-handed, almost throwing the bat at the ball.

Here was a man who weighed only 180 pounds, used one of the lightest bats in baseball, did not uppercut or, until late in his career, try diligently to pull the ball. He swung off his front foot and frequently hit homers when his power hand—the top hand—was barely touching the bat. Aaron waited well on pitches and struck out much less often than a free swinger. In other words, to baseball minds he was a logical impossibility. Lacking an explanation, experts rhapsodized about Aaron's "quick" wrists.

"Aaron didn't know any better," says Lau. "Nobody taught him the 'right' way, so he learned for himself. Ernie Banks and Roberto Clemente hit in a similar way, and Willie Mays, too.

"I began to believe what my eyes saw, not what my ears heard. I wanted explanations for things like why Brooks Robinson, my teammate, could hit with more power than I could when I was stronger than he was. I began to look at technique, and mechanics."

As soon as the twin myths of the back foot and the top hand had been dispelled, Lau looked at film with fresh eyes. Two winters working at the Royals' Baseball Academy strengthened his beliefs. The concepts familiar to golf kept sneaking in: aligning the feet, balancing throughout the swing, keeping the elbow of the lead arm straight in the launch position to maximize the arc of the swing, even keeping the front toe closed to keep the front leg from spinning open.

Perhaps only Brett was such a willing pupil that he used every Lau technique. However, even before Brett's amazing 1980 season, the game was chock-full of stars who used at least some of Lau's ideas. Rose had the crouch, the sighting over the front arm to diminish fear, the drastic weight shift, the down-chopping stroke, the arm extension and the steady diet of liners into centerfield. In '79, Schmidt was convinced to back off the plate, then charge it, Lau-style, with an inside-out, full-extension, front-foot swing that concentrated on driving the ball between the power alleys, rather than constantly trying to pull. Schmidt improved immediately. In 1980, Jackson, too, backed off the plate, concentrated on rhythm and extension and combined a .300 average with power (forty-one homers) for the first time in his career—spraying hits and homers to all fields.

"I've been tagged 'anti-home run,' " says Lau. "I think I'm now trying to find the swing and stance that combines ultimate power and consistency. The golfer doesn't want to pull, but we've got to turn and hit a home run once in a while. Heck, let's have it all. I'm emphasizing the closed stance less. I think being perfectly square is probably best. Then, if you get out in front a little, you'll pull it where the fences are shortest. I used to say that an average player could hit fifteen home runs by accident. Why not increase the accident rate a little?"

Lau believes that he has found a concept which well may have wide appeal. The average athlete has no hope of duplicating the power of Ruth or the leverage and eyesight of Williams. But what about Brett? Lau's techniques appear to bring out the greatness in the player of normal physical attributes.

"In golf, you choose to teach the theories that have the broadest applicability," says Lau. "You'd tell a young player to imitate the Sneads or the Littlers, rather than the Palmers or the Trevinos, who are exceptions to the rule."

For decades, baseball players were told to copy Hall of Famers who hit sixty homers or batted .400. Now they are following the teachings of a man who batted .255 in eleven scrubeenie seasons with five teams. The author of *The Art of Hitting .300* is a man who never did.

Nonetheless, Charley Lau is one of those men, rare in any discipline, who believed what he saw, not what he was told. Now, with the pride that becomes a second-string catcher and high-handicap golfer who has made something of himself, he says, "All of a sudden, I'm not just another .250 idiot."

And the baseball swing will never again be just a plain, old, uncomplicated baseball swing.

Another baseball myth is that the bunt is dead. What Charley Lau has done for the full swing, an old-school gent named Bunny Mick is trying to do for the game's anti-swing: the bunt.

Down in Cocoa, Florida, on a bizarre infield laced with multicolored strings in strange, crazy-quilt shapes, one of baseball's oldest and most sadly neglected skills—bunting—has had a renaissance and a reformulation.

It is the classroom of Bunny Mick, the sixtyish Houston coach the Astros call "Bunty" Mick, because he is the only instructor in the major leagues whose sole task is to teach players how not to hit a ball very hard.

Mick—a former minor-league manager who, after becoming a prosperous businessman, returned to baseball as a part-time lark —is not merely preserving an endangered species; he has, in his spring-training-only avocation, systematically reinvented the bunt, turning accepted theory on its head. In the seven-year process, Mick has transformed the old-fashioned, dead-ball-style Astros from (in one Houston manager's words) "the worst bunting team I ever saw into perhaps the best."

For years, ever since the coming of AstroTurf fields and the advent of the designated hitter, the delicate bunt has been forced toward extinction. What was once a fundamental skill suddenly has become a rare gift. Where grass and dirt were the friends of the bunt, dragging the ball to a quick halt, ersatz grass has made precision bunting as difficult as trying to chip a golf ball to a quick stop on a bowling alley. As Pete Rose puts it, "Bunting's gone from being the easiest thing in the game to the hardest. When I came up, everybody could do it. Now ain't nobody can do it."

Once, the bunt roamed the foul lines of the major leagues. Back in '17, Ray Chapman had 67 sacrifice hits in a season; last year in the AL, home of the DH, where nobody plays for one run, the average *team* had 65 sacrifices. Eddie Collins had 511 career sacrifices. Now a venal age lists among its records: Harmon Killebrew, 8,147 at-bats, zero sacrifices.

For fifty years, before George Herman Ruth waddled into the game, one of the trademarks of the sport was the deftly placed bunt, be it a sacrifice, suicide squeeze, drag or push bunt. A man like Collins, with dozens of bunts a year, was no oddity. The gentle, sneaky bunt was at the strategic heart of a game that was played one tactically crafted run at a time. Those were the days when a whole run, like a whole dollar, was a unit of measurement to be respected.

It is said that Ty Cobb spent more time laying down practice bunts, until he could roll them dead on top of a silver dollar along the third-base line, than he did working on his hitting. Even his grip—hands one to three inches apart—was designed to disguise his intentions.

Gone are the days of '08, when an average team hit 14 homers a season and scored 525 runs. Now Cobb's Tiger heirs score 840 runs in a year and still finish fourth. Breathes there a team that still values the bunt as all of baseball once did? Does the game still have one man whose sole duty is to study the bunt, refine it and pass it on?

Only Houston has a "bunting coach." That's because only the Astros think they need one. Ironically, the stadium that spawned the synthetic turf field—the Astrodome—also is the only park where the fences are so remote and the stale indoor air so dead that baseball is played much as it was before 1920.

"Some teams might not need to bunt well. But we'd be dead if we didn't. Our vast improvement in bunting is one of our major pluses," says Joe Niekro, who, during a two-year stretch, was called on to sacrifice-bunt thirty-two times and completed the mission successfully thirty-one times.

Mick is reluctant to reveal his technical secrets, but finally agrees. "I might as well tell all. I'd hate to see the bunt keep dying out. If you picked a team at random and asked what I thought they were doing incorrectly, I'd probably have to say, 'Everything.' "

How does this Ted Williams of bunting contradict current vogues?

Many teams no longer want players to square and face the pitcher when they sacrifice. Instead, to buy back the vital split seconds that are lost to turf, they simply twist their feet at the last instant, spinning to face the pitch.

"Terrible," says Mick. "You're off-balance for any outside strike."

The Astros square away earlier, rather than later. "Who cares if you tip the play?" asks Mick. "The sacrifice is no surprise. The fielders are going to be down your throat anyway. By squaring early, they may charge too much; then you can chop it past them."

Mick's men put their inside foot on the inside line of the box— "as close to the plate as is legal." That way, by flexing the legs in a squat or leaning slightly outward, the bunter can cover the whole strike zone.

"Start with the bat set level at the top of the strike zone and sight over it. That way, anything above the bat is automatically a ball. Then work down to the ball. Ideally, on a knee-high pitch, you're in a squat, still sighting over the top of the bat," says Mick. "Also, work from the outside in, being more conscious of the outside pitch, then reacting if it's closer to the body."

Many bunters chop the ball down, hoping the bounce will kill the ball's speed. "Don't bunt down," pleads Mick. "Cast the ball outward, like a soft line drive. If you bunt down, you'll hit pebbles and pock marks. A third of the time, the ball won't go where you want. We don't depend on lucky bounces."

A vice born of trying to bunt down is holding the bat at a 45-degree angle, barrel up. "The minute the bat is out of level, you're in trouble," says Mick. "I'm convinced that for every inch the bat is more than six inches below the eyes, you get about 10 percent less efficiency. And for every inch the bat is out of level, either up or down if you're stabbing at a low pitch, you also lose about 10 percent."

Now for the heart of the matter. How do you deaden the ball, kill the roll?

"First find the dead wood in the bat," says Mick. "Turn the trademark on the bat toward the pitcher, which you'd never do when hitting, so you aren't bunting with the dense, tight grain. Next, never bunt with the sweet spot: the meat of the bat, from four to eight inches from the end. Bunt with the outer four inches of the bat, where you get that hollow, weak sound.

"Finally, find the weakest way to grip the bat. The knob hand should be so loose it's almost limp. And don't let it slide up from the knob. That gives too firm a grip. The fingers up by the trademark should not be pointing out, the way almost everybody's do. Grip only the back half of the barrel with the thumb pointing out (toward the end of the bat) and the other four fingers pointing in (toward the handle). That grip is so weak that the pitch sometimes knocks the bat out of our bunter's hands. That's perfectly okay."

Mick's *piece de resistance* is what he calls "the double spring action of the arms." Most bunters instinctively use a push-pull motion with the barrel, jabbing at the ball while the knob hand pulls back to dictate the last-second angle of the bunt. Mick presets the angle of the bunt, making it no secret. "You can only bunt toward first or third. What's the mystery?" he asks.

Having preset the angle, as the ball arrives, Houston's bunters pull back *with both hands*. In essence, they try to catch the ball on the bat.

The results are lovely. The ball strikes the bat squarely and is cast outward (not downward) in a soft line, but it comes off with a thunk. The combination of dead wood on the end of the bat, a baby's grip and the pull-back spring action by both arms at the moment of impact produce a bunt that would die on glass.

The Astros are just as adroit at bunting for hits as they are at basic sacrificing. Two thirds of the lineup is ready to drag at the drop of a sign, led by outfielder Terry Puhl, who averages a couple of dozen bunt hits a year.

On drag and push bunts, all the theories are the same: preset the angle; use the trademark-side dead wood on the end of the bat, plus that double-spring arm action; catch the ball on the bat; cast the ball outward. Also, instead of running toward first base, the Astros' first step is toward the pitcher. "We sacrifice half a step getting away from the plate," says Mick, "but, because our bunt is ten feet better [more accurate], we more than make it up."

"When you drag-bunt Bunny's way," says Puhl, "it feels so soft it's like you're carrying the ball with you as you start to run to first."

To traditionalists who archly oppose the lax trends of the modern baseball age, few scenes could be better tonic than seeing the Astros labor under Mick during spring training.

"I'm amazed they listen to me," says Mick of the million-bucks-a-man Astro starting rotation, which has a larger payroll than the entire Minnesota team.

Every day here, the Astros trudge through Mick's tiny private diamond. Each must pass his daily test. Mick's infield is crowded with red, blue, yellow and black strings. Each area has a point value. If the ball's fair but within thirty feet of the catcher, that's one point. If it's down the line fair, but more than forty feet out, that's five. If it's between thirty and forty feet, that's the maximum, ten points. The Astros pepper that ten-point zone. The only penalty is the dreaded black-string area, straight back at the pitcher, the zone that leads to double plays—minus ten.

The Astros think they are merely playing a bunting game, a casual idyll of spring. But Mick knows better. He is the last protector of one of baseball's gentle, neglected arts. "Bend your knees more, Joe," he calls to Niekro, annual salary $1.1 million.

"Aw, Jeez, Bunny," grumbles Niekro, "you know the big-league rule: It's not how well you bunt that counts. It's how good you look doin' it."

Bunny Mick, keeper of the flame, gets a small hurt expression on his face.

"Just kidding," grins Niekro as he lays down a stinking dead mackerel of a bunt that would have made the Georgia Peach proud.

These days, almost nothing is sacred in baseball. Come up with notions that seem utterly preposterous and there are successful men who'll defend them.

Let's see, how about a left-handed catcher? No such creature, right?

Actually, there's a fellow named Lou Hanales who has a *school* for left-handed catchers, in Florida. Hanales claims, with reason, that in theory a southpaw has few, if any, inherent disadvantages behind the plate.

How about a left-handed third baseman?

Lenn Sakata swears he played against one in high school who was an all-star and says, "You could have left-handed third basemen right up to the college level."

Can we top that? How about a possible future Hall of Famer who practices taking bad swings more than he works on his good swings?

Million-dollar-a-year slugger Eddie Murray deliberately fills his batting practice with the worst-looking, off-balance, formless swings ever seen; he seldom hits a ball hard and looks like a bum.

"All Eddie does, except for one round of swings that he takes seriously, is to practice what we call his 'emergency swings,'" says Ken Singleton. "He's the only hitter who practices being fooled. He gets off-balance on purpose, then improvises. That's why he fouls off so many tough two-strike pitches and gets so many horrible-looking fluke hits in games. It drives us crazy watching him; then he hits .300."

In this realm of left-handed catchers and emergency swings, perhaps what we really need is a manager who loves superstitious athletes and encourages his players to believe in magic charms, voodoo, mid-game rituals and all-blue underwear on airplane flights. What myth would that expose? Why, the myth that sane players, living in the real world, are the best kind.

"I've always loved superstitious players like Mike Cuellar," says Bamberger. "You always knew that while another guy was out getting drunk, Mike was worrying about the color of his underwear, or his special game-day clothes or waking up at exactly the right time, or eating the same pregame meal.

"Superstitions can actually be a measure of how deeply a player cares about the game. Another pitcher might begin thinking about his game twenty minutes before the anthem, when it's time to go warm-up," says Bamberger. "With Cuellar, you knew he'd been thinking about nothing but pitching for twenty-four hours before he went out there. You know that the superstitious player will be mentally prepared."

In the eighties, even our assumptions about something as traditional as the batting order—the ol' lineup—are being drastically revamped.

For years, the No. 2 hitter in the lineup was supposed to be a contact hitter who could "hit-and-run" and hit-behind-the-runner. In other words, he was probably the club's fifth- or sixth-best offensive player.

Now several successful AL teams have put one of their very best hitters at No. 2—such as Milwaukee (slugging leader Robin Yount), Boston (all-around star Dwight Evans) and Oakland (Dwayne Murphy). In tandem with such a move, several clubs have strengthened the No. 9 spot in the order, using players with little power but good on-base percentages and decent speed; Milwaukee uses .300 hitter Jim Gantner, Boston has Rick Miller.

Statistics show that for every spot in the order that a man moves *up* in the lineup, he'll get about eighteen more plate appearances per season; so why not throw that modest No. 2 batter down to seventh or ninth in the order and move *everybody* up a notch? Or move one power hitter up four or five spots to No. 2 and get him eighty to one hundred more plate appearances?

What's the result? The top four or five spots in the order have undiluted punch. With the improvement of the No. 9 spot in the order—maybe you even put the old No. 2 hitter there—a lineup develops around-the-corner authority. For example, the Red Sox lineup begins with Jerry Remy, Evans, and Jim Rice. But in innings when No. 9 man Miller leads off, the order of Miller-Remy· Evans-Rice also has a potent chemistry.

Why, one wonders, have AL managers been putting the player with the *worst* chance of getting on base in the No. 9 spot just when the players with the *best* chance of driving him in—Numbers 1-2-3-4—are coming up? Old myths, with origins that go back to the playground, like "worst hitter bats last," die hard.

These are the brave new days when any conventional baseball statement is likely to be contradicted. For instance, take Bill James' *Baseball Abstract,* a book devoted to statistical analysis (called "sabermetrics" after the Society for American Baseball Research). James lives to contradict what he calls "all the stupid things people say about baseball."

So you think, as Stan Musial once said, that a player's prime age is twenty-eight to thirty-two. Well, James can prove that it's two or three years younger than that.

You think Fenway Park is heaven for right-handed hitters but hell for lefties; James can prove that it's heaven for both, and maybe even better for lefties. You think Reggie Jackson plays better before big crowds, but James can prove he plays worse before big crowds. You think star pitchers like Nolan Ryan are big drawing cards, but James can prove that the identity of the day's starting pitcher, even if it's Ryan, ranks no higher than seventh on a list of variables determining attendance.

The computer, matrix theory and slide-rule guys are scurrying around out there, and it's probably just a matter of time before one comes up with a bonafide "Eureka!"

One obscure whiz even hypothesizes that, in this era of quality four- and five-man bullpens, a team should always use a reliever as its starting pitcher until the third inning. That way, your "real" starter would never have to work more than seven innings. Also, because you could catch lineups in the left-right percentage switch, you'd supposedly have an improved chance of taking an early-inning lead.

"That would be a helluva theory," snorted Weaver, "if you had twelve good pitchers with rubber arms. The first guy [manager] who tries that won't have a pitching staff left by June."

Nevertheless, developments almost as curious as the "relief starter" are already transforming the game.

The watershed accomplishment for which the '82 season will always be remembered—Rickey Henderson's new stolen-base record (130)—has come as the direct result of ignoring old myths.

Since Ty Cobb's time, base stealing has had four fundamental precepts:

• Study the pitchers to get the best possible jump.

• Take the longest possible lead that will allow you to get back safely on a pickoff.

• Seldom take a gambling, "one-way lead," in which your weight (and mind) are leaning more toward the next base than the base you're already on.

• Slide into the bases feet first, because it's the fastest and most injury-proof way.

So what does Henderson do?

• The A's speedster admits that, at age twenty-three, he has barely begun to study pitchers' moves and, as a result, actually gets picked off first more often than he's thrown out at second. He has replaced studiousness with raw daring.

• Henderson takes a distinctly shorter-than-maximum lead. The reason? Less pickoff throws that wear you out diving back to the bag.

• That slightly shortened Henderson lead flows right into the Oaklander's next breakthrough notion. He *always* takes a one-way lead in which his whole being is focused on the next base, rather than returning whence he came. If he spots the pitcher's pickoff in time, then, well and good, his lead is short enough to let him get back. If the pitcher throws to the plate, Henderson will get a tremendous jump, because he has no doubts or inhibitions; he's been in an ultra-aggressive, one-way lead all along. He's committed to sprinting, not deciding.

And finally, if he gets picked off, he doesn't care. Henderson believes that he can steal on the pitcher and first baseman just as easily as he can steal on the pitcher and catcher. Besides, first basemen are more easily unnerved than catchers. Henderson's record-tying 118th steal came just in this way—on what traditionally would have been called a pickoff play.

Lastly, Henderson always slides headfirst. The reason is simple, although no important base thief thought of it for a century: you get there faster. Instead of decelerating into the base, like other sliders who don't want to break an ankle, Henderson actually explodes into the base and beyond it; often, Henderson slides entirely over the base and almost into left field.

Obviously, this is the better method. Why? Because every athlete, from the sprinter breaking the tape, to the golfer driving a ball, to the karate master smashing boards, is told to run or swing or strike through the target, rather than at it. So how come nobody ever slid through a base instead of merely sliding into it?

Probably because somebody in the nineteenth century said you shouldn't.

By an elegant touch, Henderson's theories are not his own, but, rather, grew out of the work of the novel and short-lived Royals Academy, directed by a slightly eccentric and occasionally brilliant man named Syd Thrift.

Thrift has a new idea about everything except the sunrise; and his Academy disciples have spread the base-running word to Henderson and Montreal's Tim Raines, who may someday steal 125 or more bases. Everything from the "measured lead" to putting the stopwatch on pitchers and catchers came from the Royals Academy.

Fortunately, not all baseball myths are in danger. San Francisco manager Frank Robinson loves to tell a story about how left-handed pitchers have the greatest pickoff tricks and how no right-hander will ever be able to match the move of a former minor-league southpaw named Frank Conger.

As the Hall of Famer tells it, he was managing in winter ball in Puerto Rico in the bottom of the ninth inning of a game with his team trailing by a run. Robinson's club got the tying run to first base. Suddenly one of his relief pitchers, named Freddie Bean, climbed the bullpen fence, screaming "Time," and ran into the dugout.

"Robby," said Bean, "this guy's a lousy pitcher, but he has the greatest pickoff move in history. I saw him pick three guys off first in one inning in AAA this year. You've got to tell the runner on first to be careful."

"Go in and pinch-run yourself," says Robinson to Bean. "You've seen his move."

Pitcher Bean went to first base, did his stretching exercises, then took the shortest lead in history: about one yard. Even with this tiny lead, Bean leaned back toward first.

Conger went into his stretch, then fired to first.

The hyper-excited Bean dove headfirst back toward first, flew entirely over the bag and was tagged out to end the game while sprawled in the coach's box.

Says Robinson, "I was laughing too hard to chew him out."

This proves unequivocally the ancient adage that left-handers have the best pickoff moves.

Well, maybe.

12

SMOKY'S CHILDREN

One day, along about the fifth inning, Gates Brown decided that the Detroit Tigers wouldn't need a pinch hitter for an inning or two, so he rounded up a hot dog for each hand. Next thing he knew, manager Mayo Smith was intoning, "Gates, get your bat." Normally, the rotund Brown, who is the premier pinch hitter in the history of the American League, might have chucked the wieners, but this day he was deep into the munchies. So as Smith stared directly at him, Brown got an inspiration.

"I turned my back and stuffed 'em down my shirt," recalls Brown, who is now a Tiger coach.

At bat, he slapped a liner in the gap to right center. "I started running and forgot all about those hot dogs." He forgot about them, that is, until he slid into second base—on his stomach. When Brown arose, his jersey was awash in colors: mustard yellow and ketchup red. "I was a mess. I drove in the winning run and Mayo still fined me a hundred dollars."

To Brown, this story sums up the tribulations of the substitute swinger's life. They give you a baseball lifestyle that would drive a saint to drink, then they expect you to play it like a straight man.

"If I had it all to do over again," says Brown now, "I wouldn't. Hell, nobody wants to be a pinch hitter. I had to do it to survive." Pinch-hitting is baseball's mission impossible.

Ted Williams says the hardest thing in sports is hitting a base-ball. Wrong. If we judge by frequency of failure and depth of occupational depression, the toughest task isn't hitting, but pinch-hitting.

To begin, the pinch hitter is a player of modest ability, or he'd be in the lineup. Next, he's rusty, because pinch hitters comprise only 3 percent of all batters. Even in batting practice, pinch hitters still must bat with the scrubeenies.

Who are these creatures who sit at the end of the bench, grudg-ingly allowed perhaps one start a week and treated, for the most part, as though they should be grateful just to get a big-league paycheck? As they sit the other six days, waiting for their fleeting, two-minute chunk of failure-filled piecework, these men on the margin have nothing to do but let their minds prey on them.

When will I get my next hit? Will I get my chance next inning or next week? A team sends six thousand hitters to the plate every season; if the pinch hitter is called on seventy-five times, he's been worked to death. His name is called peremptorily about once per hundred team at-bats; yet, in theory, the PH must be ready to jump up all those other times.

His baseball life often seems a preparation for something that never happens. But if, after a dozen years on the job, he unties his shoes or loosens his belt, then that's just the minute when fate, or Billy Martin, offers the chance of a lifetime. And if he fails, it haunts him for years.

His task is simple: Change a half-dozen games a season with one swing. "Throw in a decent pinch hitter and you've got a deal," says the GM.

Against all this, what does the pinch hitter have? Usually, he's getting old, and was never of star quality. He's probably near the bottom of the pay scale. There's no play-me-or-trade-me leverage, since the only thing a PH has to be able to do is walk from the dugout to the plate without having a heart attack. Only one pinch hitter has ever been put on an All-Star team specifically for his PH ability: Smoky Burgess.

"You may sit on the bench for ten days, then you're supposed to walk up on a minute's notice in the ninth inning," says much-traveled Jose Morales of the Los Angeles Dodgers, the active leader in career pinch hits.

"You sit for two hours, then Earl Weaver tells you, 'Get loose. You're up next,' " says Terry Crowley, who was the most productive pinch hitter in baseball for several years. "So, to make him happy, I stand up."

"Lots of times you know you don't have your stroke, but you got to go," says Brown. "That messes with your mind when you got to keep going up there cold turkey."

As if that weren't bad enough, the pinch hitter is, more often than not, the prey of the monster reliever. "I'd get only three at-bats all week," says White Sox coach Charley Lau, recalling his PH years, "and they'd be against Ryne Duren, Dick Radatz and Hoyt Wilhelm. That's a helluva way to stay in the majors."

"Very difficult, but not impossible," says Manny Mota, the Dodger coach who retired in 1980 as the all-time pinch-hit leader (150). "You have to love a clutch spot."

The naked pinch hitter takes only one thing to the plate: his raw, and somewhat irrational, confidence in himself. That this confidence is so unreasonable adds to its dignity.

"What makes a good pinch hitter?" says Murcer, who in 1981 had twelve pinch RBIs in just twenty-two at-bats. "I wish to hell I knew."

"Some guys can't pinch-hit under any circumstances. I was ready before I ever got to the on-deck circle. All I had to do to prepare was take off my jacket," says the King of Confidence, fifty-eight-year-old Burgess. Taking power (sixteen homers), durability (145 hits) and average (.286) together, Burgess was the best pinch hitter who ever lived. "If they'd let me use that aluminum bat, I'd still be playing."

Just how tough is pinch-hitting?

It's so tough it turns Hall of Famers into klutzes. Ty Cobb was fifteen for sixty-nine (.217) and Babe Ruth thirteen for sixty-seven (.194). The twenty-two players in history who had career batting averages of .333 or better—taken as a group—batted just .271 as pinch hitters. That's typical. Only six players, led by Tommy Davis at .320, are career .300 pinch hitters. In fact, only thirty-one have career pinch averages over .271. In a typical season, the major-league pinch-hitting average is in the .235–.240 range. Despite these stats, pinch hitters—because they so often come up with men on base—have a disproportionate importance. In '80 and '81, for instance, they drove in 39 percent more runs per at-bat than nonpinch hitters.

No claim will be made that pinch-hitting is the secret common denominator of champions. Yet it is true that a stable of excellent pinch hitters can get a team over the hump to the Series. Yankee, Dodger, Oriole, Phillie and Royal clubs have monopolized the best pinch hitters since 1975.

Recent postseason history is full of less-than-well-known fellows like Jay Johnstone, Del Unser, Manny Sanguillen, John Lowenstein, Benny Ayala, Piniella and Bernie Carbo, who've achieved momentary fame with a few pinch swings in October. Those glamour chances, like Dusty Rhodes of the Giants turning the '54 Series into his showcase, stand in stark opposition to the daily life.

Many PHs wonder how they got stuck in the job in the first place. Brown, for instance, had a pinch homer in his first big-league at-bat. "I'm twenty-three years old and, goddamn, I'm a pinch hitter already. It hurt me. I should have fought against it harder."

Crowley also had the poor judgment to bat .290 in the pinch as a rookie. Sometimes he wonders if that's part of the reason he's never gotten a whiff of being a regular, though his teammates respectfully call him "the King of Swing." "I was 'Old Terry Crowley' before I was thirty. Being known as a pinch hitter adds five years to your age."

Someday Crowley may think like Burgess, who initially rebelled at catching less and pinch-hitting more. "Pinch-hitting was great to me," Burgess says. "I can sit right here in my den and look at a plaque they gave me with every one of the 145 hits and who it was off, where and when."

Once a pinch hitter has accepted his lot, he must perfect his cramped craft. That means adopting an almost religious daily ritual. After all, pinch hitters get to the plate perhaps only thirty to sixty times a season. It took Burgess eighteen years to accumulate his record 507 at-bats. "If you leave the other team on the field

four or five times a year, you've done your job," says Morales. He
should know. In '76, he had a record twenty-five hits (in seventy-
eight at-bats), plus twenty-four RBIs, just one off the record set by
Jerry Lynch and Joe Cronin.

Pinch hitters prep differently. Mota ran two miles a day. Burgess, Brown and Fats Fothergill (a .300 career pinch average)
trained on hot dogs and beer. Burgess never got in shape until he
retired: "People are shocked when they see me now." Recently,
Burgess faced Duren in an old-timers game. Burgess hit a line
drive off the rightfield wall. "I had to wait until I was retired to
hit the hardest ball of my life."

Once the game starts, no two great pinch hitters seem alike.

Mota would sit alone for the first five innings, watching the
game intently, largely ignoring his teammates. Then, during the
sixth and seventh innings, he would disappear under the stands.
In Chavez Ravine, he'd run sprints in the tunnel and hit against a
subterranean batting machine. Most of all, Mota'd have one of his
eight children stand fifteen feet away and toss a softball in the air,
which he would smash, with a downward chop, into a screen.
What would Goose Gossage do if he knew Mota prepared for him
by playing softball with a ten-year-old girl?

The dutiful approach is most common, like Morales quizzing
himself aloud from the middle innings as he tries to guess sequences of pitches.

Nevertheless, some PHs simply avoid thinking. Burgess says, "I
didn't do anything." Piniella offers, "I smoke a lot of cigarettes."

"I've won a couple of games with mustard on my mouth," says
Murcer, who sits in a rocking chair in front of his locker, a symbol of composure.

The radical approach, however, was practiced by both Tommy
Davis and Brown. Both spent much of the game in the clubhouse
talking on the phone. Davis preferred his wife's voice and would
even call her long distance. Brown would simply talk to anybody
who would answer his area code.

When Detroit installed an outside line in the Tiger Stadium
bullpen, Brown was in heaven, watching the game and calling
friends simultaneously. One day manager Smith barked to coach

Johnny Sain, "Get the bullpen up." Five minutes later, Smith was
ready for a new pitcher, but nobody had thrown a warm-up pitch.

"Didn't you call the bullpen?" screamed Smith.

"I couldn't get through," said Sain. "The line was busy."

Next day, no outside line.

13.

GRAND ILLUSION

On a bluff overlooking miles of green, gently rolling plain, sits Rosenblatt Stadium, home for more than a third of a century of the college baseball World Series. To the north are the lights of Omaha, a little big town twinkling in the distance at sunset; to the south, rich farmlands and forest stretch to the horizon. This is the fruited plain of which "America the Beautiful" speaks.

On this remote stage in the middle of breadbasket America, future stars such as Sal Bando, Dave Winfield and Bob Horner—all College World Series MVPs—as well as dozens of other future major leaguers, have shown themselves sharp against the Nebraska night. This has been one of baseball's secret places, known to insiders, but a mystery to the public. Usually, the only non-Midwesterners who've found their way to this feast are a box-seat section full of major-league scouts.

Baseball here is different, and in a sense, better, than anywhere else. Last year, for instance, PA announcer Jack Payne told the record crowd of 15,333: "Let's give the umpires a surprise. Let's give 'em a standing ovation." And the fans—some sitting on the warning track—obliged, their cheers bringing two of the grateful umpires to tears.

Once, when Cal State-L.A. got to this eight-team, double-elimination tournament, the underdogs delighted the crowd by going through a phantom infield drill. All the fungoes, throws and catches were made, but with no ball. When the miracle team of 1982, Maine, hit a homer, the Black Bears formed a greeting line of high fives for their hero from third base to home plate. "We're not bad," Maine's coach, Dr. John Winkin, said, "for a bunch of snowbirds and potato pickers." After games, both teams always form lines to shake hands. When Miami wins, it calls a postgame team meeting in left field. "Heck, we've got no locker room," Coach Ron Fraser says with a shrug.

Little of the ugliness that fouls big-time college football and basketball has gotten here yet. The national champion, for example, gets only fifteen thousand dollars above expenses for its victory. Not a single Division I school is on probation because of baseball. Here, finally, is amateur sport with little cheating or twisting of values. "When I was hired," says Miami's Fraser, "I was told, 'Do the best you can, but don't spend any money.' That's typical of college baseball."

Before one game this week, Coach Cliff Gustafson, of No. 1-ranked Texas, had a problem: one of his practice balls was stuck in the top of the batting cage. He wrestled for five minutes until the valuable horsehide was salvaged.

Instead of relying on big-time scouting, players here stay up until 4 A.M. to see center-field-camera replays of their next opponent's game on cable TV.

For once, teams actually draw their players from within their state, and coaches have the look of their locale. Texas' leather-skinned Gustafson could have come in from branding cattle; he says dryly of his club's 59-4 record: "We hit a slump in mid-season." Maine's Winkin could be an honest-John lobsterman.

The mood here is defiantly old-fashioned. One of the dozens of billboard signs on the fences reads: SOMEBODY STILL CARES ABOUT QUALITY. Another sign proves bounty-hunting isn't dead yet: "Put an arsonist away—for pay."

The tangy language in the park is that of farm country. An extreme example: "The outfielders' ain't any too skeered a this fella. They ain't agin the fences yit."

The PA man, reading a license plate, says: "Move it or lose it. You're in a heap a trouble now, boy."

"It all seems like what I knew of baseball growing up," says Dick Bergquist, the NCAA baseball committee chairman who coaches at Massachusetts. "The game's still something you can be proud of. Most of the college baseball coaches aren't drawn to the pros. They enjoy it right where they are. They're real teachers of the game. They know there's more to life than baseball."

In the box next to Bergquist's are four little old ladies. "They come every year, arrive an hour before the games and keep a box score of every play," he says. "One of them is a Texas fan and she's converted all the rest."

These are the good old days for college baseball. Everywhere that the principal actors in the College World Series turn, they find themselves being shaken by the hand and congratulated on the upright, healthy and growing state of the game.

Their subsist-on-a-shoestring sport, so long consigned to the status of intramural hopscotch, has come of age; on the horizon, the pioneers of today's high-quality college baseball can even begin to see a prosperous maturity. The day has finally arrived when the low minor leagues—long the underpaying, youth-eating, career-killing disgrace of the pro game—no longer are a necessary evil for the teenager who dreams of playing in the major leagues.

"It kills me to see a young man, just out of high school, go into that pro jungle," said John Winkin, coach of the Maine Black Bears, who finished tied for third in 1982. "It's not necessary anymore."

"We're proud that the colleges can now make a very convincing case to the top high school players—except, perhaps, to the first- or second-round draft choice who gets a bonus of $100,000 to $150,000," said NCAA chairman Bergquist.

"It's reached the point where I'm surprised when a promising young player, provided he has any academic ability at all, decides not to play in college," said Miami coach Fraser, whose Hurricanes won the championship in 1982, beating Wichita State. "Yet it still happens. We had six recruits signed away from us by the pros in the last year."

"Minor-league baseball is the most unsupervisable, begging-for-trouble situation I can imagine for an eighteen- to nineteen-year-old," said another prominent coach in the final eight. "As a parent, don't you have to wonder, 'What are they doing with all those empty hours?' "

It's old news that the overwhelming majority of big leaguers have played at the college level. At the moment, more than 70 percent of all American-born major leaguers have played in college. And that figure keeps rising every season. For instance, of the players signed from last summer's pro draft, more than 80 percent were college, rather than only high school, players. That's not a trend; it's an established, irreversible fact of baseball life.

Once, the route to the majors was to quit school after high school, accept a signing bonus and head to the bus rides and bad hops of the bush leagues for a five-year-or-more education in the school of hard knocks. Too often, the player got a few thousand dollars, a new car and fifty years of remorse. Now the majority of high schoolers good enough to get a pro offer are forgoing the minors for at least one year of junior-college ball, and more likely, three or four years of major-college baseball.

Throughout the sixties and deep into the seventies, one of baseball's recurring knee-jerk laments was the sorry state of the shrinking minor leagues. Now it's become apparent that the winnowing of the minors may have been, in the long view, a bonanza for the game. As the minors—especially leagues below triple A—have receded, college baseball has come to flood tide as baseball's prime source of future major-league players.

"The better college teams, like the ones here, could compete with AA pro teams in a short series," said Fraser, whose Hurricanes beat the Baltimore Orioles in a spring training game. "In a ten-game series, however, I think their deeper pitching would prevail. Most of the younger players who turn pro are the promising pitchers. We [colleges] only have one or two 'pro quality' pitchers.

"In general, I think the good college teams would be winners in A-ball," continued Fraser, a modest appraisal with which few pro scouts would disagree. "Many of our players are, of course, not professional prospects, because many lack one or two conspicuous skills. They aren't signed, because it's obvious they lack something that would keep them out of the majors. But they're still excellent athletes.

"Also, I think the college game stresses proper instruction, in-

dividualized teaching, weight training, fundamentals . . .
There's more emphasis on team play, smart play, hustle and winning in college. In the minors, individual stats are very important."

From the first clank of aluminum bat against the ball, it's obvious that the college game is geared toward offense and brains.
Because the two most difficult skill positions in baseball—pitcher
and catcher—are spread thin in college, many clubs wisely em-
phasize long-ball hitting lineups and speed.

The 1982 runner up, Wichita State, was a good example. When
coach Gene Stephenson arrived in 1978, the Shockers didn't have
a baseball team. "There hadn't been a bat or glove on campus in
eight years," he said. Now the Shockers are a club of staggering
stats that epitomize the college game. In eighty-seven games in
1982 (the most ever played in a spring season by an NCAA team),
they outscored their foes 858–274. Wichita State hit 101 home
runs and stole (gulp) 333 bases.

It's a mark of the depth and increasing balance of power in
college baseball that the best major-league prospects no longer are
bunched on a couple of teams, like eleven-time NCAA champ
Southern California or five-time champ Arizona State. In fact, for
the first time in twenty-eight years, no California or Arizona team
reached the final four in '82.

Final proof of college baseball's balance of talent is the fact that
finalist Miami doesn't even have a star; its best player—pitcher-
catcher Sam Sorce, who played all nine positions in one game this
season—wasn't taken until the draft's twenty-fourth round, by
Texas. Sorce is hoping that having helped his team to the national
title, he can talk the Rangers into a bonus of "maybe three thousand dollars."

Each year, the popularity of this game of metal bats and bright
double-knits is increasing, although all guesstimates of national
crowd figures—about 5 million in '79, 7 million in '80, 8 million in
'81 and more in '82—are unofficial, since the NCAA doesn't keep
attendance stats.

"Even though Miami's drawn 160,000 people each of the last
two seasons, we still only have about seven to ten schools that

average a thousand people a game," said Jim Wright, series publicity director. "The rest draw in the hundreds."

The quality of play in college ball is respected and its relationship with the major leagues is cordial, thanks largely to fifteen-season Commissioner Bowie Kuhn, whom Fraser calls "the college game's best friend. None of us will forget his work in getting the [annual] January draft abolished. That saved us by bringing some stability to the game. Now we at least know we'll have our players for three years, even though I'm sure most coaches wish it were all four years."

On the one hand, college baseball programs, since they aren't revenue producers, get only a paltry thirteen scholarships and are run on skimpy budgets. On the other, both cable and national TV deals have arrived in the past couple of years—the first whiff of potential local and national cash.

"I hope that with the pressure of the battle with pro ball for the good players, and with the increased pressure to win now that we're starting to get media recognition, we don't reach the level of recruiting ills that fester in college football and basketball," said Maine's Winkin. "Frankly, I feel that's a world of animals."

For the present, though college baseball has become the breeding ground of future major leaguers, the people in its World Series are like characters out of John Tunis. Each season provides fresh tales full of a gentle charm.

After his Black Bears were eliminated here Friday night, Winkin, sixty-two, was troubled. "They were all crying. I was at a loss for words. I don't know if I handled it well or not," he said. "I told 'em, 'Boys, the coach had a bad night. Everything I tried backfired on us. I'm sorry I let you down.' Then I handed each one his plaque, shook his hand and thanked him for helping us have such a great year."

Two years ago, Miami's Mickey Williams heard a neighbor screaming for help; the man had been robbed, beaten and tied up, and his house had been set afire. Williams jumped a fence and saved the man's life. But he slipped a disk and ended any big-league chances. He has warmed the bench since. Finally, on Thursday, he got to play because of a star's injury; he got a hit and scored the winning run as Miami beat top-ranked Texas, 2–1. "Been waiting a long time," said Williams. "Now it's worth it."

Last year, the Omaha beauty queen assigned to the Michigan team ended up marrying the Wolverine centerfielder. This year, the world series' "princess" is having a storybook romance with the Maine shortstop. "Those Maine guys must not get out of the woods too much," quips Miami's Fraser. "When they came down to play at our place last year, one of their players ended up marrying our ball girl."

Although there are future major-league stars here, they don't dominate the tournament. History says that, from these eight teams, perhaps three or four players will become national names, another couple of dozen will play pro ball and the large majority will have their finest hour here, then retire.

So they play till they drop. Miami shortstop Bill Wrona claims to have two impacted wisdom teeth, a case of tonsillitis and canker sores in his mouth; he's been living on soup, milkshakes and penicillin for a week. Hurricane fans say, "From the neck down, Wrona's perfect." He's lost eight pounds, but he's playing.

Omaha loves all this. As in '81, the fifteen-game series will probably draw more than 120,000 fans. Some cities buzz about world affairs. Here, talk is about two aluminum bats riding alone in a taxi. You see, Miami's star Sam Sorce left two favorite bats in Florida. In a trice, the bats were put on a jet, lost for a day in St. Louis, rediscovered and put on another plane, put in a taxi and sent to the park. A Miami coach grabbed the bats just minutes before the game. Naturally, the Hurricanes won, 4–3, as Sorce hit a homer.

In all Omaha's third of a century as host, however, there has perhaps never been one play that capsulized this event's clean amateur ambiance, its charm and saucy spirit as well as Miami's marvelous Grand Illusion this week.

On Sunday, Miami's Fraser put in a farfetched trick play. "We only practiced it twice, because everybody was laughing too hard."

But it worked. With Wichita State star Phil Stephenson (eighty-six steals) on first, Miami's pitcher stepped off the rubber and faked a throw to first. As Stephenson dived back, the first baseman dived over him, pretending to leap for a bad throw. A dozen Miami players screamed and pointed, telling their teammate where to retrieve the ball. The players in the Miami bullpen down the rightfield line scattered to get out of the way of the wild throw.

Stephenson headed for second base. Where, of course, the pitcher's lob throw had him out by twenty feet.

Wichita State's coach, Gene Stephenson, was livid, possibly because he was the tricked player's older brother. After the game, he complained that Miami had broken the rules, because their bat girl had been pointing toward the imaginary ball too. "She was in on the play," said the coach, "and that makes it against the rules."

Said a grinning Fraser: "I've always said the bat girl was the key to that play. We always tell our runners, 'Never go for the extra base until you've checked to see what the bat girl does.'"

14.
THE BEST
OF ALL TIME

Amid the daily welter of chatter about today's "superstar," how are we to identify the performer who is unique, who may someday hold a place in baseball history?

We managed to overlook Henry Aaron until he was almost forty, had the beginning of a Hall of Fame gut and couldn't run the bases or play the outfield. By the time we realized who he was, he wasn't that man anymore.

We almost missed Johnny Bench. If he hadn't been in the World Series four times in his fleeting, eight-season prime, we might not have known we were watching the greatest catcher in the history of the game.

As it was, by the time we acknowledged Bench's stature—around the time the Reds won those back-to-back titles in '75–'76 —the record book says Bench was already aging, slipping back to the level of all the other merely marvelous catchers, like Dickey and Cochrane and Campanella.

When we're old folks, sitting around naming our all-time team and trying to remember how many of them we saw, we'll rattle off the nine hallowed names, like a roll call on Mount Olympus: Babe Ruth, Willie Mays and Ty Cobb will make a nice little outfield; on the right side on the infield, let's have Lou Gehrig on first and Rogers Hornsby on second; for a battery, how about Walter Johnson pitching and Johnny Bench catching. And on the left side of the infield, Mike Schmidt at third and Robin Yount at shortstop.

Mike Schmidt and Robin Yount?

There, that's the point. We don't think of them that way yet, and by the time we do, it may be too late to consider them in the glow of their prime, see them as our grandchildren will assume we had the wit to see them—full and fit and glorious.

First, let's not shilly-shally. Schmidt is a virtual certainty to retire with combined batting and fielding credentials that leave no room for argument about his place as the all-time third baseman. Those few men who could hit like him couldn't field like him, and vice versa. Eventually, when such teams are made, we'll say, "Well, start with Ruth and Schmidt, since they're the only two all-time positions nobody ever debates." Then we can start fighting about Cobb-versus-Aaron and the rest.

As for Yount, it says here the day may soon arrive when he's acknowledged as the most valuable shortstop since World War I. What other shortstop in the lively-ball era has excelled in the sport's five basic skills: running, fielding, throwing, hitting and hitting with power? Not one. Although, if 210-pound Cal Ripken, Jr., doesn't soon grow too physically big for the position, he could join Yount's class.

To be seemly, we'll let Robin have ten more fine years before we get worked up and compare him to Honus Wagner, the Flying Dutchman, who won eight batting titles, six slugging crowns and five stolen-base titles.

However, when a Gold-Glove shortstop has 1,500 hits by his twenty-eighth birthday, while also cracking 85 extra-base hits a year, then it's not farfetched, just farsighted, to wonder if he'll someday surpass Wagner's 3,430 hits and 1,004 extra-base hits.

One of the great baseball charms for the rest of the eighties will be watching Schmidt and Yount as they try to play themselves up into the All-Time Nine. By 1990, we'll know. Then Schmidt, who has already won six home-run titles, plus back-to-back MVP's, will be forty years old, with a home-run total approaching six hundred. As for Yount, he'll turn thirty-five that year; by then we'll know if his fabulous batting seasons of '80 and '82 were to become his norm, or whether his nagging back miseries were to derail him.

What will make Schmidt and Yount so fascinating to watch is that they've both recognized that they must face a dual task; while they battle to fulfill their athletic potential, they must also try to survive the public eye, which fixes on MVP's and Series heroes.

Schmidt is the rarest of all baseball cases: the player with "unlimited potential" who actually becomes as good as the graybeards thought he should be. Each spring, the Grapefruit League is filled with young players burdened with the weight of their potential. More often than not, they self-destruct, victims, in a sense, of their own abilities or the expectations of others. Hardly a year goes by that some Clint Hurdle or Kirk Gibson isn't consumed by his own promise. Schmidt remembers seven seasons when he played under a cloud of anxiety about whether he could live up to his physique. It wasn't until he turned thirty that he took the final step in an apotheosis of which few would even dream. The great change came during batting practice before the 1979 All-Star game.

Before recalling that moment, let Schmidt talk about the bad old days in the '70s when, despite averaging thirty-three homers and 105 RBI in one 5-year span, he still found the game a mystery.

"When I got in the box, the idea of what was expected of me, what I could be, affected the way I swung the bat, every time. There were smatterings of success that excited people, and excited me, to the point where I really never found the time to develop a real batting stroke. It's a hell of a lot easier to stand up there and whale away at everything and make a lot of outs, and occasionally hit home runs. That's easy. One game-winning homer would wipe out a week of strikeouts . . . but I always knew that I could be better.

"I didn't do well in the playoffs, because hitting under pressure was a problem for me . . . I was pitched inside and consistently missed that ball or hit home runs foul. Seeing a steady diet of that pitch, and wanting to swing at it, created an [early] opening of my [left] shoulder and a vulnerability to the breaking ball. I hated just being 'dangerous.' I hated being the guy that could be an easy out if pitched properly. It's not fun to have to battle that anxiety constantly, every at-bat."

Then, that evening before the All-Star game, the dickering Schmidt experimented with turning his whole hitting theory inside out. He moved well off the plate, charged into every pitch and tried to hit the ball to center field, instead of pulling. His conscious model: Roberto Clemente. "I got two doubles in that All-Star game, both to right center field, one off Nolan Ryan," recalls Schmidt, who hit over .300 in his next thousand at-bats and won those two MVP awards as well as a Series MVP. "I've gone from a dangerous hitter to a good one. Now I'm less slump prone and better under pressure. I can hit according to game situations, and that's the way baseball should be played."

Schmidt's latest career stage is often attributed to more ethereal causes: a stable home life, the birth of a son and daughter, a rediscovery of Christianity. While all this is true, it amuses Schmidt. "I used to be accused of being too cool. Now it's seen as 'intelligence.' Then I had no emotion, lacked desire, thought too much for my own good. Now people flock around to try to figure out what I've been thinking."

When Schmidt slugged .832 in the '80 World Series, he was "the thinking man's ballplayer." When he slugged .050 in the '83 Series, he was back to "thinking too much."

Schmidt is an interesting hybrid: an introverted extrovert. He broods; then, when he's out of his funk, he can't stop talking about it. In his dozen seasons Schmidt has grasped one rare moral: he thinks a hero has a duty to speak directly to those who idolize him—in his case, teenagers. This is unusual, to say the least, among big leaguers.

What other future Hall of Famer with an $8-million contract goes to junior high schools to get his points across? Because Schmidt has always been something of a jock-hip fashion plate—the first with the blow-dried hair, the gold chains, the open-necked silk shirts, the designer blue jeans with lightning bolts stitched down the sides, the maroon Ultrasuede sports coat (don't laugh, it looks great on him)—he doesn't get too many snickers.

"Grade school kids are experiencing now what I didn't experience until college. If a kid in the eighth grade has run the gamut of experiences from sex to drugs to hard liquor, if he's gotten in the habit of altering his state of mind as often as he can, is he going to grow out of that by the time he's twenty? I don't see a lot of kids nowadays who like themselves. When I was growing up, I followed the crowd. That's why it bothers me to go to schools and see there's no respect for hygiene, no respect for the way you look, no respect for teachers, no respect for the mind. There's only respect for whoever has the most fun.

"That," he says, enjoying the irony of saying it, "is wasted potential."

Schmidt and Yount have bodies that look as if they came out of the same crate: long, tapered and sleek, with big, bodybuilders' veins that seem to be working doubletime. These guys have the sinewy, built-to-inflict-damage look that would seem fitting if they lined up at strong safety. Schmidt and Yount look one level tougher and more serious than other ballplayers; they're pure athlete, ready for a decathlon.

They also share a distrust of the great mulching machine of celebrity. Yount, in particular, distrusts all the right things.

For instance, when the Milwaukee crowd in County Stadium began to chant "MVP" in his honor during a 1982 playoff game, Yount didn't like it. He resists, distrusts, withholds himself from all the twisted perceptions that surround athletes. Perhaps he senses how those external distortions can somehow, with time, become internalized. The curse of a public image is that, sooner or later, it starts showing up in the mirror. Robin Yount has no public face.

"Robin has no pretenses," said Brewer catcher Ted Simmons. "That chant is almost embarrassing to him. Maybe embarrassing isn't exactly the right word. But it's close. You can see his jaw kind of clench."

"The attention, I don't need it," Yount said not long after he became the first player to twice get four hits in a game in the same Series ('82). "I'm just a human being gifted with the ability to play baseball. I'm nothing special. I'm just another person."

What Yount resists most is the cult of personality that surrounds many American athletes. And because he's been a regular since 1974, starting at the age of eighteen, he has had more than enough time to make a considered decision on the subject. Almost nothing about Reggie Jackson's life would appeal to him.

When he's asked those open-ended, puffball questions that seem to say, "Come on, kid, say anything even half smart, half funny, half controversial, and we'll make you a star," Yount gives back nothing. Yount refuses to chip off pieces of himself for the public's consumption.

During his first World Series, in '82, fans chanted so long that Yount's own teammates forced him to give a tip-of-the-cap to assuage them. "That wasn't me," said Yount after his millisecond appearance. "I've done it once before and I hope I don't have to do it again."

"Robin gets through all this a little easier than most other guys would. It doesn't frazzle him," said Simmons during the '82 Series, as he watched Yount—with a gentle, becalmed sea of reporters lapping at the foot of his locker—talk quietly and disinterestedly while looking lazily across the room. "It's like he's sayin', 'I'm going to have a little fun with this, but I'm not going to let it impress me, because it's not all that important. I'm not going to let it frazz me . . .'

"He's much more mature than his age. You gotta remember, when he was eighteen to nineteen, he was living in a world where the tone in the locker room was set by guys twenty-seven to thirty-five years old."

"This is even better than I thought it would be," said Yount of that Series, recalling his early, struggling years on a bad expansion ball club. "The only drawback is all the exposure." Or, as they say in the Caribbean, "The higher the monkey climb, the more he expose."

Yount, who seems taller than his six feet, broader and stronger than his 170 pounds and years older than his age, has that middle-distance look about him most of the time. It's an American frontier look that is undeniably strong. It's tantalizing to imagine him, with his hair and mustache out of the mid-nineteenth century, as a stoic Pony Express rider about to be sent off through Indian lands.

If Yount were not an athlete, Simmons thinks he knows just what Yount would be. "Just what he is in the off-season," says

Simmons, "a freewheeling motorcycle person." Not motorcycle *gang* member. Motorcycle *person*. Alone, eating up the road, getting away from the beaten trails. As a teenager, back in the suburb of Los Angeles where he grew up, Yount and his buddies used to hunt jackrabbits in the desert. On motorcycles. Pitting their speed and reflexes and agility on their bikes against the rabbits' quick cuts. "We wore those jackrabbits out."

For Yount, it's still the game that matters most. Whether it's cycles or baseball, it's the hunt, the challenge, the hard work that's appealing. Not the fame or the money. Watch Yount on a hot, sleepy August night before a game in Oakland. He's playing catch. He's in heaven. He and Gorman Thomas compare curves at twenty paces until Thomas cries uncle. Simmons is next in line and Yount snaps off a few dozen more crackling pitches to him. Back in the clubhouse to change to his game uniform, Yount has a little boy's radiance. "Had a great breaking ball tonight. Gorman couldn't hold me."

So, for a while, forget all the numbers and evaluations when Yount and Schmidt take the stage. Don't bother to strain your mind looking a decade down the road to foresee a day when Yount might retire with the thirty-five hundred hits, and Schmidt with the six hundred homers, that would make them the greatest shortstop and third baseman in history.

Let's be content to watch them as they are now, when even the greatest challenges of their sport are still just the hardest and best kind of play.

15.
PALMER
VS.
PALMER

In the Jockey ad, half of Jim Palmer's princely, brooding face is fully lighted, the other half is masked in shadow. This chiaroscuro portrait, intended only to sell underwear, comes alarmingly close to capturing the man. Or rather, it hints at how elusive a clear view of the dichotomous Palmer can be.

Ever since he pitched a shutout in the World Series seventeen years ago, at the age of twenty, beating Sandy Koufax in Koufax' final game, Palmer has been as glamorous, as bright, as gifted and as public a figure as baseball has had to offer. Yet today Palmer forlornly describes himself as so "completely misunderstood" that he has given up hope of ever being appreciated rightly. His teammates go further, doubting whether anybody fathoms the consistently contradictory Palmer—least of all Palmer. In one breath his fellow Baltimore Orioles call him a true Hall of Famer; then, in the next, denigrate him as a hypochondriac, borderline paranoiac, prima donna and even quitter.

Outside the clubhouse, the inner circle of baseball, Palmer is regarded as one of the dozen best pitchers in the history of the game. Even his remarkable resurrection, in 1982—a 15-5 record, eleven victories in a row, runner-up in the American League's Cy Young voting—seemed just another step in his inevitable stroll to Cooperstown. After all, he is fifth *in history* in twenty-win seasons (eight) and Earned Run Average (2.79); he owns three Cy Young awards and the best winning percentage of any active pitcher (.651).

To the public eye, Palmer is an American ideal made manifest: a certified major-league master who is as well a sensationally handsome and successful ABC sportscaster, male model and national sex symbol. This Palmer stands for elegance and sophistication: the embodiment of natural gifts, both athletic and personal. He stands, in short, for perfection.

Strange as it may seem in an age of manufactured images and cynical opportunists, all the buttery praise for Palmer is basically deserved. His courtesy and common touch are rare and genuine. He gives his time—some would even say squanders it—on charities both famous and obscure. As though this weren't enough, Palmer is a doting father to his two teenage daughters and a man of principles so lofty as to seem anachronistic. He's never gone free agent and consequently plays for a salary that is half that of players who've had half his career. He's scrupulously clean-living. Some ballplayers snort coke; Palmer won't even drink one. Unpretentious in his clothes, car and home, honest to a fault, fanatically punctual and responsible, Palmer is old-fashioned and moral.

At thirty-seven, Palmer should be basking in the glow of a brilliant career, taking the sweet, lingering bows to which an athlete is entitled as he faces the curtain of age. But always, for Palmer, with the spotlight have come the shadows. Instead of savoring those final bows, he says, "I'm tired of opening letters that say, 'Go to hell, Palmer.'" Instead he faces fans and teammates every day who feel ambivalent toward him, respecting his talent and labors yet often disliking, even disdaining him; to some Orioles, he's an acquired distaste. Over the past several years, there has been more sniping at Palmer than at all other Orioles combined. The recurrent criticism from players like Rick Dempsey, Doug DeCinces, Mark Belanger and Ken Singleton is that Palmer has great gifts but is often hors de combat at the first sign of pain or pique. "Palmer has earned the right to be a hero here," Orioles general manager Hank Peters once said. "It's a shame he isn't one. He's badly damaged his reputation in this community."

In Memorial Stadium, where catcalls are rare, the players most often booed are Reggie Jackson, who defected to New York, and Palmer, who's won 263 games for Bal'mer.

The sudden shifting of light and shadow in Palmer's life was never more apparent than on the morning of the last game of 1982. Baltimore—the town that booed him and team that doubted him—needed Palmer more than at any time in the club's history. The Orioles had won thirty-three of forty-three games, to tie Milwaukee for first place on the season's next-to-last day. Before that final game, the Birds suggested that Palmer take a cortisone shot in his shoulder, which, that week, had become sore. With a pennant, a season, at stake, many pitchers would have taken the shot unhesitatingly. Palmer balked. "I'd never taken a shot *the day of a game,* although I'd taken them the day before. I didn't want to take that chance."

The Orioles didn't press, partly because they've come to believe that pregame excuses are essential to Palmer. As Al Bumbry puts it, "When Jimmy's got his alibis all lined up, he's tough to beat."

This time, Palmer lost.

He was stunned, partly by the 10–2 defeat, but also by a fifteen-minute standing ovation after the game, which left Palmer and many others in tears. That same night, just hours after the most disheartening loss of his career—and the most precious ovation—Palmer flew three thousand miles to Los Angeles so he could see his orthopedic specialist the next morning.

Diagnosis: nothing wrong.

Is this neurosis, narcissism or the farsighted wisdom that allows a fellow to win three hundred games? If, upon examining the Palmer conundrum, the answer occurs to you, call (301) 243-9800. That's the Orioles switchboard. They've wanted to know for nineteen years.

Jim Palmer, as it happens, is one great unresolved dialectic in which every thesis is coupled with a ready-to-hand antithesis—with not a synthesis in sight. Any list of his conspicuous qualities turns out to be a recitation of opposites. Palmer's inability to reach a synthesis in almost any area of his life is what makes him exasperating. This is a guy who has gotten on a few nerves. Within the baseball world, the glossy view of Palmer—his public image—is seen as a sort of strange joke. To his peers, he's an all-star eccentric who is pitied or clucked over protectively as often as he is envied. Yet, in the long run, it is Palmer's determined complexity, his refusal to embrace shabby compromises and blunted principles, that gives him dimension.

At times, Palmer seems mellow. During the season, he regularly takes a dugout seat where he can work on his tan. In warm-ups, he lopes where others run. In or out of uniform his motion is languid, his voice relaxed and mellifluous, his movements deliberate, confident.

"I'm easygoing," he says, sitting in the spotless, stylish living room of his suburban Baltimore home. If *Gentleman's Quarterly* comes by for a photo spread, Palmer won't have to put a single sock in a hamper. The house, like every obvious manifestation of Palmer, is ready for a full-dress inspection. Asked to describe how Palmer played golf, his long-time manager, friend and nemesis, Earl Weaver, said, "How do you think? Like he does everything else: perfectly." If Palmer seems easygoing, it may be because that's how a "perfect" person should appear. In fact, he's completely manic, known, among other things, for mowing his lawn at 6 A.M. "I'm really hyper," the "easygoing" Palmer says sheepishly.

A lazy off-season afternoon in Palmer's house is like being trapped in a Rube Goldberg cartoon. In three hours, the phone rings nearly twenty times. Each time, Palmer answers it before the second ring so his message machine can't take control. Every call delights him. He's polite and amusing, inventing comic voices to deceive friends. He confirms appointments, makes appointments, critiques past appointments. ("It was *supposed* to be terrific. You wouldn't have had me if you didn't think it would be terrific.") The front door stays unlocked, because Palmer is in heaven when, while talking on the phone to one person and being interviewed by another, he can lean around the corner and welcome somebody new into the house.

First, Palmer's girlfriend of long standing, Paula, drops by. She's a businesswoman, smart and not particularly deferential toward him.

"How'd you like the Mozart I left?" she asks.

"Not much," says Palmer.

"Great taste," she says.

She's slim, blond and healthy-beautiful, but makes no attempt to be flashy. She wears jeans and knee boots—the rubber kind you wear to work in the yard.

"Just write good stuff about my pal," she says.

"That'll be the day," says Palmer.

Next to appear are his pretty, teenage daughters, whom he calls the apples of his eye. Kelly, thirteen, plops herself in his lap, and Jamie, sixteen, makes a split-second decision to join her father on his trip to California the next week. The girls will be back later for dinner, which Palmer can't wait to cook. That, like gardening, is among his ardent hobbies.

Although he is a believer in the close-knit, old-fashioned family, Palmer got married at eighteen, and, in what is surely the most easily comprehensible of broken marriages, found that he and his wife grew apart. Talk of a divorce has gone on for years, but nothing has ever been settled. So, wanting to give his daughters love while still allowing both himself and his wife some freedom, he has bought a house on the other side of the hill from theirs. An unusual, but decent, arrangement.

"My wife and I have been married for nineteen years," says Palmer, mulling the stress-fracture in his family life. "It got to a point where neither of us could be our own person. But many of those nineteen years were very happy ones. I don't really see it as a failure . . .

"The kids know that they're loved . . . my wife did an excellent job of preparing them so they'd look at me as their father and not a celebrity, the way other people do. They know there isn't anything in the world I wouldn't do for them. My job allows me to have two houses, so they all live right over the hill.

"My wife and I never argue . . . but there's been anguish. I had to go back there, to the other house, at the beginning of the year, for legal reasons. Talk about psychosomatic injuries. The minute I got back out of there my neck stopped hurting. I was relaxed again," says Palmer, his white poodle, Holly, curled up at his feet, soft jazz on the stereo. "My wife says the separation is not my fault, it's hers. She doesn't feel good about being Mrs. Jim

Palmer. 'Oh, glad to meet you. You're Mrs. Jim Palmer' . . . people in their thirties sometimes want to change the course of the ship. I guess she's in that now. I hope to do it in my forties."

The all-afternoon open house continues with the entrance of a striking blond neighbor who just happens to be wearing her ankle-length silver mink. When women go to Palmer's house for a cup of sugar, they don't wear their hair in curlers. The man's life is one long female audition. Mostly, they must settle for a smile. "I don't date that much," Palmer says. "It's work. I have to make a great effort as far as straightening people out about their preconceived ideas about me."

Palmer's need for a kaleidoscopic environment is so ingrained that, as he talks, he changes position in his chair as exotically as a little boy, at one point even getting his feet above his head. Every few minutes he switches the music coming from the tape deck. "I *never* watch television," he says, then corrects himself: "Well, sometimes Carson's monologue." That's about as long as he likes to sit still. Nevertheless, Palmer is one ballplayer occasionally seen in the company of long, heavy novels. They feed the mind, to be sure, but also help him get through the interminable hours he spends on planes. Once, seeing Palmer reading *Dr. Zhivago,* teammate Steve Stone said, "It must be about an elbow specialist."

Partly because he can't stay put, Palmer is among the best-conditioned of major leaguers. In a day, he'll play basketball and racquetball, lift weights and run, then throw. And that's in January. "He has the best twenty-year-old body in baseball," says Weaver. "When rookies ask what to do in spring training, I say, 'Follow Palmer.' Not one has ever kept up with him."

Just as Palmer, taken in sixty-second doses, seems relaxed, so, measured over hours, he seems in need of a sedative. "My wife always said to me, 'You fit everything in,' " says Palmer, "meaning I was fitting her and the children in around a lot of other things. But I'd say to her, 'Yes, but I fit *everything* in.' Meaning, I did get around to all of it."

Not surprisingly, this laid-back ball of nerves is also both intensely rational and explosively emotional. On the one hand Palmer is the man with a passion for logic. That may be his greatest strength as a pitcher. "Nobody's got as many theories as

Jim. He'll use a whole game just to prove he's right," says fellow Oriole hurler Mike Flanagan. "One year he was convinced we'd thrown too many curves in spring training. So, on opening day, he threw 120 fastballs out of 124 pitches to beat the White Sox. Another time, Earl was on one of his kicks about starting hitters off with breaking balls. Jimmy told us, 'Forget Earl. He knows baseball, but all he knows about pitching is that he couldn't hit it. He gives the hitters too much credit. The key is to get ahead with a first-pitch fastball for a strike.' So Palmer started all thirty-three hitters that game with fastballs, thirty-two for strikes," recalls Flanagan.

"It's amazing how predictable he is, but the hitters can't do anything. Every batter, it's a fastball for a strike or pop-up, then a change-up for a ground out. We look at each other and say, 'Don't they *know?*' "

"Jim calls his change a BP [batting practice] fastball," Flanagan says, "but it's really a helluva screwball. We never tell him, 'Great screwball,' though, because then his elbow would hurt.

"When Palmer is on a roll, the innings go so fast they're a blur —always ahead, no trouble, minimum of pitches, always working around the good hitters. We can call every pitch he throws. Maybe once a game he crosses us up. When he gets back to the dugout he'll tell us why before we can ask. Usually it's 'cause he's thinking three batters ahead."

After years of studying Palmer in action, Coach Ray Miller simply calls the six-foot-three, 194-pound right-hander the game's best situation pitcher.

"You must accept that you'll give up runs," explains Palmer. "The pitcher who gives up runs *one at a time* wins, while the pitcher who gives them up two, three and four at a time loses. I've given up long home runs that I turned around and admired like a fan. But the ones I admired were all *solos.*"

With the bases loaded, the ultimately rational Palmer *always* throws every pitch at a corner—even with three balls on the batter. In his career, he's walked home many runs, but in more than thirty-eight hundred innings, Palmer has *never* given up a grand slam. Not one.

This level-headed man of logic, however, is also a creature of moods and funks. Once, he walked off the mound in the eighth inning of a 1–0 game after right-hander Pat Kelly dropped a flyball, prompting a furious Belanger to say, "Palmer has always begged off under pressure." Palmer hardly makes friends when he calls his outfield "our Bermuda Triangle" or when he stares at offending defenders; when he fires his glove off dugout walls and hrumpfs between innings or when he asks an umpire for a new ball seven straight times, knowing an umpire carries only six in his pouch; or, finally, when he repositions his fielders between pitches. ("I have to move my outfielders ten steps to the right," Weaver once said, "so that after Palmer moves them back five steps to the left, they'll end up in the right place.")

Yet Palmer can't forget any slight ever done to him. His memory is encyclopedic—a curse for a man who feels persecuted. Palmer can remember sequences of pitches from games fifteen years ago; ask him, out of the blue, how long reliever Don Stanhouse has been married and he says, "October 27, 1981." Unfortunately, Palmer also recalls that "in 1966 I was 15-10 and got fifteen thousand dollars the next year, while Jim Lonborg [of Boston] was 10-17 and got twenty-two thousand dollars." He can't help it. "I just can't forget any of that stuff," he says. "I'm very logical but also very emotional." He says it as if they went hand in hand.

To appreciate the Palmer paradox, it's important to understand that Palmer's childhood and young adulthood were dichotomous. He was adopted at the age of one week, yet grew up with a silver spoon in his mouth. He says he has never wanted to know who his natural parents were. His father, Moe, a dress manufacturer, was Jewish; his mother, Polly, was Catholic. Growing up, his name was Jim Wiesen. The family lived on Park Avenue and in Rye, New York, summered on Lake George and had servants in the home. Then, one morning, the boy noticed that lots of cars had pulled up in the family driveway. His father had died of a heart attack in the night. Jim was nine years old.

His mother moved Jim and his sister, also adopted, three thousand miles to California. The family's style of life went from upper to middle class. Polly Wiesen eventually remarried, to Max Palmer, a Hollywood character actor in shows like "Playhouse

90," "Dragnet" and "Highway Patrol," who also managed the bars at Hollywood Park and Santa Anita racetracks. Next the family moved to Scottsdale, Arizona. One of the first children Palmer met there was a girl named Susan. They dated through high school, then married after graduation. As Palmer was venturing through the minors in the early sixties, his sister became a child of the times, a hippie, and embarked on the first of six marriages. They seldom see each other anymore. "I always wondered how two people so different came from the same environment," he's said.

No sooner did Palmer make his bombshell appearance in the majors at twenty, winning fifteen games and becoming the youngest man ever to pitch a World Series shutout, than his elbow blew out. He spent two lost and traumatic years in the minors, getting shelled in Miami and Rochester. Many thought his career was over. The Orioles scarred Palmer by insinuating that his problems were in his head. Palmer learned a bitter lesson early: "Your arm is all you are."

Put that first twenty-one years of life in your David Copperfield pipe and smoke it. Palmer's view is that it was basically idyllic: loving parents, no wants, lived on the lower acreage of the Jimmy Cagney estate across the street from Tony Curtis and Janet Leigh in Beverly Hills. What's the big deal? Next subject.

With this as background, perhaps it is easier intuitively, though probably not clinically, to sense how one man can be so many things—and also their opposites.

For instance, this putative prima donna whom baseball colleagues swear is often selfish and immature, is notably charitable and responsible. His one stipulation before okaying a poster of his Jockey ad, for example, was that all proceeds go to cystic fibrosis. Well known for his inability to say no to worthy causes, Palmer has always been a whirlwind of good works. One day during the off-season he offered himself as a luncheon partner to anybody who would donate a hundred dollars to the Baltimore Symphony. The next day, he spent the morning at Memorial Stadium pouring cokes at an Oriole party for a hundred poor children. That night, Palmer was a "celebrity bartender"—again for charity. ("They didn't know what they were getting into," he says. "I'd never mixed a drink in my life. If it wasn't white wine or draft beer, they were in trouble.") The following day, at the request of his estranged wife, Palmer spent ninety minutes playing tennis with people he'd never seen before in order to raise nine hundred dollars for another charity.

And all this was during Christmas week.

Palmer turned out to be so dependable in his public appearances that Jockey was shocked. "You tell Palmer when and where to be, and he's there. That's one reason we made him the company's spokesman," says a Jockey official. "We've had to do amazing things to get players—even Pete Rose—where they were supposed to be. Sometimes a limousine isn't enough. You need somebody to wake the guy, get him dressed and in the limousine."

At his dozens of Jockey shows, often on mornings after he's pitched, Palmer signs his name a thousand times without missing a smile. Sometimes when a woman asks him to sign her briefs, it turns out she's still wearing them. On a hot day in Milwaukee once, Palmer quietly asked the assembled admirers, "Mind if I take off my jacket?" Soon a thousand women were shouting, "Take it off!"

"I go out for Jockey, and people—guys in sales and vice-presidents—they're amazed at how I can get along with people," Palmer says. "Well, my politeness definitely comes from my parents. My mother was one of six kids and her father died when he was forty. She went to New York and got a job in a small dress shop and put her brother through Juilliard School . . . When she met my father, it wasn't like she didn't know the value of a dollar . . . She would give her last dime to anybody who asked for it. She was certainly aware of how other people live, because she'd gone through it . . .

"What's life all about," he says, "except using your experiences to figure out how you want to conduct yourself? I've seen too many ballplayers go to dinners where they're getting fifteen hundred dollars or two thousand dollars and not want to sign autographs. I mean, why are you there?"

There are those, however, who don't equate sangfroid and good manners with maturity.

"Many people grow up late," says Weaver. "But Palmer *still* hasn't grown up . . . [pause] . . . but he's getting closer.

"Jim has a hard time making difficult decisions. For instance, is his divorce final? No? I didn't think so. It's been up in the air for years. He hasn't faced that," says Weaver. "He's still got his security blankets. He hasn't let go of any of them, has he? Once he stands in front of that judge and hears him say what the alimony is and what the child support is and how much he can see his own children . . . when he starts facing things like that, he'll start finding out what it means to be an adult."

True to form, Palmer is ambivalent about Weaver, with whom he does commercials and TV commentary. "It was great to see Earl humble. He was in awe of the pros," crows Palmer, looking back on their TV work during the playoffs last October. "He even told me I did a good job. That's when I knew he was nervous."

Palmer compares their Odd Couple relationship to "a marriage where each partner knows exactly what to say to make the other one mad." Certainly Weaver has been the burr under Palmer's saddle for almost his entire career. It's a considerable compliment to both men that they could sincerely like, and sincerely dislike, each other—yet coexist. In a strange sense, it was a model for human relationships. To be sure, opposites attract. But there were also many times when either Palmer or Weaver could have written the other off as an incorrigible pain in the ass. Yet each saw in the other a winner who possessed native intelligence. Such foils could not willingly part.

"The only thing I ever asked from Earl," Palmer says, "was that he treat me the way I would have treated him—that he just be fair and polite and compassionate. Of course, that's just not Earl. That doesn't mean I would rather have had Earl be compassionate and thoughtful than be a winner.

"With Earl, enough is never enough. He has never been satisfied with my performance, not in my best year. It goes back to that series of great expectations, the Jim Palmer syndrome. The years after I went 16-4 (in '69), he had me winning thirty games before I had ever won twenty. And when I've been hurt, they've never been able to accept it. I don't think I'm a hypochondriac.

It's always been the same: Tim Stoddard has a sore arm and they believe him. Jim Palmer has a sore arm and it's in his head.

"I was a baby when I came up here and Earl made it very difficult, listening to him complain about everything. Lee May used to make a joke out of it. There'd be Earl—we'd have a man on third with one out in an early inning and a guy would pop up, and you know Earl, he'd have his head between his knees, going, 'Bbbrrrrrr.' He's sure we've blown the game; he's seen his omen. Lee would say, 'Well, the Little Genius has given up again.' And we'd laugh and go on and play our own game. And we'd win.

"I just think a lot of the ways that I acted, and the misunderstandings that came out of it, were caused by Earl Weaver. That sounds like a cop-out. But it's true."

One episode, out of dozens, gives the true Odd Couple flavor.

In '81, Weaver was so incensed by Palmer's five-year-old habit of missing starts with mysterious injuries, begging for relief help at the first sign of trouble and generally second-guessing everybody, that, on the mound in Seattle, Weaver screamed at Palmer, "I'm sick of your crap. Come on, let's fight."

"I plan to scream at Palmer the rest of the season, 'cause that's the only way I can get his attention," Weaver announced. "But, knowing Palmer, it'll go in one ear and out the other. His problem is he won't listen to anybody. When I want him, I'll just send Ray Miller to drag him back by his diaper."

Palmer retaliated with medical journals, supporting his new self-diagnoses: an injury "to the suprascapulous . . . my career is probably over."

This was old news to Weaver, the man who once said, "The Chinese tell time by 'the Year of the Dragon,' 'the Year of the Horse.' I tell time by 'the Year of the Shoulder,' 'the Year of the Elbow,' 'the Year of the Ulnar Nerve.'"

That a man as fanatical as Palmer about good health should have spent his career performing the most unnatural act in sports —throwing a baseball—deserves a cosmic snicker. A pitcher's life is one day of deliberate self-injury, followed by three days of healing, then a fresh injury. Ask a narcissistic perfectionist, who's pretty sure he knows more about sports medicine than most doctors, to endure in this job, and the result is "the Year of the Ulnar Nerve."

Finally, Weaver gave his true diagnosis of the slump Palmer suffered from '79 until '82—a period in which he was 34-26, with two dozen missed starts: "We've got to find out how much Palmer has left. He's got to get rid of all this emotion he wastes on blaming other people for everything that goes wrong," said Weaver. "He has to say, 'That's my fault' or 'I can overcome that.' Now he's always pitying himself and taking himself out of games and asking for help."

Pitching coach Miller added, "Palmer has reached the stage of his career where he has to bite the bullet. I don't know if he's ever really had to. Palmer can't keep putting Earl on the spot with all his antics."

In response, Palmer tried enough advice and remedies for a whole pitching staff. He changed sliders three times until he found one that didn't hurt his elbow. He adopted Steve Carlton's hand-in-a-bucket-of-sand exercises. He practiced the pregame meditation methods of Steve Stone. (Said Flanagan: "It's a good thing for Jimmy that Stone didn't stand on his head.") Palmer also went on a small-weight-lifting program prescribed by one doctor and a general strengthening scheme devised by another. He consulted with specialists in Los Angeles, Boston and Baltimore.

The result: nothing.

By May 1982, Palmer had reached the lowest point in his career. His ERA was 7.44. His stock in the organization had bottomed out. "I think Palmer can win those sixty games he needs to reach three hundred," said Weaver, "but I doubt if he can do it here. He needs something to completely shake him up."

As a last resort, Palmer's twin bêtes noires—Weaver and Peters—decided on shock treatment. First Palmer was sent to the bullpen. Not for rest or rehabilitation, but indefinitely. "I got the word," says Palmer, "that Peters had said, 'I don't want Palmer to start another game here this year.' "

Contending that he was being used as a scapegoat, Palmer asked for a trade. To his amazement, he got an answer he'd never heard before: Great. Give us a list of teams you'd approve and we'll work something out within *two weeks.*

Peters and Weaver had decided that, underneath everything, Palmer was utterly attached to Baltimore—both town and team. To their minds, he was like a child trying to test the limits of his family's patience and affection. So they let the little boy run away from home; then they didn't go look for him.

Within two days, Palmer decided he didn't want to be traded, that he wanted to finish his career in Baltimore, because the dislocations of a trade would be too cruel for his family. Next he walked into Weaver's office and, according to Weaver, said, as he often had in the seventies, "Earl, my arm feels good. I think I'll win seven or eight in a row."

"Palmer always keeps his word," beamed Weaver, putting the right-hander back in the rotation. This time, Palmer bettered his word. From that day, in late May, until September—from before Memorial Day until after Labor Day—Palmer went unbeaten, winning eleven in a row and equaling the longest streak of his career.

He wasn't lucky. He was good. Often overpoweringly good. Once again he could throw his fastball for strikes with impunity— for six or seven innings at least. His combination of a rising fastball, that nasty new slider, a rainbow curve and two change-ups (one a screwball), gave him a paralyzing combination of pitches.

To Palmer, the coincidence of his bullpen exile and his return to form was galling. "I did all the work to get my fastball back, to rehabilitate my shoulder," he says. "Of course, *they* think it's in my head."

"I think that sending him to the bullpen and agreeing to trade him was a kick in the rear end to him. It spurred his pride," says Peters. "I think it was the catalyst." But then, if a clear line of causality could be traced, we wouldn't be talking about Palmer. This, after all, is the winner who's been called a quitter. This is the hypochondriac who averaged 288 innings a season for nine consecutive years, the sex symbol who lives the clean life, the baseball paranoid who can't forget, the responsible adolescent, the urbane sophisticate who is, in private, a Gordian knot of fascinating kinks.

Finally, this is a man who is trying to live up to his own personal conception of "the good," both in his pitching and in his life. His charitable works, his attention to responsibilities, his forbearance with strangers, his concern for his children bear no evidence of being the machinations of a fellow with ulterior motives: an eye on politics, perhaps, or public favor.

At the risk of applying a word out of fashion, no enterprise is *nobler* than this striving after a life that will bear up under the strictest scrutiny—not just the scrutiny of celebrity, that is, but of our own internal eye. Palmer has tried to conduct an examined life, to arrive at his own precepts and live by them. That this hardest, and most universal, of tasks often leaves him at odds with himself—in apparent contradictions—isn't surprising.

Palmer is, of course, just as tangled up, as human, as everybody else—*and he knows it.* Given his advantages, that's not an easy insight. When Palmer pleads that he's misunderstood, he means people don't understand that despite his wealth-looks-talent-fame, he finds life just as troubling as anybody else. With him, it takes us a little longer to appreciate the shadows in a glittering life.

Surely some of the paradoxes in Palmer can be credited as virtues. Attempting to lead a decent and reasonably reflective life while trying to win three hundred baseball games along the way is full-time employment. Palmer takes some "bearing with," and, like us all, has his weaker side. However, once we take the trouble to meet him whole, he draws us toward him with a human link we would not want to break.

"In the little things, Jim can get on your nerves," says teammate Flanagan. "But the longer you know him, and the better you know him, the more you like him. He's a really fine man.

"I talked to 'Cakes' on the phone one day," Flanagan says, using Palmer's nickname (short for the pancakes he eats before pitching), "and told him I was going to have a patio built. He said, 'Don't do that.' Next thing I knew, he and Rich Dauer are out back pouring concrete and building my patio while I'm 'supervising.' I had the most expensive landscape gardner in America. That's typical of Palmer. He just has to find something to do every minute. And nothing makes him happier than helping somebody else."

But, of course, it could hardly be that simple. Palmer's desire to be loved is large, his need for proofs of appreciation considerable. Those who neglect or mistrust him may be punished—indeed may deserve to be. "Fans are front-runners," he says, for instance. "I've won 250-some games and I get booed. They announce my name and a third of the people boo. I go out there and get booed. I win, and no cheers. That's the way it is. I'm never going to be understood. But that's all right. It really is.

"When I walked out after the final game last year, I just knew that fate dictates," says Palmer. "Here you've got Don Sutton, who's a good friend of mine. He leaves L.A., which I never could understand because his family lives there and it's a nice place to play. He goes to Houston for a lot of money and he gets tired and doesn't want to play down *there* because they never score any runs. So he goes to Milwaukee. And it's Sutton and me in the last game. Here I am, played here for nineteen years, I'm the one who *stayed*. If there's any justice in the world, we'd win.

"But life doesn't work that way. It just doesn't.

"The true fans are the ones who came out afterward—how wonderful . . . The people were still there waiting after the game, and they were calling for us. Now, those are the real fans, those were the fans who came up to me when I was 7-8 and said, 'We don't care. We appreciate all the things you've done.' Not that I'm somebody who lives in the past, but I do think that counts.

"It's like Rudolf Nureyev. We saw him in *Sleeping Beauty* in Washington. People say he's not what he used to be. Well, who gives a shit? He's still good."

Like you?

"Yes," says Jim Palmer.

16

NINE AGAINST ONE

Defense is baseball's visible poetry and its invisible virtue.

Defense is also the vital, but easily torn, web of order that runs through the game, giving a team a sense of itself as more than a motley of individuals. Above all, fine defense is the often ignored common denominator of champions.

It took a bloody Englishman to teach me these lessons.

I once took a British soccer writer, Brian Glanville, of the London *Sunday Times,* to his first major-league baseball game. He'd never clapped eyes on the sport at any level. Beyond a few Americanisms like "three strikes and you're out," he may have known less about baseball than I knew about soccer. Our arrangement was that I'd explain this colonial fuss about rounders if, on some dim future day, he would introduce me to the mysteries of Manchester United versus Leeds, should I find my way to England.

We saw a first-rate game beween the Yankees and the Orioles. Those aspects of the game which I most wanted him to appreciate were entirely lost on him.

Explaining strategy was, naturally, wasted breath. That would take years.

The pitching didn't much impress him either. He wasn't surprised that one fellow could throw a ball fairly fast to another man twenty paces away. Nor did he doubt a ball could be curved; spin bowling, it's called in cricket.

Base running barely fazed him. Englishmen can run quickly, on occasion.

Glanville was even oblivious to home runs. He knew that a muscular being with a large stick could crack a ball a considerable distance; golf, don't you know. A home run might be a curiosity, but, to a cosmopolite, hardly a marvel.

Yet, all in all, my English opposite number was agog at baseball. Loved it.

All he could talk about was the defense.

"My God, look at how wonderfully they can catch the ball and throw it," he marveled. "Almost more than you'd think humanly possible."

To my jaded eyes, the game barely contained a single play that would rise above the routine. Yet it was the routine, or, the routinely excellent, which yanked this Brit out of his seat time and again.

When a shortstop went in the hole for a grounder and threw out a fast runner by half a step, his jaw dropped. "Was that entirely deliberate?" he asked. "Is it done often?"

When an outfielder made a knee-high catch at a dead run, the visitor went into transports. "Remarkable intuition! How does he judge its flight?"

When an infielder dove parallel to the ground to snag a line drive, he thought his eyes had deceived him and that the ball had not really been caught. To him, it seemed that both the ball and the man who caught it were a blur.

When a pop-up, as high as the light tower and barely visible at its apex, came down squarely into the glove of a nonchalant and unmoving catcher, the Englishman was beside himself with surprise that a thing so patently difficult should be done in such an obviously offhand manner.

"Good Lord," he said, "the man trotted to *the very spot.*"

Don't try to imagine his reaction to a double play. He saw its balletic quality before I could drag up the cliché. Luckily for Glanville, neither Willie Mays nor Ozzie Smith was on the premises. He'd have had a coronary.

In fact, every difficult ground ball and throw to first base enchanted him.

An infielder gliding toward a grounder; then—all in the same instant—skidding to a stop, fielding the erratically hopping ball cleanly and casually, planting himself to throw, then delivering the ball a hundred to a hundred fifty feet, precisely on target, with a snake-tongue flick of a throw—was a skill so foreign to his European experience that it seemed superhuman.

Just as the Brazilian, no doubt, comes to take Pele's heart-skipping footwork for granted, so we often forget to be thrilled by those defensive gifts in baseball which take a lifetime to perfect.

We forget that an American child's first baseball pleasure is catching a ball. Hitting comes later, pitching last. First, we learn the magic of plucking a speeding object out of the air; eventually, we do it with graceful certainty. Throw a child a ball and watch his look of amazement the first time he stabs his arm in the air and actually discovers the ball has lodged in his glove. He can barely believe this act was his own doing. Playing catch is one of our first innocent forms of mastery over the recalcitrant objects of the world.

Because defense—apprehending the ball and heaving it to a target—is the skill we learn earliest, we forget the years it took to judge the flight of a fly or the thousands of balls we flung off stoops until every hop and spin of a grounder became familiar. Who knows the exact process by which the crack of impact, and the first flash of the ball departing the bat, tell us where to run to make the catch? Every sandlot player has marvelous skills he's half forgotten that he owns.

Whether we consciously recognize it or not, we judge a player's basic athletic ability, as opposed to his acquired baseball skills, by his gifts on defense. The outstanding hitter who is also a Gold-Glove shortstop or centerfielder, like Robin Yount or Andre Dawson, is another athletic species from a clumsy slugger like Dave Kingman.

Since that game with Glanville, I've begun to suspect that, like many fans, I've gotten a false slant on the value of the glove and arm.

Fielding is treated with knee-jerk disdain in the baseball community. There's no more damaging insult to a player than "Good field, no hit." "Gloveman" is not a description but a pejorative. A special position, designated hitter, has even been created for players who, let's be honest, aren't good enough athletes—too fat, too clumsy, too old—to play in the field. Just try to find the weekly fielding stats in the Sunday paper next to the batting and pitching averages. Who's Who in Baseball contains not one solitary fielding statistic.

Perhaps we only recognize the true difficulty and validity of defense in those youthful days when we are still trying to be players ourselves. The search for a proper position is a baseball identity crisis.

For instance, I would play any position before I would venture into the outfield. Out yonder, your sluggish servant was in charge of too much space. It's lonely in the outfield, especially if your teammates nickname you "Speedy Gonzalez." No doubt Joe DiMaggio looked on the great acreage of Yankee Stadium's outfield as a canvas for his art. To me, every outfield looked like one vast landing area in which the ball had an almost infinite number of discrete points on which it could alight before I could get there.

In the infield, alertness and practice and intuition, that knack of getting a rolling start as we see the stride and swing in progress, can give even a slow runner a chance to be respectable. Brooks Robinson was one of the slowest runners of his era, and Rich Dauer, who has the highest fielding percentage of any second baseman in history, is even slower.

How many joys in sport are comparable to finding our natural position?

I was a first baseman.

You snickered. Don't say you didn't. I heard you. It's not little pitchers, but first basemen, who have big ears. We know what you say about us: that we play first base because they're afraid to put us anywhere else. It only hurts because it's true. First base is the easiest position. That's why I called it home. The lowest step is the safest. Yet the very difficulty of becoming even a decent first baseman shows the larger difficulty of defense in general.

The problem in evaluating defense is that statistics provide little help. For instance, what is the quantitative difference between two shortstops on different teams? There is just no precise way to tell. In 1982, shortstops Ozzie Smith and Tim Foli led their leagues in fielding percentage. Both played in 139 games for division champs. Smith had 103 *more* assists than Foli (while making only three more errors). Does this mean Smith threw out a hundred runners on ground balls on which Foli could not have made the same play?

Is the difference in defensive value between Smith and Foli as great as the gap between two hitters whose offensive stats are different by a hundred total bases? I think so, but I couldn't prove it.

Inferior defensive players are hard to differentiate statistically from superior players. The subtle gradations we make among hitters and pitchers are impossible among fielders.

Could any fan confidently rank the defensive value of these AL second basemen: Frank White, Lou Whitaker, Willie Randolph, Bobby Grich, Jerry Remy, Rich Dauer, Damaso Garcia, Jim Gantner, Julio Cruz and Tony Bernazard? I doubt it. Most general managers probably couldn't.

This empirical despair leads fans and baseball executives to throw up their hands concerning the niceties of defense.

Of course, no one likes errors, and a fine glove is usually appreciated. Defense isn't ignored. It just isn't studied in the sense that pitching and hitting are dissected. Baseball is uncomfortable with mysteries; the passion to calibrate is ingrained. So defense—a realm of pure opinion—stumps us. Yet intuitively we are nagged by the knowledge that defense must be vital. We pay lip service to the virtues of the leather.

As evidence, look at the '82 world champion St. Louis Cardinals. When did a team ever win a world title with less-impressive talent? A dozen teams had better hitters and several had better pitching. But the Cards had the best defense in baseball. The Cards led the NL in fielding percentage, and Mark Belanger, then of the Dodgers, declared them the best fundamental team he'd seen in years.

When Whitey Herzog took control of the Cardinal operation, in '80, he said, "We need three things: left-handed pitching, right-handed pitching and relief pitching." His method for improving that pitching was, as much as anything else, to improve the Cards' defensive range.

Compare the '80 and '82 St. Louis lineups and you will find that, through trades and position changes, Herzog improved his team's range *at every position.*

In '80, St. Louis allowed the *most* runs in the NL. In '82, the *least.*

It's also interesting to note that the Cards were supplanted as World Champs by the team which has—for the past twenty-five years—been the best, and most defense-conscious, team of glovemen in the game: the Baltimore Orioles.

Gold Glove Awards were inaugurated in 1957. Through '82, the Orioles had won forty-six such awards, seventeen more than any other team in the AL. The National League coleaders were Cincinnati and St. Louis, with thirty-seven. It's been assumed the Orioles' success has been built on pitching. But Baltimore's first tenet of pitching is, Make 'em hit it at our defense.

Look at the best teams of the past fifteen years. One of their common qualities was exceptional defense.

The '69–'71 Orioles were the best defensive team of their period. The A's of '72–'74 were strong up the spine, with Campaneris at short, Green at second and North in center. The '75–'76 Reds had one of the greatest up-the-middle defenses in history, with Bench catching, Morgan and Concepcion around second and Cesar Geronimo in center. The '77–'78 New York Yankees were a class outfit with the glove: the infield of Chambliss, Randolph, Dent and Nettles was smooth, Munson could catch and Mickey Rivers could chase in center.

"I coached for Baltimore, Kansas City and New York before I came to the White Sox," coach Charley Lau once said. "At all those previous places, where we always won, I didn't know what we had. Those teams took good defense for granted. You don't miss the Aparicios and Belangers and Dents, and even Freddie Patek, until you get to a team that can't catch the goddamn ball."

The motto of the '81–'82 Chisox, who spent a fortune on free agents and new stars but couldn't field a ground ball to short, should have been: "Millions for tribute, but not one cent for defense."

Broadcaster Jimmy Piersall said, "They're amazing. I'm surprised they don't miss the dugout when they run in." White Sox managers endured insults, like the jeer of one fan who yelled, "Hey, [Tony] LaRussa, it's ten o'clock. Do you know where your outfielders are tonight?"

"I looked around and said, 'What the hell is going on here?' " said Lau, recalling the '82 season, when the Sox made 154 errors and allowed 92 unearned runs. "We were ridiculous. When you start giving five outs in an inning, there's no club in baseball bad enough not to take advantage of you."

"I would place defense considerably higher on the list of things that a team needs than I would have when I began managing, in '79," said LaRussa. "Your confidence as a club gets sapped most quickly by defensive mistakes. If the out is there to be taken and you don't get it, that can make your club droop. Then the mistakes multiply.

"If you analyze ten big innings, in eight of them you could pick apart the inning and see where the defense could have done some simple, fundamental thing to limit the damage or end the inning."

In '83, LaRussa lived by his own advice. In midseason, he revamped his whole infield to go for defense; weak-hitting Julio Cruz, Vance Law and Scott Fletcher all played at once. Suddenly Chicago blitzed its division and won ninety-nine games, as its pitching improved overnight from good to great.

Often, it is this conviction of fundamental solidness and collective mental discipline that gives a team its sense of itself as a team. The most common glue in an excellent club is pride in cohesive defense. Only on defense do nine men act as one: backing up bases, setting up cutoffs, arranging a relay from the most remote fence to home plate.

The team which seldom errs on routine plays, which rarely embarrasses itself in the eyes of its opponents with mental lapses, quickly acquires a belief in itself as an entity. When it's said that a team "knows how to win," what is often meant is that the club in question has, with experience, learned the knack of "staying in the game," seldom falling behind by more than a run or two, until it can find some way to win, or let its opponent discover a new way to lose. Flashy and acrobatic defensive plays are welcome but not essential to this adhesive process; they are a bonus, an inspiration.

As a perfect contrast, consider the "inexplicable" Montreal Expos. From '79 through '83, the Expos had enough pitching and hitting to play in a World Series; in fact, masked gunmen broke into my home four consecutive years and forced me to write stories picking them to win their division.

In retrospect, all the Expos lacked was an infield. Everywhere you looked, converted outfielders were trying to play the infield on a lightning turf field. In all five of those years, Montreal was last or next to last in turning double plays. The culprit of culprits was Chris Speier, utterly inadequate as a turf shortstop. Over five years, from 1978 through 1982, Speier played 643 games at short and averaged 2.91 assists per game. In the same span, Ozzie Smith averaged 3.71 assists a game, while L.A.'s Russell averaged 3.25 assists a game for the first fifteen hundred games of his career. Over a season, Speier probably reached fifty fewer ground balls than a mediocre shortstop like Russell and nearly 125 fewer grounders than a great one like Smith. Leaving Speier at shortstop for four years cost the Expos a couple of pennants.

Even after we've convinced ourselves that defense is important, we still haven't begun to answer the quantitative questions that nag us. Sooner or later, even the worst defenders will make enough plays to end every inning; the balls they failed to reach *will never show up in the stats.* When we analyze the defensive statistics of the great team and the awful one, they will certainly look similar, and *they may look identical.*

Finally, we are left with defense as baseball's irreducible matter of faith. You either believe it's as important as hitting and pitching, or you think it's hooey.

With the years comes wisdom. Once, John Lowenstein, in an oh-for-twenty-four slump, returned to the dugout, took his seat and began counting how many defenders the other team had on the field. When he reached "nine," he nodded with satisfaction.

"What are you doing?" a concerned coach asked.

"Just checking," said Lowenstein. "Sometimes it seems like Abner put too many of 'em out there."

17

THE FOURTH DIMENSION: BASEBALL AND MEMORY

Why, awakened at dawn on a winter morning by rowdy star-lings, do we catch ourselves thinking of Florida? Has baseball set its roots so firmly that, even asleep, the sound of birds means spring and spring means spring training and that means Florida?

When the birds arrived that dawn, and sleep would not return, Pete Rose's face came up like sunrise in my drowsy mind and I saw him in his prime, back in Tampa, when he was still a Red. He was telling a story, his eyes merry in his craggy face and his voice full of earthy devilment. The day had been made glorious by his brother, David, who'd whaled the tar out of a fan who'd been heckling Pete.

"The fan's yelling, 'Rose, you bum,'" intones the jolly Rose. "He turns around and the guy behind him looks just like me but is fifty pounds bigger. That fan's gotta ask himself, 'How bad is my luck? I gotta sit in front of Pete Rose's *bigger* brother.'

"Dave's a paramedic and his ambulance was out in the parking lot," said Rose casually, "so he knew just how long to punch the guy and still get him to the hospital in time."

And so back to winter dreams.

Even while we are still relatively young, our baseball recollec-tions begin to well up within us, nudging their way to conscious-ness at odd times, knitting together the decades of our life. Baseball exists in four dimensions: height, width, depth and memory. The diamonds in our minds, the fields of reverie, often rival reality. Of all American sports, none can match baseball's passion for the past. From the wooden stands at a spring training game, to the veranda of the Otesaga Hotel, in Cooperstown, to the dugout at an Old Timers Classic, baseball has many venues for its veneration. Wherever we go in the interwoven world of baseball, we feel the tug of the game's history and the affection toward traditions and former heroes which runs through the sport like an unspoken code of honor.

Because baseball is the mind game, it is also the memory game.

As many a fan has realized, no sport is so well suited to vivid and almost completely satisfying re-creation within the fences of the mind. That's why no game is able to imbed itself so firmly in our memories. Baseball is the only game that can be disassembled, broken into its composite pieces, then put back together an hour or a century later with almost no loss of detail or drama. Sometimes the game is actually better digested the second time around.

To illustrate, would a football fan listen to one hundred games a year *on radio?*

Many a baseball fan does, and thinks it a great pleasure. It's common to find sensible folks who, when they aren't in the park, would prefer to hear a game on radio, rather than watch on TV. The tube seems to shrink baseball, fade its colors, slow the sense of pace, dilute the accumulation of tension and generally stultify the sport. Radio lets the imagination do its proper work of re-creating the sweep of the stadium and the anxious susurrations of the tidal crowd; the game comes to us over radio as it really is: a loosely connected succession of crisis points. TV makes all moments, all pitches, seem monotonously equal, which they aren't; radio lets the innings flow along at their own pace, while we wash the car or read a book, until the game reaches its inevitable moments of internal leverage—two on, none out, pitcher in a hole, bull pen warming in a hurry, cleanup man on deck. It's all about to break open; we lay down the book or wring out the sponge, and relish the moment.

In memory, only those vivid settings continue to exist. The meaningless two-hoppers to the second baseman are erased. In our minds, Floyd Bevens is always pitching to Cookie Lavagetto, Carl Yastrzemski is facing Goose Gossage, or Willie Mays has just turned and headed for the 463-foot sign. All the dross is wrung out. Even moments that happened fifty years before our birth have an almost tangible reality for us. The foul lines never move, the bases stay ninety feet apart and a windblown pop-up drifts today just as it did when Rabbit Maranville made his first basket catch. We are told that when that big, bowlegged Flying Dutchman, Honus Wagner, dug out a grounder in the hole at short, he sometimes scooped up pebbles and dirt in his huge meat hooks and seemed to throw a small cloud of debris toward first base along with the ball. He was part of our great-grandfathers' time and no newsreel exists to document such a moment, yet we possess it and can even hand it around among ourselves; in baseball, memories are a negotiable coin of the realm: we can deal in them like a legal tender which never devalues.

A man's gestures, his tone of voice, the acts and anecdotes that typified him, all are handed down through the baseball generations along with his statistics and his bronzed testimonials. Every ballpark, every midsummer gathering at Cooperstown, every Old Timers Day is a bartering ground where memories are legal tender. Here, at least, we have a currency which always seems to appreciate.

They sit together now as they sat together then, sixty years ago and more. In their long lives, almost nothing has stayed the same. Except baseball. The three Mazotas brothers have changed, but the game, the marginalia of their common lifetime, hasn't. It was there at their start—they remember the dead ball and Babe Ruth —and it's still there, a kind of gentle chamber music, at the last.

Shoulder to shoulder in the third-base stands, the two burly fellows—Red and Leo—are bookends around thin Ted, who looks like actor Don Knotts. All wear floppy baseball-style caps and have the rumpled, self-sufficient look of a harder but simpler age. They're senior citizens, retired, no wives left.

These three Connecticut Yankees migrate to Florida from Hartford as soon as the ballplayers arrive. In the morning, they play golf. Then they head to the Yankee ballpark here, in Fort Lauderdale. They come early to catch the bargain days, when workouts and calisthenics and drills and rookie B games are free. They've got tickets to nine Yankee spring training games but resent paying five dollars for an exhibition. "Fifteen years ago, you got a real program. Now they hand you this lousy piece of paper," says Red, looking at the flimsy, tissue-thin scorecard.

Long ago, in their bygone playing days, they watched Jim Thorpe when he came through Hartford, playing in the Eastern League. And they spotted that kid from Columbia University who played under a fictitious moniker so he wouldn't lose his amateur status. Sure they remember him: Lou Gehrig. Matter of fact, Red played semipro ball against Gehrig one summer. Or, at any rate, figures he probably did, seeing as how Gehrig was born in '03 and Red in '04.

"I'd have to say he [Gehrig] was pretty damn good," says Red, a tough man with a compliment.

Has anybody since hit the ball like Gehrig?

Red Mazotas chews this over, then decides that maybe one upstart was worthy of comparison.

"Hack Wilson," he says, naming the ex-Cub dead for thirty-three years.

To sit with the Mazotas brothers is to be reminded of why ballparks are one of our last, best community gathering spots. In few of our public places do our differences of age, race and the rest give way so readily to our common tastes.

Says seventy-eight-year-old Red, referring to the strike of 1981, "They about soured me with that strike. But they couldn't drive me away. The game pulls you back. The game is strong."

"The strike was just a temporary annoyance. Oh, I still enjoy the game," says Leo, seventy-three, a former lawyer, as though the mere thought of abandoning the game were the extreme of cutting off one's own nose. "The players are more intelligent now. There's more finesse. Baseball's just got a lot more to it than other sports, more substance."

"Game's just as good as ever, I guess. Some ways, better. More speed now," says the youngest, Ted, seventy, whose words are clipped and pruned—partly by a life in New England, partly, perhaps, because he was a telegraph operator. "Best part is, the game's there for you every day."

One minute, the talk is of Hank Greenberg and Warren Spahn —the way they looked when the Mazotas clan (seven brothers and two sisters) first spotted them as minor leaguers. The next instant, a Yankee pitcher named John Pacella has just given up a long home run to Atlanta's Dale Murphy; "He'll be back in triple A again," says one brother. The whole process of sifting a young crop is being done again, this time with Pacella failing to fill the shoes of Spahn.

On each new baseball subject, the brothers' opinions run the gamut, no two exactly agreeing—although not absolutely disagreeing—on anything. It's as though, through all the back-porch discussions during advancing age, they have, by convenience as much as conviction, each staked out a slightly different position, the better to while away the hours.

In this sense, they are perhaps typical of any group of lifelong fans. For instance, Red, a flight maintenance chief who was with the Flying Tigers in China in World War II, didn't like the players' position during the strike one bit; he sees all that fresh green money being stuffed into their young pockets and figures it's being taken from his old pocket. "The fans are the suckers," he says. "Oh, I guess I shouldn't say that, since I'm still one."

Leo's no flaming liberal, but he likes to point out that "all that TV income today helps the owners now. The old owners didn't have that . . . There's more money from advertising and everything else. Salaries are bound to be higher. More power to them if they can get it." Then he pauses. "I just hope it doesn't kill the game."

Like all who care for the sport, they'd rather talk the loyalties of the heart than the economics of the wallet.

"There's Yogi Berra," says Red, spotting the Yankee coach. "Gets fifty- or sixty-thousand dollars a year to count the baseballs."

"Bill Dickey was better," says Leo.

They all nod agreement.

Next case.

Chris Chambliss steps to the plate.

"Dignified," says Red.

"Journeyman," amends Ted.

"A top journeyman," says Leo, getting it precisely right.
Next case.

"The Babe was my all-time favorite, an authentic showman,"
says Ted, who's such a Yankee fan that he says he drinks Ruppert's (beer) in honor of Roaring Twenties Yankee owner Jake
Ruppert. "Never compare [anyone] to Ruth."

"Ted Williams compares to all of them," demurs Leo, giving
the perspective of the lifelong suffering Red Sox fan.

Since Hartford is midway between Boston and New York, the
Mazotas are part of that town's historic schizophrenia regarding
the Red Sox-Yankee rivalry. As a consequence, Hartford has, for
decades, been bombarded with TV broadcasts from both clubs,
making it a fans' paradise.

To the Mazotas brothers, baseball is the whole package: spring
at the Yankee camp, minor-league ball around Hartford, an occasional pilgrimage to Yankee Stadium or Fenway Park, plus all
those radio and TV games.

How often do the brothers figure they'll be in the ballpark?

Red, the old Flying Tiger, answers for all of them, as he would
have any summer since before World War I.

"In a sense," he says, "every day."

They gather each year—none of them young, some very old, a
few in wheelchairs—on the veranda of the Otesaga Hotel at sundown.

This particular summer, spry Stan Musial led the laughter.
Dapper Burleigh Grimes, eighty-five, told tall tales. Cool Papa
Bell said he could score from first on a sacrifice bunt when he was
forty-five, and Robin Roberts answered, "yeah, without touching
third." Stan Coveleski shifted a 1925 Washington Senators World
Series ring from his scrawny ring finger to his middle finger to
keep it from falling off. And Rube Marquard—yes, Rube Marquard, of the John McGraw Giants—held a baseball in his huge,
gnarled hands and meticulously signed an autograph for a child.

There were moments of silence in honor of Red Faber, the last
legal spitballer, and Phil Wrigley, day baseball's best friend, men

who would never join them on the veranda again. And there were toasts—for Ernie Banks and five others on the eve of their induction into the Hall of Fame.

Jim Galvin, a grandfather himself, watched them from a short distance and thought of his own grandfather, Pud Galvin, who won the first of his 361 major-league games in 1879. Five generations of Galvins were on his mind. "They're happy and they're sad," Galvin said knowingly, looking at the celebrating Hall of Famers. "They feel rejuvenated tonight, but in the back of their minds they don't know who'll be back next year."

Baseball commissioner Bowie Kuhn said, "This Hall of Fame induction is the greatest day we have. Opening Day, the All-Star Game and the World Series are all special. But this is the premier event of baseball's life. Cooperstown makes it so."

To those who have never been here, such statements might seem disingenuous. What can a tiny, inaccessible village and a museum stuck next door to a five-and-ten-cent store have to offer?

A new inductee, Joe Sewell, spoke for many a former player and many a fan when he said, "I've never been here before. I can't believe what I've missed. If I live, I'll be here every year."

The modern world has aimed at Cooperstown and missed, much to Cooperstown's benefit and delight. The village, which has one traffic light, has been bypassed by every harbinger of progress from nineteenth-century canals and railroads to recent interstates; it has no industry but beauty, no operating principle but the preservation of an affluent civility. Every lamppost in Cooperstown has a scrolled iron crossbar from which flowerpots are suspended like balance-scale pans. Ubiquitous red geraniums grow up, and small-leafed English ivy grows down. Induction day at Cooperstown looks like the Fourth of July, as the five-square-block downtown has almost as many American flags as potted lampposts.

This is Cooper country, home of Natty Bumppo's cave, Blackbird Bay, Mohican Canyon, Glimmerglen Cove and Leatherstocking Falls. This is a haven of antique shops, art galleries and quiet restaurants.

The village of Cooperstown manages to be both quaint and grandiose. "This area is an oasis of wealth and cultivation in what is really a very poor rural county," pointed out Hall of Fame curator Peter Clark. "Cooperstown is a gorgeous, historically preserved village because the Clark family [heirs to the Singer sewing machine fortune] make sure it stays that way."

The Otesaga, the huge old fortress of a hotel that sits with its toes in spectacular Lake Otsego, is the symbol of Cooperstown's relaxed, poignant marriage with baseball. For the lifelong baseball person, the Otesaga is a well of memories, an unchanging touchstone. From its back porch, generations of Hall of Famers have looked up the nine-mile length of the lake, the body of water that James Fenimore Cooper called "Lake Glimmerglass." The hills on either side, including Sleeping Lion Mountain, have trails down to the edge of the water. The Leatherstocking Golf Club runs along the lake's left bank, with its finishing hole—a duplicate of Pebble Beach's eighteenth—curling to a conclusion at the very steps of the veranda.

If baseball has a common room, it is the Otesaga lobby. On induction eve, the old-timers assemble, names on lapels ("We change so much, we need a little help," explained Earl Averill), to chat and sign autographs. In one corner, the gregarious Grimes flirts with the young women and puffs on a sinfully big cigar. A handsome middle-aged woman, his wife of two years, asks gently, "Honey, isn't the ash going to fall on your suit?"

Grimes regards the precarious ash sagely and announces, "No, it ain't."

Lloyd (Little Poison) Waner also rules a corner. He is a living testimonial to sit-ups, Grecian Formula, three hundred dollar suits and a briar pipe. He looks thirty years younger than his seventy-six, and he knows it. This is his yearly showcase. Age? What age?

Perhaps most delighted is Joe Sewell, signing everything in sight. "This is the greatest thing that ever happened to Dad," says Sewell's daughter, Mary. "It's come at just the right time of his life to give him an enormous boost. He gave up making the Hall years ago, when his old friend Ty Cobb died. Ty was doing everything to help Dad get in, but after that . . . nobody."

The mood of each summer's induction is, to a large degree, determined by the identity of that year's dominant new Hall of

Famer. When it's Ernie Banks, whose Chicago fans live a thousand miles away, and the ancient Sewell, then the gathering is
polite and small, barely causing Cooperstown to bulge at its cozy
seams. When Mickey Mantle is the showpiece, then a gang of
almost ten thousand show up, bringing the accents and manners
of the five boroughs to upstate New York.

And if the year is 1983 and Brooks Robinson is the enshrinee,
then the biggest celebration in the history of the Hall breaks loose.
By the time the forty-two charter buses, twelve airplanes and
thousands of private cars—many decked out in Oriole orange—
arrived in Cooperstown, the hamlet's population quintupled from
its normal twenty-five hundred, and the Mantle Mob's attendance
record was down the drain. All that weekend, the interstates from
York to Harrisburg to Scranton to Binghamton to Oneonta
looked like a "No. 5" caravan.

Before the ceremonies could even begin in the rolling park behind the Hall, the crowd—which swept over knolls, spread itself
under maple trees and stretched almost out of sight—had conducted its own singing of the national anthem, complete with an
ear-splitting "O" at the appropriate "Oh, say can you see" juncture. The gleeful throng, fresh from a Sunday morning of lay
services at The Bold Dragoon Saloon, followed unofficial team
mascot Wild Bill Hagey in spelling "B-R-O-O-K-S" and passing
the cold beer on a hot afternoon.

Bed-sheet signs and placards dotted the sea of orange-and-black
humanity, their slogans perhaps more heartfelt than literary. One
Yankee couple chose to demur, she carrying a topical pine-tar
protest sign that read, "Suspend Brett, Impeach MacPhail," and
he wearing a sandwich board which read, " 'Backwoods logic be-
gets backwoods vengeance'—The Tombs."

Perhaps the beloved Robinson, with his sixteen gloves and one
heart of gold, was the perfect Cooperstown inductee—a suitable
marriage of person and place. His closing remarks that summer
day seemed, without saying so, to explain why his life has been so
exemplary in private, so patient in public (even when he went
bankrupt, in the late (1970s), so seemingly guided by a stronger
principle than winning games. "From the beginning, I was committed to the goodness of this game," he told his congregation. "I

think my love for baseball has been the biggest thing in my life
. . . This is a day for my giving thanks. This is a [blessed] life
from which I want to give [something] back."

Cooperstown's central attraction, the Hall of Fame itself, has a
hard time competing with the splendor of the century-old man-
sions and the winding streets of the town and the ambience of the
emotional inductions in the shady park. In recent years, the reno-
vated and expanded Hall has begun to hold its own against the
splendidly high standards set by its surroundings.

A sly mind, for instance, was at work behind the Ted Williams
display: the three photos of "the Splinter" show him (1) missing a
pitch and accidentally sailing his bat into the stands (homer on
next pitch); (2) striking out slugger Rudy York in a 1940 stint as a
relief pitcher; and (3) hitting a homer in his last at-bat, with the
photo showing unequivocally that both his eagle eyes are closed.

For every meat-and-potatoes exhibit there seems to be a delightful surprise; for example, a four-picture sequence of Mickey Mantle missing a flyball, a photo of Woodrow Wilson's wife laughing
hysterically as her intellectual husband struggles with his "first
pitch." Catfish Hunter's one artifact is the thirty-nine-cent pen he
used to sign his $5-million contract.

Major leaguers and the sort of devoted fans that the Dutch
originally called baseball "kranks" find the Hall most rewarding.
"I never dreamed that Cooperstown was such a beautiful place,"
said Rod Carew. "I like the museum exhibits. It's amazing that
they could catch the ball with those old pancake gloves."

The museum's tasteful climax is the Hall of Fame gallery. The
86 × 43-foot room of brick and steel with its black Vermont marble columns and 25-foot-high ceiling seems suitably imposing, but
not gaudy. The room is first of all designed to be child-proof.
Dennis the Menace himself would need a jackhammer to do a
nickel's worth of damage in this galley. Little boys tugging with
both hands on Mickey Cochrane's nose in bronze relief are overmatched. Nothing here can break. Some say that the more recent
bronze likenesses could not be any worse if the noses were torn
off. Ted Williams was so incensed by his nonlikeness that he demanded a new plaque. Nevertheless, no baseball player would

turn one down, no matter how homely it made him look to posterity.

Jim Kaat, here for the annual Hall of Fame game, admitted, "As I get older, I think more about the Hall. I don't want to keep my hopes too high even if my stats are of Hall of Fame caliber. My career has been one of obscurity. I know that. I've been a workhorse, not a Seattle Slew. I hope there's a place here for a nag like me."

All fall and deep into the winter, seventy-five-year-old Luke Appling got up each morning, went to his writing table, reached into two huge cardboard boxes and began opening thousands of letters of fan mail. When a man has been retired for a third of a century and has been in the Hall of Fame longer than some ballplayers have been alive, it's nice to discover that, right smack dab in the middle of your old age, you're hot again.

"My wife started to get pretty mad at me. She told me, 'Morning, afternoon and night, all you do is answer those darn letters,'" recalls Appling. "It took me most of the off-season, but I finished 'em around Christmas. Must have been about four thousand letters. The first boxful were all real friendly. They'd mostly start off, 'My grandfather tells me you were a pretty fair ballplayer. I saw you on TV when you hit that home run in the old-timers game in Washington. Please send me your autograph.'

"By the time I got to the second box, it was 'round Thanksgiving and darned if I didn't get cussed out about a hundred and fifty times. You see, the second box was chewin' me for not answerin' the first box sooner. Oh, I got some snotty ones."

Appling, sitting in the dugout of the Atlanta training complex here in West Palm Beach, Florida, spits his tobacco juice in the direction of the young Braves whom he coaches in hitting. "Guess they think I'm a retired old coot with nothin' to do but answer letters. I've got work to do, travelin' around to Richmond, Durham, Pulaski, Anderson, Bradenton and Savannah to look at these hitters and troubleshoot," says Appling, a Braves organizational instructor.

Some players are burdened for the rest of their lives by one event in their careers. A single deed, even a heroic one, can become an albatross, given enough time, enough retellings; who wants to spend fifty years lingering over one split second from the deep past? Appling is the opposite case. With one swing at the age of seventy-five, "Old Aches and Pains" was reborn.

When Appling led off the first inning for the American League with a home run into the leftfield seats off that youngster Warren Spahn in the Crackerjack Old-Timers Classic in the summer of 1982 in RFK Stadium, the former Chicago White Sox shortstop never guessed what he'd done. Videotape of Appling's picture-perfect swing, his swat a dozen rows into the seats and his comic circuit of the bases (with Spahn chasing him and swatting him in the rear with his glove), became an overnight slice of Americana. The breathless Appling, all ham, feigned a heart attack as he reached the dugout.

"The reaction was, oh, tremendous," says Appling, still stunned. "You know, I got more action and more publicity from that one swing than I did in twenty-one years in the majors. I'm not kiddin' about that. Nobody interviewed us much back then, or put us on TV," said Appling, who played shortstop from 1930 to 1950 with the White Sox, batting .310, winning two batting titles and reaching base over four thousand times.

The endless retellings of the tale might burden a man in his prime, but they've spruced up the salty Appling no end; he's stored up a lifetime of stories and opinions that nobody bothered to ask him. Now he's holding court.

"Oh, no, here comes Luke," says Braves manager Joe Torre. "I won the pennant and got a two-year contract. Appling hit one home run and got a new three-year deal . . . What nice thing can I say about Luke Appling that he hasn't already said about himself?"

"They've been blasting me ever since I hit that home run," moans Appling delightedly, knowing that when the young stars think you're worth needling, it means you must be twinkling a little yourself. "They told me it probably went two hundred feet and the wind blew it the rest. They said, 'By the time you get to camp next season, it'll be five hundred feet.' I tell 'em I've got thirty thousand eyewitnesses who know I hit it pretty good.

"I loved playing," continues Appling. "Shoot, these guys don't have fun. They worry. They don't even know how to agitate . . . I teach 'em hitting, but I probably spend more time trying to show them how to enjoy the game . . ."

More than anything else in the modern game, Appling is appalled at the deterioration of the personal relationship between players and fans. "When I was playin', it seemed like every night I was home I was goin' to some [civic or club] dinner for a piece of ham and some peas. I went all the time. Now they want five hundred dollars to cross the street. They're crazy about money.

"The players even get paid to give autographs now," says Appling, aware that some players are paid about five dollars a signature by professional autograph dealers—the game's new middlemen. "They put on [autograph] shows in Atlanta. They wanted to pay me to sign autographs in my own hometown. I said, 'The hell with that.' I'd just rather not do somethin' like that. I'm gonna eat anyhow. Long as you don't owe anybody . . . long as you got enough. A guy that's a millionaire is always tryin' to get another million and that's how he goes broke," says Appling, who claims it doesn't bother him to have missed the game's financial bonanza. His only curiosity, he says, is over exactly what a team would pay "a shortstop who hit .388," which is what Appling did in 1936.

Out of Appling's boxes of four thousand letters, he remembers one in particular because it had a sour, contemporary taste. "A fellow sent fifty pictures and I personalized each autograph," says Appling. "A month later, he sent me fifty more with a note saying, 'Please, do not personalize.' The SOB was selling 'em, making a living off autographs. I sent him back a note saying, 'All pictures you send me in the future, I will consider my own.' "

Appling attributes his good health ("I've never been sick or passed out in my life") to his wife's cooking ("I guess it must be good. I ate it.") and his chewing tobacco ("They told me, 'Boy, you better quit that,' but I've chewed every day for sixty years.") As for his batting stroke, that needs no tending. "I hadn't swung all [last] summer," says Appling. "Once you've learned how to do it, you can always do it."

"This year," says Appling, who wouldn't miss Crackerjack II for the world, "I'll pinch-hit and probably strike out. The publicity is too great. I can't take it."

Thus will end a magic year that has brought happiness into many of an old man's winter nights.

Why are fans, as well as the greatest of former players, so attracted to old-timers' games? In an age saturated with sports, how can such a cheerful nonevent draw thirty thousand people?

In recent years, an oldsters' circuit has developed, with retired players building their summers around visits to various cities for reunions, charity work and goofy games. In Chicago, more than twenty-six thousand fans paid to watch an old-timers' game on the eve of the fiftieth All-Star Game. Plenty of modern stars thought the oldsters' game outshone their own.

Perhaps Americans are merely celebrity-struck and can't resist a marquee with names like Aaron, DiMaggio, Killebrew, Kaline, Banks, Wynn, Spahn, Marichal, Drysdale, Feller, Roberts and Brock. Old-timers aren't no-shows. Also, it's possible that names like Kell and Rizzuto, Kluszewski and Kiner, Ashburn and Dickey conjure up an innocent age when players didn't threaten to go free agent unless they got a $10-million contract.

Enos Slaughter never demanded a bonus for *not* being overweight. Vinegar Bend Mizell never said, "I don't give interviews." Allie Reynolds never charged a fee for his autograph. Mickey Vernon never missed a month so he could get a drug monkey off his back and then, when his pay was docked, had his union file a grievance to get what he never earned.

However, it's unlikely that mere stargazing or nostalgia is at the root of the eighties old-timers revival. The seats are filled with fans of all ages and descriptions. Many, perhaps most, in these crowds are seeing these players for the first time.

Every sport has its sense of tradition, but nowhere is that affection for what is past and passing so strong as in baseball. It's one of baseball's blessings that the game can be played at half speed with little distortion. Of course, when Spahn tossed a pitch to Appling in Washington's Old Timers Classic, everybody knew a ten-year-old could have caught the ball bare-handed. But that didn't detract from the sight of Appling hitting the ball into the leftfield stands.

In Spahn's delivery and Appling's swing, all the lineaments of their youth were present. Because baseball isolates its players on the mound and at the plate, we become intimately familiar with each man's face and form. When Spahn kicks now, we can see enough to remember the rest. When Aaron cocks his wrists, or Brooks Robinson goes into his preparatory crouch at third, we are thrilled. Something we thought had disappeared still exists. Old-timers games are, as much as anything, a celebration of a particularly American individualism that stands at the core of baseball. We often say baseball is "an individual team game" and thus pretend that teamwork and the fate of the group is what concerns us primarily. But that's not true.

Baseball draws forth the exceptional man from the group, celebrates his uniqueness, glorifies his deeds and makes indelible even his casual gestures.

We are moved by these old heroes partly because of our soft sorrow at seeing them grow older, but it's just as true that we are pleased to see them, at last, in proper human proportion. Once, perhaps, we wanted them to be myths, but before we say goodbye, we'd like to see them simply as our fellow men.

A fifty-five-year-old Hall of Famer looks much like any other middle-aged man. And he's much less forbidding, and usually more gracious, than a current star. These oldsters appreciate their public, having been denied it by retirement. Even those like Aaron and DiMaggio, Maris and Brock, who, in their prime, grew disgusted with the public eye, now find that gaze warm and easy to take.

An old-timers game is one long communal rejoicing at all our commonly held memories. When Stan Musial comes out for his introduction at such games, he doesn't wave; he goes into that coiled stance which, 'twas said, looked like a kid looking around a corner to see if the cops were coming. The crowd loves it, because it is one of our ways of reasserting that a man can leave his signature on the world. Such a signature cannot be erased from the pages of our memory by so powerless a force as age.

Yes, powerless. For one night, we insist that arthritis and fading

vision cannot damage the record a man has left beside his name. If
we once found his work good or even if he met the standards of
our fathers and grandfathers, then that measure of him stands for
all baseball time.

18

THE RIPKEN TEAM

Baseball has been part of the grain of the American family for more than a century. But never has there been an American baseball family like the one raised by Baltimore Oriole third-base coach Cal Ripken and his wife, Vi. Since 1957, when the sweethearts from Aberdeen, Maryland, were married and hit the road to live in fifteen minor-league towns in twenty years, the Ripkens and their four children have struggled and, eventually, flourished in a life saturated and defined by the game.

Perhaps it speaks well for the sport, certainly it speaks splendidly for the Ripkens, that their difficult and sometimes tormenting affair with baseball has, after twenty-seven years, borne such proud and promising fruit.

The Ripkens have always been old-fashioned—dignified facing the world but full of foolishness among themselves. They foster the simple virtues that the common-sense essayist Montaigne wrote about long ago: "We must show what there is that is good and clean at the bottom of the pot."

As the peppery Vi says of her salty husband, "He's never really been in touch with the times, but then that may not be so bad, because the times aren't so good."

Now, after a lifetime of enforced modesty, the Ripkens have begun to harbor a dream so preposterous it almost qualifies as a fantasy. After all their laboring in the vineyard, they wonder if, having sowed, they may not also reap.

This is what the Ripkens hope will happen in the near, and not implausible, future. The year is, let us say, 1988.

Fade to the Future

Cal Ripken, Jr., the American League's rookie of the year in 1982 and its MVP in 1983, is twenty-seven and at the peak of a career that may take him to Cooperstown. A free agent after the '87 season, he's re-signed with the Orioles—a multiyear deal for $10 million. He could have gotten more elsewhere, but everybody knows why he wanted to stay.

As Cal said back in 1983, "I enjoy playing shortstop. But, like I've told my brother Billy, I'll be glad to move back to third base when he's ready to take over short." Now he's ready.

Bill Ripken was signed by the Orioles as an eleventh-round draft pick in '82, played in Class A in 1982 and 1983. Some folks laughed, or muttered "nepotism" when he hit .244 in rookie ball. That was before he hit the typical Ripken late growing spurt. Just five foot eleven and 160 pounds when he signed, Bill was already 6-1 and 175 by '83. Just as his mom predicted, he ended up 6-2 and 190 pounds.

Cal needed four years in the minors, but Bill, now twenty-three and full-grown, took longer. His big brother had more tools. That never bothered either Ripken, since they'd always been each other's biggest fans. "Cal's Cal and I'm me," said Billy. "I'm not going to mess myself up by comparing myself to that big horse. I'm just going to be as good as I can be."

Cal at third and Billy at short? Or Cal at short and Billy at second?

It would be a tough decision for the Orioles' new manager, their father.

After a dozen years as third-base coach, Ripken had replaced Joe Altobelli, who'd retired. It was the logical choice, since Ripken, then fifty-two, was one of three finalists for the managing job after Earl Weaver retired, in '82.

The baseball world came to Baltimore to behold this miracle.

Only two fathers ever had a son play on the team they managed or coached: Connie Mack and Jim Hegan. And neither of their sons was a star. Now, brothers side by side in the same infield, playing for the managing father. How did it happen?

"Well," says Big Cal, a man of few words, "it's a long story."

Jim Palmer was a rookie in the Northern League twenty seasons ago, when he first met a tough cuss named Cal Ripken, his manager for the Aberdeen Pheasants, in South Dakota.

This wiry fellow with a face like a ratchet seemed like a hard-boiled old coot to Palmer. He'd played six years as a minor-league catcher and was in his fourth as a manager in the bushes. Married, with three kids and a fourth on the way, Ripken was only twenty-eight; he'd been an adult for a long time.

One day, the Pheasants were on a thirteen-hour bus trip from Duluth to Grand Forks—a typical trip. When the driver tired, Ripken took over the wheel in the middle of the night while the team slept. Finally, after driving from midnight till almost noon, with Grand Forks still a way off, the bus broke down.

Sometimes Ripken could fix a bus and sometimes he couldn't. This time, he couldn't. A player was dispatched to a farm to phone for help, while Ripken figured out what to do with a busful of rookies who were tired, stiff and bored.

Once before, Ripken had held batting practice in a cow pasture. This time, there was spring wheat in all directions. Then Ripken noticed his golf clubs.

"He had us go out into the fields," recalled Palmer. "When we get six hundred feet away, he starts hitting these long tee shots. We're running through the wheat like little kids trying to shag golf balls in our baseball gloves."

Ripken and his family have come a long way since he fungoed golf balls to his Pheasants in the wheat.

Ripken became an Orioles coach in 1976, after thirteen years as a minor-league manager. He and Vi thought that was the end of the rainbow. They'd return each fall and winter to the hamlet north of Baltimore where they'd grown up, but now they could settle down and watch what was left of their kids' childhoods. They had no ambitions beyond that. They'd made the bigs at last.

Too often, lives start brightly, then dim with the years. The poet Yeats, recalling the friends of his youth, said, "Not a finish worthy of the start." That applies to baseball, too. Even the most gifted baseball men of Ripken's generation have left behind stories that make us want to cry. Mickey Mantle and Willie Mays, contemporaries of Ripken, now work as casino handshakers; both are barred from baseball.

Ripken, so small that nobody offered a contract till he was twenty-one, has reversed this process. After a quarter century as the good servant, the hitter of fungoes and fixer of buses, the dutiful man always worrying that he was shortchanging his family, Ripken has discovered that—sometimes—bread does return on the waters.

Ripken uprooted his family nine times as a player, then nine more as a manager, taking them to every town. Yet, through all these dislocations, the family grew together, not apart. "We made friends with each other because we were moving so much that we were always leaving our other friends," says Cal, Jr., now.

To the Ripken children—Ellen (25), Cal (23), Fred (22), and Bill (19)—their parents represented a strict world that blended love with discipline and order; they were strict on vices, demanded respectful manners, hard work. "My dad really did say, 'Drink your milk, Cal!' " says Cal, Jr.

Fred Ripken tells a favorite Ripken story to show his father's temperament and the tone of his household. A groundhog had been eating squash in the family garden, so "Pop got up before dawn three days in a row and sat in the garden with his shotgun in his lap. He took his lunch and he wouldn't move 'til it was time to go to the park, in the afternoon. The third morning, before we were out of bed, that gun went off one time. That was the end of the groundhog."

How many days would his father have waited for the groundhog to return?

"As long as it took."

The perfect complement to the taciturn Cal is the vivacious Vi, who's full of good cheer, common sense and conversation. She's seen her husband mellow. "It used to be when he said jump, you jumped. Now he's loosened up."

The cause for that may be the needling inflicted on the great groundhog slayer by his wife and her two most gregarious children: Cal and Billy. "Their father will finally get exasperated and say, 'Will you stop it? I don't have anything to smile about,' " says Vi. "That playfulness is with Junior twenty-four hours a day."

Calvin and Billy are close in temperament: innocent jokesters, intensely competitive, poised in public but bubbling over with foolishness in private. For instance, the brothers were notorious for their homemade tape recordings: satires and insults in the form of "commercials" directed at their peers. "Cal and Billy would sit in the basement by the hour, making those tapes, just laughing at each other's jokes like two ignorant fools," says Ellen.

When did this form of amusement end?

"Oh, we still do it," says Cal, Jr.

Cal and Billy have shown parallel talents as well as temperaments. Both were shortstops and pitchers in high school. Both arrived in the minors too spindly to hit a homer in their rookie season (Cal hit .264 at Bluefield, Billy .244). Both came on thereafter. This spring, when Billy reported to the Orioles training camp, Cal, Sr., asked Cal, Jr., "Who's that new kid over there?"

"That's Billy, Dad."

"Can't be. Much too big."

"I just want a good start wherever they send me, says Billy, who has planned for a baseball career "since I was eight or nine. It's always seemed right to go to the yard [ball park] and put on a uniform."

Billy, who is his own best critic, says he's comfortable at short and has a strong arm. "I run pretty well, but our family's not noted for its wheels. My hitting's been slack. I see a fastball and my eyes light up, but I still have trouble with the curve. Like Cal, I call Dad when I'm not hitting. Even though I'm a thousand miles away, he can tell me what I'm doing wrong."

If Cal is the pride of the family, Billy is the darling.

"After three children, I wasn't so happy about having Billy," says Vi. "But Cal, Sr., insisted, 'He'll be the joy.' When we've been in a restaurant and Billy has done something, Cal would write on a napkin, 'He's a joy.'"

"There *is* a difference between Calvin and Billy," she continues. "Just give me a second and I'll think of what it is . . .

"Billy is more vociferous. He lets everything out," she decides. "If things bother Cal, he pouts."

Vi Ripken worried that Cal's moodiness would hurt him as a pro, until her husband assured her, "It won't last. Ballplayers catch a flaw and needle you until, out of self-preservation, you correct it."

"But," insists Vi, "I still think Cal puts on the pout sometimes."

Naturally, mothers know. Scott McGregor loves to agitate, saying, "J.R., why are you so moody? What do you have to be unhappy about?"

"I am moody," says Cal, who's bouncy compared to most players. "But I disguise my moods well."

He has never disguised his desire to play ball. "When he was in Little League in Asheville, he'd sit on the bench and study the game, not just play it," says his mother. At thirteen, Cal was in his father's oversized catching equipment, handling 80-mph pitches during batting practice for the Double-A Asheville team.

"I felt like I was hiding inside all that big equipment," he says. "When I started out, I did things to please my dad. I remember those clinics on Saturday morning in Rochester. He'd come in my bedroom, shake me and ask me if I wanted to go with him. I'd say, 'Sure I'll go.' And I'd be bored to death. But I could see that it made him happy.

"Years later, when I was playing in the minors, I'd do some little pro trick and Dad would say, 'Where'd you learn that?' and I'd say, 'From you,' and he'd say, 'When?' and I'd say 'At one of those clinics.'

"Maybe I started doing it for him, but then it got to be for me."

Ironically, Cal's drive not only to play but to study the game may have stunted his brother Fred's interest. Ellen calls Fred "the best all-around athlete in the family," and Cal says, "He could be as good as I am.

"I always try to figure out why Fred stopped playing," says Cal. "I was a year older, but we always played on the same teams. I always had to edge him out, because he was younger . . . Maybe he was looking for his own identity."

Fred Ripken's love now is motorcycles—riding, building or fixing them; he works for a Suzuki dealership in Aberdeen and is the family's free spirit. "As free as they get," says Billy. Adds Ellen, "Fred's the type of person who'll give and give, and not expect much in return . . . He's a natural at everything. He stands in the woods where you can't even see him and throws a ball a hundred yards and hits you in the glove . . . But Fred only loved the games. He never liked to practice. He always had better things to do."

"I'd rather sit in the stands and drink beer," says Fred, whose blunt speech matches his father's and who, like his dad, has a soft heart. When a slightly homesick Billy headed to Bluefield last year, Fred drove his young brother all the way and, in Billy's words, "gave me a seven-hour pep talk."

"Dad never pushed any of us in anything," says Ellen. "I don't think he even expected Cal or Billy to play beyond high school." In fact, Ellen is the one who often wishes she'd had the baseball opportunity Fred passed up. She'll tell her mother, "If I'd been a boy, you'd have three playing [pro] ball now," says her mother.

"When I made the high school varsity," says Cal, "Ellen still had the best arm in the family."

Now Ellen plays third base on a women's fast-pitch softball team. She was all-region on a team that went to the nationals in Colorado last season. "I saw her play last summer. I was very impressed," says Cal, Jr. "She plays third and she can really pick it. She was in for a bunt and some girl hit a hot smash and she backhanded it like it was nothing. First time up, she hit a seed [i.e., line drive] over the leftfielder's head for a home run."

"Ellen's gotten her accolades [as an athlete]," says her mother. "Unfortunately, for women, that's as far as you get."

Ellen Ripken has played in fast-pitch tournaments where she was booed and taunted because of the family name. Sometimes she prefers friends to introduce her as just "Ellie," not "Ellie Ripken." Still, when she went into a batting slump before the nationals last year, she knew where to go for help. Back to the family. Her father pitched batting practice, while her fiancé,

David Bonsal, who was a star on Cal, Jr.'s, high school varsity baseball team, shagged balls. "Dad's a natural teacher, because he's so patient. He had a game that night and I thought he'd spend a few minutes with me," she says. "We worked for an hour and a half."

The two Ripkens stand beside the batting cage in Memorial Stadium, Little Rip almost a head taller than Big Rip.

"Come on, lunkhead. Line drives up the middle," Little Rip barks at Rich Dauer, breaking the quiet with a perfect drill-sergeant imitation of his dad. Big Rip has to put his head on his arm to hide his laughing. He's been yelling at Dauer for years, since they were all in Asheville. "Guess if you say something often enough, some people learn," says Big Rip.

Little Rip has turned his cap bill up in front, instantly transforming himself from the six-foot-five matinee idol who inspired "Cal's Gals" signs in the bleachers into a Gomer Pyle type. His father looks away. He's told the kid a million times, "That doesn't look like a ballplayer." But the son keeps doing it " 'cause he hates it and I love to agitate him."

"I read in the paper today where Eddie Murray hasn't hit a home run in a long time, but that he hit two *foul* home runs yesterday," says Ripken. "I guess when you get rich and famous, like Eddie, you start getting publicity for your foul balls."

Eddie Murray tries to pretend he isn't listening. All the veterans around the cage snicker.

A year ago, Little Rip was as quiet as a rookie should be. After a home run on opening day, he went one for thirty and looked lost. Then he got hit in the head with a 91-mph pitch. The helmet had a hole the size of a half-dollar in the temple.

After one day off, he was back in the lineup, started hitting and never stopped. He finished with twenty-eight homers and ninety-three RBI. "I got mad after I was beaned. Maybe it got me going."

Like a chick breaking out of its shell, young Ripken showed more of himself, his true shape and skills, with each month. At midseason, Weaver put Ripken at short, a spot he hadn't played since high school. In July, he struggled. In August, he'd adjusted.

In September, he led. His fielding was steady, his brain was the central switchboard for a defense that lacked smarts till he took charge.

These days, Little Rip can say anything he wants to anybody.

"My [fourteen-year-old] daughter says she's going to join your fan club," says Jim Palmer, thinking this will embarrass Little Rip. Palmer has miscalculated.

"She's good-looking, isn't she?" says Little Cal. "And I hear her old man's got a lot of money. Hey, can I marry her in seven years?"

"Hey, Cakes," says Little Rip, his voice rising in victory as Palmer flees to the showers, "can I marry into your family?"

No family could be more at ease with a potential superstar son than the Ripkens.

"I'm amazed when people want Cal's autograph or talk about him like he's so special. He's just a guy doing his job well," says his mother, a three-sport high school athlete. "When Cal makes a good play and everybody claps, I think, 'Don't they know that's what they're supposed to be doing?' People say, 'Oh, but you live with them,' like we go around wearing golden shoes . . .

"Cal knows he's good. You can tell he wants the game to come to him, so he has a chance to win it. The success stories are the ones who are very comfortable with themselves . . ."

It's Ripken, Sr., who's sometimes a bit uncomfortable with his son's fame. "I get more attention now than I ever did before, because of Cal, Jr. Now they're aware that there is a Cal, Sr.," says the father, according to the mother.

The elder Ripken is an explosive man who keeps his feelings deeply concealed. His eruptions at umpires are genuine furies. "When something goes against his grain," says Vi, "he just completely loses it."

Once, in 1979, after having had too much to drink on a road trip, Ripken, Sr., fell asleep sitting against a wall in a Detroit hotel lobby. When a couple of cops roused him, thinking he might be a vagrant, Ripken saw blue—the color of umpires—and blew his cork. An Orioles official had to bail him out of the hoosegow the next morning.

Vi Ripken wishes her husband could moderate his assertiveness a little more. For instance, she wishes he'd pushed harder for the Orioles' managing job. "I felt very hopeful," she says. "Cal said, 'I've been interviewed. There's nothing to campaign for. Either they want me or they don't.' I'd tease him and say, 'You tell 'em, "This kid of mine is going to be a free agent in a few years. You better keep *us* happy." ' "

That, of course, is not his style. You can barely even get him to say he's proud of his son. He insists he's taught Dauer and Murray more than Cal. "I don't like it when he starts that speech, and how you have to judge a player over his whole career, not a couple of years," says Vi Ripken. "That seems very cold, doesn't it? Like the kid's not going to be allowed to the dinner table unless he's in the Hall of Fame.

"I've asked Cal, Sr., to phrase that differently."

Nonetheless, that long progression toward Cooperstown is going nicely.

For one so gentle in temperament, Little Rip is extremely resilient. His gypsy childhood has left him independent, self-reliant and tough. He can't, for instance, remember if he went to school that year in Miami, and his only recollection of Dallas is "brave mom" capturing a real poisonous scorpion—alive—so he could keep it in a jar. Those qualities have proved useful. In the minors, he started doing his own cooking and hasn't stopped. "Everything I've tried, I've made a mess of the first time, but I've never burned anything so badly I couldn't eat it." Ripkens don't throw good food in the garbage.

Typical of his no-foolishness approach is his advice to Billy: "Be yourself and prove yourself." Cal has always been aware of the charges of nepotism that follow the family, as well as the jealousy. Wives of minor-league teammates talked about his father-son pull until "I felt like taking a stat sheet with me to parties." When he and Billy are having a boisterous time in public, "I've heard people say, 'They're Ripkens. They think they can do anything they want.' I guess I have enemies that I'm not really responsible for."

Though his roots are in little Aberdeen, with its one-block business district and a community point of view that his mother describes as "not modern but not naive," Little Cal seems to have a leather-skinned immunity to the distortions and entrapments of budding celebrity. Again, it is the family that provides ballast. Talk to the Ripkens for hours and not once does the financial windfall in Cal, Jr.'s, future get mentioned. "I'd like to act the way Eddie [Murray] does," says Cal, when asked about a future megacontract. "He's just the same person he was before."

For the Ripkens, dreams are about other things. They worry about Bill making the hard climb up through the minors. They know the odds against having two big-leaguers in one family. How much does managing in the majors mean to their father, and will he get his chance? Will Little Rip stay healthy?

"When I think about baseball, I think about the sport of it, not the glamorous life," says Cal, Jr. "I'd like to play every game, every inning, every day for twenty years, like Brooks Robinson and Pete Rose. I'd like for little kids to emulate me. To hear some kids playing and have one say, 'I'm Cal Ripken'; that would be the ultimate degree of success to me."

Some say that a decent, hardworking, common man, a man with a high school education and no great gifts, has little chance to leave a mark in the world. Some say a strong, caring woman who marries such a man and bounces among fifteen towns, scrimping to stretch each dollar, raising a passel of kids while her husband labors at an obscure job—some say such a woman has wasted her life.

Some say the American family is an endangered institution. Some disagree.

19.
INDECENT
EXPOSURE

Baseball has traditionally possessed a wonderful lack of seriousness. The game's best player, Babe Ruth, was a Rabelaisian fat man, and its most loved manager, Casey Stengel, spoke gibberish. In this lazy sport, only the pitcher pours sweat. Then he takes three days off. Nobody much gets hurt, unless you count sore arms. Spring training is a gentle boot camp of aches without pains. Where else do foes crack jokes in battle as at home plate?

No other sport can truly say it is so close to being play. Yet the 1981 season seemed to put that playfulness in danger. Baseball seemed to replace its easygoing ways with gravity, with a foolish seriousness.

Nothing focused this shift in tone better than the World Series, won in six games by the Dodgers over the Yankees. This wasn't an October celebration, the harvest of a ripe season. Rather, it was the tense, inflamed stuff of tabloid headlines. Even the weird comedy was dark.

These events shadowed the Yanks and the Dodgers during the busy playoff month of October:

—Two New York players were put under protection against death threats.

—Two Los Angeles earthquakes (4.5 on the Richter) hit on a Series game day.

—Yankee owner George Steinbrenner wore a cast on his left hand after, he says, punching out two Dodger fans in an L.A. elevator.

—An alleged thief was shot by guards in the Chavez Ravine parking lot.

—The Yankee Stadium interview room went up in flames at 1 A.M. and firemen evacuated the press room.

—A fan in New York charged and tackled an umpire, the first such on-field attack in the majors in forty years.

—A woman was found strangled in the L.A. press headquarters hotel.

—Rich Cerone interrupted a chew-out/pep talk of the Yanks by George Steinbrenner to tell the owner, "Go screw yourself."

—Yankee Graig Nettles celebrated his selection as MVP of the AL playoffs by fulfilling a five-year fantasy: He punched Reggie Jackson at the team's victory party and reportedly decked him.

—Minutes before the start of the Dodgers' pennant-clinching game, snow was falling in Montreal's Olympic Stadium.

—So many objects were thrown at visiting players in New York, including a ball that hit Tony Armas in the back, that the Yankees implored their fans to govern themselves. Bleacher fans responded by pointing en masse at the next offender, then chanting, "Asshole, asshole," as police led the miscreant away.

—A player with a $23 million contract, after starting the Series oh-for-sixteen, called time-out after a single to collect the ball for a souvenir. Dave Winfield finished the Series one-for-twenty-two.

—Perhaps the least-known player in the Series became its central figure: George Frazier became the first man ever to lose three Series games.

—The only team records set were also negative: the Dodgers walked more batters and the Yanks left more men stranded than any clubs ever in a six-game Series.

—In the end, the world championship was between two teams that finished fourth and sixth in the "second season," while the sport's only .600 team—the Cincinnati Reds—never made the playoffs.

—The last game of the Series was played on the latest date in baseball history—October 28—in a stadium with a power failure, on Bowie Kuhn's birthday.

—Finally, Steinbrenner, the Dodgers' most valuable player, wrote a grim, graceless public apology for his team's performance. In fact, he was the Yankee who needed to apologize. Instead of letting the Dodgers be remembered as the gallants who surmounted deficits of 0-2, 1-2, and 0-2 to beat Houston, Montreal and New York, Steinbrenner did his worst to make them live in lore as recipients of Yankee incompetence.

This five-alarm blend of violence, danger, bad blood, bad manners and the bizarre may be typical of modern life, but it is alien to baseball. Once, Urban Shocker was a Yankee pitcher. In 1981, "urban shocker" was a baseball headline.

Usually, each season leaves a specific aftertaste. Recently, these have been easy to identify, and savory, too. From the star-crossed 1975 Red Sox to the Yankee-Red Sox playoff of 1978, from the Pirates' family to the Phillies' anti-family, that lingering baseball aftertaste has been sweet—or at least bittersweet.

But in '81, sourness curdled our appreciation. Baseball's one blessing was that—from its two-month strike to its sham-and-shame split season right through its World Series—every black-guard trend in the sport came forward, brashly and proudly identified itself for what it was. This was truly a season of indecent exposure.

This season will be recalled as the year when baseball mimicked the discredited example of pro basketball and hockey by expanding its playoff format to eight teams.

For its first century, baseball was a summer-long test of an entire team over more than a hundred fifty games. If 1981 is prologue, that may all change. After all, one year before baseball celebrated its centennial, in 1969, the postseason still meant two teams in the Series. Just thirteen years later, we had an eight-team, three-week stampede. That's what you call a trend.

While the notorious split season is dead for good and all, it introduced us to a sad novelty: meaningless regular-season games involving the sport's top teams. Ask fans of the Yankees, Dodgers and Phillies how exciting they found August and September as their teams coasted into the playoffs. That's what may happen in the future when more and more teams realize that they have a playoff spot locked—thanks to the largesse of a wild-card system —with weeks, even months, still to play.

The regular season of the future will seem interminably long. After all, the point won't be to prove which team is the best in the league, but simply to decide who's fourth best (and therefore in the playoffs) and who's merely fifth best (and therefore out of the playoffs).

On the day baseball becomes primarily a playoff sport—and that's what an eight-team system is—there will be many a season when everybody goes home without a clear sense of who baseball's best team really is. Lest we forget, Los Angeles' success was built on a fluky, playoff-style, three-man starting rotation of Cy Young winner Fernando Valenzuela, Burt Hooton and Jerry Reuss, which had a collective postseason ERA of 1.78. If those Dodgers seemed like a jerry-built, it-could-only-happen-in-the-playoffs bunch, just wait.

In a season defaced by a strike by rich players against rich owners, it was appropriate that the Dodgers and the Yankees met in the Series. Once, the Dodgers epitomized scruffy underdog class while the Yanks were overdog class. Now they just represent old greed and new greed: Dodger franchise-jumping rapacity and Yankee free-agent grabbing. No teams approach these two for sober self-importance. The world champions invoke the Big Dodger in the Sky. Other clubs have chickens as cheerleaders. Only the Dodgers would appropriate God for a mascot. Meanwhile, the Yankees have taken secularity to a new high.

As much as any man, Steinbrenner embodies the ambiguous tendencies afoot in baseball. He's a first-and-ten capitalist in a bunt-and-run world.

In constructing the Yankees over the years—with a huge scouting and minor-league network, with canny trades and free-agent grabs—Steinbrenner has been at his best: a smart, daring long-range conceptualizer, one of the few leaders in baseball worth the name.

In guiding his team through a crisis, Steinbrenner is at his worst and ugliest. It's not that he's the rotten, jack-booted Baron von Steingrabber of caricature, but that his business and football notions are destructively out of place in baseball. Football is an adrenaline game. Baseball is a sport of properly balanced metabolism. Steinbrenner hasn't a clue as to the difference.

In football, you can fire the coach and threaten the players, bribe and intimidate with instant rewards and punishments. A coach must manipulate emotions on this ultraviolent end of the behavior spectrum. In baseball, a sense of moderation is almost a philosophical precept.

This World Series, which was lost more than won, was the testing ground where Steinbrenner's joyless practices came to grief on the rocks of a temperate game. By the final four losses, the Yanks had become disoriented and passive, the victim of too many fired managers, too many public rebukes, too many vague threats, too many capricious benchings and obtuse strategies that smelled like half-baked notions cooked up in an owner's box.

In the clutch, bats grew slow and tentative. On the bases, veterans found their instincts gone haywire as they inexplicably ran in the wrong direction. The worst of all contagious baseball diseases —pressing under pressure—became epidemic. Journeyman players, made confident by their reincarnation in pinstripes, suddenly reverted to humbler pedigrees. Like clowns at a masked ball removing their masks, folks like Rick Reuschel, Larry Milbourne, Aurelio Rodriguez and Jerry Mumphrey began resembling the lowly Cubs, Mariners, Senators and Padres they once had been.

Unable to reason clearly in the heat of big innings, manager Bob Lemon froze at the switch. He was torn between his own, ingrained baseball judgment and that of the boss looking over his shoulder.

The glazed look of panic sometimes seen on football sidelines, with assistant coaches in earphones scampering everywhere and doing nothing, eventually gripped the Yankees. It took the form not of pandemonium but of blank-faced disbelief. When icy Tommy John was yanked in the fourth inning of a 1–1 tie in the last game (his Series ERA at that moment was 0.69), his face was a portrait of stupefied anger. As John's poise crumbled in curses, the Yankees' characteristic cool professionalism died with it. Seven Dodger runs in the next two innings had the finality of a "Q.E.D." at the end of a geometry proof.

Even Winfield, perhaps the best natural athlete in his sport, became a parody of a player in full choke: by gritting his teeth with gridiron intensity, he became completely useless. On one final-game pop-up swing, Winfield found himself knocked flat in the dirt as though he'd been punched by the Invisible Man.

Of course, that invisible man was Steinbrenner, who had drained all pleasure from the playing of the game and replaced it with tension.

This drift toward angst goes beyond Steinbrenner. Too many in baseball are learning that football expression: "Put on your game face." Baseball is rarely played at its best unless it is an immediate pleasure to the performers. From Ruth to Mays to Rose to Brett to Valenzuela, the thread that runs through the game's best players is a tough but still light-at-heart enthusiasm that would seem out of place in a football huddle.

Nonetheless, the opposite theory of baseball, perfected by that brilliant psychotic Ty Cobb and practiced by Billy Martin, suggests the game can be played as guerilla warfare. In the Year of the Clenched Jaw, Martin taught his Oakland A's the virtue of baseball vice. They called it Billyball.

Maybe only a team like New York, which had been exposed to Martin, could be so successfully indifferent to his tactics. No, not double steals, suicide squeezes and other niceties designed to unnerve opponents. What really unsettles Oakland's foes are their outlaw gambits: greaseballs, scuffballs, beanballs, high-spikes slides, obscene bench jockeying, field-filling brawls, corked bats, hotdogging and—the A's trademark—perpetual stylin' and stallin'.

It was a playoff pleasure to watch the A's crumble in a three-act play of self-exposure. In their first loss, Cliff Johnson knocked out hyper reliever Ron Davis by stalling for eight minutes in one obnoxious at-bat. Davis got so furious he couldn't come within a foot of the plate. The Yank antidote was reliever Goose Gossage, who said, "I spent last night anticipating Billy's little tricks. I wouldn't put anything past him."

In the next game, Martin, an unsurpassed heat-of-battle tactician, blew his cool by going against standard operating procedure twice in a seven-run Yankee fourth inning. First he gave the quick hook to ERA champion Steve McCatty while he still had a 3–2 lead. Then he refused to give Lou Piniella the compliment of an intentional walk, because the two are feuding. Piniella hit a three-run homer. Those textbook examples of overmanaging unnerved the young A's, who were outscored 16–0 over the last fourteen innings of the series sweep.

By the final game, the A's were so tight, so out of sync with the spirit of their sport, that both Rickey Henderson and Dwayne Murphy disabled themselves while merely swinging at pitches.

The tendency toward dawdling—"stylin' "—has been growing for years, as players are tempted to believe they're as important as their salaries. The 1981 A's turned it into an art form.

"Guys, after one decent season, make an epic out of getting into the batter's box," says Baltimore coach Ray Miller. "If Rickey Henderson, Mike Hargrove, Disco Dan Ford or Carlton Fisk ever leads the league in hitting, we'll never finish another game. They'll have to turn off the stadium lights and turn on a spotlight as each guy comes to the plate."

For aeons, baseball was a two-hour game. Each decade, the pace has slowed. The infuriating A's, however, made the latest quantum leap, averaging 2:55 per game. Can the age of the three-hour, football-length game for every team be far away?

The player with an inflated opinion of himself who, before every pitch, will step out, call time, adjust his batting glove, re-dig a hole for his back foot, adjust twelve parts of his uniform and anatomy, then imperiously signal to the umpire that he is ready to proceed, will show himself in other ways.

He will, if he is Garry Templeton of St. Louis, make indecent gestures to his home fans if they have the impertinence to boo him for loafing to first base.

He will, if he is Steve Carlton of Philadelphia, refuse to speak in any public forum for years at a time, since he's indifferent to whether the fans who cheer him and provide his pay get to share what he thinks and feels.

He will, if he is Dave Parker of Pittsburgh, gain thirty pounds, until he looks like a Parker roll, so that he can chastise his team for not treating him respectfully and teach his critics in the grandstands a lesson for throwing debris at him. And so on.

Multi-year multimillion-dollar malingerers aren't as common-place as resentful owners maintain. The player who's made it to the top in baseball's meritocracy is, by athletic natural selection, an overachiever. Nevertheless, in 1981 bad apples seemed easier to spot.

Reggie Jackson once talked about "the magnitude of being me," and the burdens attendant on such a responsibility. A more common case is The Importance of Being Us. Most players can still get their hats on, but plenty of teams have a collective big head.

To wit, the ex-world champion Phillies. For several years, the Phils, with some such exceptions as Rose, Tug McGraw and Mike Schmidt, have adopted an attitude that they're important fellows doing vital world work, who shouldn't have to brook any nagging criticisms. Supercilious in defeat, vain in victory, the Phillies make themselves hard to like.

How hard?

Hard enough that manager Dallas Green quit his job after a tolerably successful season to become GM of the Chicago Cubs. Green couldn't wait to get in his final licks, either. On the morning of their fifth and final mini-series playoff game against Montreal, the Phillies awoke to discover that Green had laid the wood to them—in toto and at length—in the Philadelphia *Inquirer*. "A lot of these guys think they're real human beings, but they aren't," said Green in a memorable managerial sendoff to a team facing its biggest game of the year. The Phillies lost.

Much of what is worst in baseball commanded center stage in '81. It would take the compassion of Albert Schweitzer to summa-rize this lost season in cheerful tones. We can only wish to forget quickly:

—Ray Grebey, Bowie Kuhn and Marvin Miller. Hang 'em all up by their thumbs—especially Grebey, who did what the owners hired him to do: cause a strike. Only Grebey seemed to relish the strike and his sudden notoriety. It was his show and he enjoyed it too much. Given his druthers, Grebey would have preferred that the strike last till Christmas. It was neither his money nor his game.

—The split season. The vote of one club—Montreal—brought

into being the second season and the eight-team playoffs. "It came down to us, we were the pivotal vote," said Expo president John McHale. "We're traditionalists and firmly opposed to the plan. But we didn't want to thwart the will of the majority, so we went along." Rebutted Cincinnati president Dick Wagner, "That's why you have minorities: so they can stop the majority from doing stupid things."

—The hilarious Integrity Question. A trivia question in the twenty-first century will be, In 1981, if the same team had won both halves of the season, its wild-card opponent would have been: A) the second-place second-half team, B) the second-place first-half team, C) the team with the next-best full-season percentage, D) the Mormon Tabernacle Choir, or E) a team of fixers chosen by Tony ("We'll forfeit if we have to") LaRussa and Whitey ("Me, too") Herzog. For bonus points, outline twelve playoff plans better than the one that was adopted.

—The Kuhn system of temperature conversion, discovered by reporter Dan Shaughnessy. Question: When the temperature in Montreal on November 1 for the last game of the World Series is 0 Celsius and 32° Fahrenheit, what is the temperature in degrees Kuhn? Answer: The postseason is always 72° Bowie.

Despite all of that year's dross, the game's tradition of decency and good spirits was visible below the shabby surface. The best folks and most appealing teams seemed to be in the wings, acquitting themselves adequately but waiting for a more seemly setting before stepping forward.

For instance, Herzog was the NL manager of the year for bringing home the Cardinals (who didn't make the playoffs) with the best full-season record in the NL East and the third-best overall record in baseball. However, Herzog could have won the award the day he dragged Templeton off the field and suspended him. "Everybody's so afraid they'll get sued that they get petrified," said Herzog. "We can't get too scared to do what's right. What Garry did was typical of the sort of thing that's tolerated in our society. But I'm not tolerating it here."

Milwaukee, strengthened by a trade that brought Pete Vuckovich, Ted Simmons and Cy Young reliever Rollie Fingers, rallied from 0-2 to force a fifth game in its playoff with the Yankees. That was a fitting reward for Brewer team builder Harry Dalton, who was fined fifty thousand dollars by Grebey's player relations committee for these voice-of-reason words before the strike: "I hope that management is really looking for a compromise and not a 'victory.' I hope we're not about to witness another macho test of wills." The price for telling the truth, and being right, can't get much higher. Fortunately, Dalton's fine was rescinded after the season.

The most refreshing moment of this season didn't even take place in the United States. On the final day of the National League season, in a stadium built for an Olympics, a Mexican pitcher on a team with a Spanish name took on the entire nation of Canada in a thoroughly American game played before a crowd of French-speaking fans to see who would get to play a team called the Yankees in the World Series.

The innocence of the twenty-year-old Valenzuela facing the thirteen-season-old Expos in a parkful of gleeful, undemanding novice baseball fanatics who kept singing "The Happy Wanderer" ("Vol-der-eee, Vol-der-aaaah") in full-throated harmony, was in many ways the highlight of the season.

It's a lovely baseball paradox that this season of corroding seriousness should also prove to be the Year of Fernando. It's as though this child of burgeoning myth with the Ruthian physique and the thousand-year-old Buddha face was sent to remind the game of its true purposes and the source of its power. His chubby face always wore an expression of wry amusement, and his strange, slow, utterly confident sea chantey of a walk seemed agelessly sage.

At every step of the Dodger championship odyssey, Valenzuela was there. In the first six weeks, when a fast start cinched a playoff spot, Valenzuela had the best start of any rookie in history: eight consecutive complete-game victories with five shutouts and an 0.50 ERA. More important, his ebullient presence seemed to change the tone of the whole Dodger clubhouse as he took the weight off an aging, oft-disappointed team.

In a club that knew itself and its limits almost too well, Valenzuela was as welcome as an unsullied horizon. The name on his jersey was "Possibility." Wherever he was, there Dodger spirits were lifted.

Valenzuela was the Dodgers' ticket back to the big time from day one. He blended perfectly with the Dodger veterans, particularly the stubby, dogged overachievers in the long-running L.A. infield: Garvey, Cey, Russell, Lopes—and catcher Yeager. In 1974, 1977 and 1978, they had come up short of the world title; always, they'd lacked the indefinable something extra—that hint of destiny or mystery—that lets a team play through its spells of nervousness and lost confidence.

Valenzuela, a seventh son from dirt-poor Etchohuaquila, clearly had a corner on the destiny market.

In the final, pennant-clinching victory over Montreal—the unprecedented fifth sudden-death, win-or-go-home victory for the Dodgers in the playoffs—Lasorda kept looking at the youngest player in the majors and thinking, "He can't lose. It's his year." Then Lasorda added an Italian saying: "If you threw Fernando in the river, he'd swim out the other side with a fruit stand."

In the third game of the World Series, when the Dodgers caught their wind and began their brave reversal of their 1978 Series fate, it was Valenzuela who was again nailed to the mound, with Lasorda unwilling to remove his ace. Never had Valenzuela been more superb than on that balmy evening, winning 5–4 with as little stuff and as little control as he had ever taken to the mound.

"I did not feel the two earthquakes today," said Valenzuela slyly. "I thought they were tonight. Everything was shaking."

Ultimately, the World Series was won by the right team for the right reasons. While the Yankees played joylessly, trying to escape blame, the Dodgers played for the sake of the game itself, and for each other.

In the end, Yeager spoke for all of them. Long after the pivotal 2–1 fifth game had swung back to L.A. because Yeager had backed Pedro Guerrero's homer in the seventh off Ron Guidry with a blast of his own, the veteran catcher talked about the not-as-good-as-we-used-to-be, but better-than-ever Dodgers.

"We're all on that edge, gettin' too old, they say," said Yeager, still in full uniform in a nearly empty dressing room two hours after the final pitch had been thrown. "But the older we get, the more we play for each other. Maybe that's maturity. As long as these guys are proud of me, the world can go to hell."

Only a few old codgers were left: Yeager, who was co-MVP of the Series along with Cey and Guerrero. Rick Monday, whose ninth-inning homer in Montreal had broken a 1–1 tie, won the pennant and made October 19 a blue Monday on the Canadian calendar. Jay Johnstone, the Dodger DH (Designated Humorist), whose pinch homer had ignited a comeback victory in Game Four. Reggie Smith, Lopes and Lasorda hung back too, tasting the tang that stays in a clubhouse after a Series victory.

Yeager started the screaming: "Where the hell are my glasses that hit my damned home run?" And then Lasorda started hollering about how the legendary spectacles had already been taken to the Hall of Fame. Everybody bellowed in, Johnstone sarcastically offering Lopes a pine-tar rag for his slippery, error-plagued glove and Monday proposing toasts to all noble old Dodgers, such as he and Yeager, who knew how to hit clutch home runs.

Soon the half-dozen men had created their own bedlam. They screamed until they were screamed out. They laughed senselessly until they were laughed out. In the end, they just sat there, tired and grinning like kids.

They still had to fly to New York for one, final game.

Unlike the Yankees, they would play for fun—just as baseball always has been played.

20.
WHY TIME BEGINS
ON OPENING DAY

Why baseball?

Millions of us have wondered. How can baseball maintain such a resolute grasp upon us? My own affection for the game has held steady for decades, maybe even grown with age. After twenty-five years of attachment, I have no sense of wanting to be weaned from this habit. What seems most strange is the way so many of us reserve a protected portion of our lives for a game which often seems like an interloper among our first-rate passions. What is *baseball* doing here, tucked on the same high shelf with our most entrenched emotions?

If asked where baseball stood amid such notions as country, family, love, honor, art and religion, we might say derisively, "Just a game." But, under oath, I'd abandon some of these Big Six before I'd give up baseball. Clearly, a game which becomes one of our basic fidelities is something more than "sport." Perhaps the proper analogy is to our other joyous, inexplicable addictions.

A thread runs through all these idle loves. Each, like baseball, brings us into a small and manageable world chocked with intriguing and unambiguous details; we are beckoned into tiny universes where the areas of certainty are large, where the regions of doubt are pleasantly small. The cook must wrestle with tarragon and basil, the gardener agonizes over his pruning. The baseball

fan knows every batting average, down to the *thousandth* of a
point. What steady ground on which to stand, if only in one corner of our lives! Each pastime has its own unstated set of values.
That part of us which is a fly fisher or a curer of hams or an
habitué of the bleachers shares fragments of a common viewpoint
with others of the same tastes.

When we meet a bona fide fan—and baseball fanciers can be as
snobbish as wine sippers or prize rose gardeners—we start from
an assumption of kinship. Implicit is the sense that you endorse a
whole range of civilized modern tastes; if you'd lived in the sixteenth century, you would probably have liked Montaigne. By
and large, baseball fans tend to prefer pastoral, slyly anecdotal,
proven-if-slightly-dated things over those which are urban or pre-
tentious or trendy. We choose the gentle grandstand conversations, beer in hand, on a soft spring night over the raucous forty-
yard-line scream, whiskey-in-fist, on a brisk autumn afternoon.
Our presumption of comradeship is considerable. Anyone who
shares our range of wise opinion must do dastardly deeds to lose
our good will.

In sum, what baseball provides is fact. Fact in a butter sauce of
tone. Fact as in the sense of detail and concreteness. Tone as in
style and spirit.

In contrast to the unwieldy world which we hold in common,
baseball offers a kingdom built to human scale. Its problems and
questions are exactly our size. Here we may come when we feel a
need for a rooted point of reference. In much the same way, we
take a long hike or look for hard work when we suspect what's
bothering us is either too foolish or too serious to permit a solution.

Baseball isn't necessarily an escape from reality, though it can
be; it's merely one of our many refuges *within* the real where we
try to create a sense of order on our own terms. Born to an age
where horror has become commonplace, where tragedy has, by its
monotonous repetition, become a parody of sorrow, we need to
fence off a few parks where humans try to be fair, where skill has
some hope of reward, where absurdity has a harder time than
usual getting a ticket.

In those moments when we have had our bellyful of abstractions, it is detail, the richness of the particular, which restores us to ourselves. There are oceans of consolation, seas of restored appetite, in as humble a thing as a baseball season. This great therapeutic wash of fact and anecdote draws us back to ourselves when we catch ourselves, like Ishmael, water-gazing too long.

In part, our attachment to the game stems from a persistent feeling that major-leaguers tend to give the best of themselves to their game, even at peril to other parts of their lives. One big-leaguer, known for his drinking as well as his fear that the bottle might be mastering him, once told me, defiantly and proudly, that in his whole career he had "never had one drink from the time I woke up until the game was over." Of course, sometimes this future Hall of Famer didn't wake up until the afternoon.

His point, ambiguous as it may have been, was that, as long as he could function, the game would get his best. Not because he owed it to the sport, but because he assumed that the baseball part of him was the best part, the piece he'd fight longest to hold. Many creative people see their talent in this light; whatever else must be pruned or neglected, their painting or writing or compos-ing will be given a full chance to prosper. Part of the power of baseball is this sense that ballplayers tend to be obsessed with their work. It is this that gives them added stature as well as an intimation of tragedy. An air of danger and courage surrounds anyone who devotes himself to the long shot of art, who has burned the bridges back to a conventional life. In their uncompro-mising confidence, in their sometimes stunningly inaccurate ap-praisals of themselves, ballplayers are linked—though they might never recognize it—to others of their generation who are living on the edge.

The notion that such internally driven people can become slip-shod overnight just because they're stupefyingly overpaid, is bo-gus. By the time a man is established in the majors, his personality has been in place for a long time. For every player who counts his money and "retires" while still playing, there are more who are doubly motivated by the promise of greater wealth or by fear of public embarrassment or simply by a feeling of responsibility to live up to those fleeting gifts which distinguish them from other men.

The career athlete who is perceived to have fulfilled his potential is, within the jock community, given a sort of lifetime pass, a character reference that can never be revoked by misfortune. And the athlete whose peers believe that he wasted his talent is, in a way, never forgiven, no matter how hale a fellow he may pass for to the rest of us.

In baseball today, the twin internal dynamics of competition and artistry are still much stronger than the degenerative effects of riches. Consequently, we can still truly enjoy baseball. If we feel that the performers care deeply, genuinely judge themselves by their acts, then the game is worth watching. Craft is the surest proof of sincerity.

Once, I sat next to Gaylord Perry, three-hundred-game winner and curmudgeon, at a winter banquet. Initially he despised me, as I assumed he would, since I was one of those slimy reporters who nag him about his spitball, his feuds with teammates, his undermining of managers and his love of a dollar. But the only thing Perry really loves to talk about, besides his tobacco crop, is baseball, and that link soon erased our differences.

"During games, I'll sit alone down at one end of the dugout and talk baseball," said Perry, then forty-four and an ancient Seattle Mariner. "Pretty soon, the young players would kinda gather around me. If anybody brings up any other subject, I just say, 'We're talkin' baseball down here. These are working hours. You wanna talk about something else, go the hell down to the other end.'

"It was amazing what those kids don't know, and I enjoyed watchin' their eyes get big. I can tell a hitter's weaknesses the first time I ever see him, just by watching him take his stance. Like, if a hitter carries the bat high and wraps it back around his neck [giving a casual demonstration of the cocked wrists], well, then you know he can't hit the fastball in on his hands. It takes him too long to get the bat started and clear his hips out of the way.

"And if the hitter holds the bat low or lays it out away from him, then he can't hit the outside pitch with authority, especially the breaking ball. You can get him to pull the trigger too soon.

"Also, you gotta watch their feet. The good hitters, like Rod Carew or Eddie Murray, they've got a half-dozen different stances and they'll change 'em between pitches. That's how you tell what they're guessing."

"What if they change stances," I asked, "as you're winding up?"

Perry raised one eyebrow.

"Oh," I muttered, "you drill him."

"I hope so," said Perry.

If one quality distinguishes baseball as seen from a distance, from the game as it is at point-blank range, it's just this sort of ambiance which mixes constant technical analysis with an equal amount of prickly agitating. My favorite clubhouse was that of the '77–'78 New York Yankees. Those world champs were perhaps the most acid-tongued, thick-skinned, insult-you-to-your-face team that ever spit tobacco juice on a teammate's new Gucci loafers. A perfect Yankee day came late in '77 when Steinbrenner decided the item he needed to complete his circus was reclusive Dave Kingman. "We already have Captain Moody [Thurman Munson], Lieutenant Moody [Mickey Rivers], Sergeant Moody [Ken Holtzman] and Private Moody [Willie Randolph]," said third baseman Graig Nettles. "Now Dave can be Commander Moody."

The heirs to that tradition were the '82 Brewers, led by Cy Young winner Pete Vuckovich. When it's time to form a new musical-chairs group called Down with People, or if you want a cover photo for a new book called "I'm Not O.K. and Neither Are You," start with Vuke.

Catching sight of Gorman Thomas' great mane of shaggy hair, his unfriendly mustache, his chaw of 'baccy, his third-world teeth and his dirty uniform, the glowering Vuckovich accosted his roommate, saying, "You are the ugliest."

"No, *you* are the ugliest," said Thomas, running his eye over Vuckovich's pockmarked skin, his mass-murderer hair, his beer belly, his whole cultivated mien of mayhem. "In fact, you are the absolute worst in every way."

Most people might take offense at such perspicacity. Not Vuke.

"Well," he said proudly, "somebody's got to be."

Men with personalities as flinty, minds as sharp and tongues as tart as Perry, Nettles, Vuckovich and Thomas are the sort who define what we might call the big-league point of view. When I covered my first major-league game, in 1972, I assumed I had a respectable knowledge of the subject. Now, after a thousand and one nights in the ballpark, I may know half as much as I thought I knew then. I stepped into the dugouts of the major leagues with an outsider's approach to the sport. With the years, I've gradually altered that angle of vision until, while still half outsider, I'm also half insider.

What *is* this big-league point of view?

In many ways, the pros watch a game, a season, just as we do; when a flyball is heading for the fence, they root exactly like the folks in the bleachers. However, more often than not, the ballplayer sees things much differently from the rest of us. If we truly want to taste the facts of the game, get the flavors right, then we must add this insider's perspective to our own. Let's have a preliminary Ten Commandments of the Dugout:

• Judge slowly.

No, even more slowly than that.

Never judge a player over a unit of time shorter than a month. A game or even a week is nothing; you must see a player hot, cold and in between before you can put the whole package together. Sometimes, in the case of a proven player, a whole season is not enough time to judge, especially if there are extenuating circumstances. In '81, Fred Lynn, traded from Boston to the Angels, batted .219 with five homers; the quick judgment was that Lynn was a Fenway Park hitter who would never be an All-Star away from it. In '82, Lynn was healthy, made his technical adjustments at the plate and saw his stats go back close to their .300-with-power, Fenway levels.

The rush to judge is the most certain sign of a baseball outsider. When, in '82, George Steinbrenner tried to *run* his Yankees, as well as own them, he made all the sort of shoot-from-the-hip judgments of a guy in the cheap seats who's had one beer too many; the results were a disaster. Steinbrenner, with his football and business backgrounds, didn't have the patience to come to sound, fully digested decisions; why, the man made judgments of players based on just one game—absolute proof of not having baseball sense. The baseball person is usually the last to work his way to a firm opinion, and also the last to abandon it. Steinbrenner is always the first on the boat and the first off.

• Assume everybody is trying reasonably hard.

Of all the factors at work in baseball, effort is the last to consider. In the majors, you seldom try your hardest; giving 110 percent, as a general mode of operation, would be counterproductive for most players. The issue in baseball is finding the proper balance between effort and relaxation. Usually, something on the order of 80 percent effort is about right. Few players have trouble revving that high. Many can't get down that low. Physical sluggishness, called "jaking," is relatively rare, except among heavy drug users whose heads are temporarily on call to another star system.

• Physical errors, even the most grotesque, should be forgiven.

On good teams, the physical limitations of players are nearly ignored. The short hop that eats an infielder alive, the ball in the dirt that goes to the screen, the hitter who is hopelessly overpowered by a pitcher—all these hideous phenomena are treated as though they never happened. "Forget it," players say to each other, reflexively. It's assumed that every player is physically capable of performing every duty asked of him. If he can't, it's never his fault. His mistake is simply regarded as part of a professional's natural human margin of error.

Even if a player consistently makes physical blunders, it's *still* not his fault and he's never blamed. It's the front office's fault for not coming up with a better player; the assumption is that while stars are rare, there is always an abundance of competent professionals. Or it's the manager's fault for putting a player in a situation beyond his talents. You don't ask Roy Howell to hit Ron Guidry. And if you do, his strikeout is your fault, not his.

• Conversely, mental errors are judged as harshly as physical errors are ignored. The distinction as to whether a mistake has been made "from the neck up or the neck down" is always made.

Mental errors, however, can cover a wide range. Failure in any fundamental—laying down a sacrifice bunt, hitting the cutoff man, covering or backing up bases, receiving or relaying a sign, even catching a windblown pop-up—is considered a sort of quasi-mental error. Why? Because, with the proper mental discipline, you could have learned to master those basic skills.

As an extreme example, a pitcher who walks home the winning run is guilty of a grievous mental error, because a major-league pitcher is assumed to be able to throw a strike whenever he absolutely must. If he can't, the problem usually has more to do with poise or preparation or proper thinking on the mound, than with the physical act of throwing the ball.

• Pay more attention to the mundane than the spectacular.

Baseball is a game of huge samplings. The necessity for consistency usually outweighs the need for the inspired. In judging any player, never measure him by his greatest catch, his longest home run, his best-pitched game. That is the exception; baseball is the game of the rule.

• Pay more attention to the theory of the game than to the outcome of the game. Don't let your evaluations be swayed too greatly by the final score.

The most common error of novice reporters is their tendency to watch what happens, rather than study the principles under the action. You don't ask, "Did that pinch hitter get a hit?" In a sense, that's a matter of chance. The worst hitter will succeed one time in five, while the best hitter will fail two times in three. Instead ask, "Given all the factors in play at that moment, was he the correct man to use in that situation?"

Only then will you begin to sense the game as a team does. If a team loses a game but has used its resources properly—relieved its starting pitcher at a sensible juncture, used the proper strategy during its rallies, minimized its mental and fundamental mistakes, had the proper pinch hitters at the plate with the game on the line in the late innings—then that team is often able to ignore defeat utterly. Players say, "We did everything right but win."

If you do everything right every day, you'll still lose 40 percent of your games—but you'll also end up in the World Series. Nowhere is defeat so meaningless as in baseball. And nowhere are the theories and broad tactics that run under the game so important.

• Players always know best how they're playing.

At the technical level, they seldom fool themselves—the stakes are too high. Self-criticism is ingrained. If a player on a ten-game hitting streak says he's in a slump, then he is; if a player who's one for fifteen says that he's "on" every pitch, but that he's hitting a lot of "atom" balls ("right at-'em"), then assume he's about to go on a tear.

There are exceptions: Jim Palmer always thought his arm was about to fall off and once alternately begged and cursed his manager in hopes of being taken out of the last three innings of a game in which he ended up pitching a one-hit shutout. Al Oliver, owner of the game's best superiority complex, believed the only reason he never had a hundred-RBI year until his twelfth season was that "I always seem to hit in bad luck."

• Stay *ahead* of the action, not behind it or even neck and neck with it.

Remember, the immediate past is almost always prelude. Ask hurlers how they go about selecting their pitches and they invariably say, "By watching the previous pitch." The thrower plans his game in advance; the pitcher creates it as he goes. A veteran pitcher usually doesn't know what he'll throw on his second pitch until he sees what happens to the first. "Don't judge your fastball by those darn radar guns," says Perry. "Judge by how the hitters act."

Was that batter taking or swinging? Was he ahead of the curveball or behind the fastball? Was he trying to pull, to go to the opposite field, or simply "go with the pitch"? Was he trying for power or contact? And just as important, how has he reacted to these factors in the past? Does he tend to adjust from pitch to pitch (which is unusual)? From at-bat to at-bat (which is more common)? Or is he so stubborn that he has a plan for the whole game and will "sit on the fastball" or "wait for that change-up all night" in hopes of seeing one pitch that he can poleax?

That's how baseball has been watched in every respectable dugout for as long as the oldest hands can remember. And the closer you come to that sort of reflective, sifting, tendency-spotting habit of viewers, the more enjoyable and open the game will seem. Of all our major sports, baseball comes closest to rewarding the spectator in direct proportion to his effort.

Pay particular attention to the first inning. Study the starting pitcher and study him hard. Both he and his foes are trying to figure out what he's got that night; his first dozen pitches will often set the tone for the first half of the game. Don't ask, "Does he have his control?" Instead, go through this checklist: Can he get his fastball over for strikes? Can he throw his fastball to *spots* within the strike zone? Is he throwing his breaking ball for strikes, or just showcasing it? Does he trust his off-speed pitch enough to throw it when he's behind in the count? Is he tempting batters into getting themselves out on borderline pitches or balls?

What does he tend to throw on each of the sport's most important counts: 0–0, 2–2 and the cripples (2–0 and 3–1)?

In other words:

What does he rely upon to *start* hitters—i.e., 0–0?

What "out pitch" does he use to *finish* hitters—that's the moment-of-truth, 2–2 pitch. Players call the 2–2 pitch "the end of the line," because pitchers hate to go from 2–2 to 3–2. *Never* take a nap on a 2–2 pitch. That's when you're most likely to find out the pitcher's true opinion of both his strength and the batter's weakness.

Finally, what does the pitcher select when he's nibbled himself into a corner: the 2–0 and the 3–1 "cripple" pitches? What is his tight-spot pitch?

As an almost clinical example, the '82 Cy Young winner, Vuckovich of Milwaukee, was often two different pitchers in the same game.

He'd go through the lineup the first time, when he was still fresh, like an utterly conventional "power" pitcher. He'd "pitch the counts," as it's called.

That means on neutral counts—like 0–0, 1–1 and 2–2—he'd use his bread-and-butter—the fastball or hard slider—trying to stay ahead of the count and "challenge the hitters."

On all the "hitter's counts"—like 1–0, 2–1 and 3–2—he'd also bravely confront the hitters with hard stuff, often on a corner or the fists.

On all the "pitcher's counts"—like 0–1, 1–2 and 2–2—he'd throw tormenting breaking balls at the corners. On cripples, he'd go macho, throwing hard strikes; on waste pitches, he'd also play fair, bouncing curves in the other batter's box or coming up and in.

Then, sometimes in the middle innings, Vuckovich—having established that he could succeed with old-fashioned, no-imagination power pitching—would begin to "contradict the counts."

That's upsetting to hitters, because they're taught to believe pitchers won't change tactics until they're forced. Vuckovich would occasionally mix in breaking balls on neutral counts or even on hitters' counts. When he was ahead, and presumably didn't need to challenge hitters, that's when he'd show the fastball, though just off the plate. Suddenly the cripples would be change-ups, and the waste pitches would be smoke on the black.

Finally, by the late innings, Vuckovich would be "reversing the counts."

Neutral counts and even cripples would, almost invariably, be nasty off-speed pitches, always nibbling; often, with men on base, Vuckovich would, almost deliberately it seemed, fall behind in a count, then "reverse the count" and get an inning-ending double play.

When he got ahead of the count, Vuke would do anything, including throw his best remaining fastball for a high strike in hopes of a fly out.

Milwaukee general manager Harry Dalton was like a kid with candy watching Vuckovich at work constantly playing mind games with hitters. "A lot of pitchers, like Nolan Ryan, can perform," said Dalton one night. "Give me Vuckovich. He competes."

Vuckovich could be several contradictory pitchers all wrapped in one for two unique reasons: First, though he weighed two hundred fifty pounds and played the role of mound thug, he was actually more a curveball control pitcher than a fastballer. Second, for some reason, Vuke felt comfortable pitching behind in counts or with tons of men on base. The more a hitter thought he had Vuckovich backed into a corner where he would have to throw either a fastball, a strike or both, the more likely Vuckovich was to throw a breaking ball just off the corner—and get the hitter out with it.

Vuckovich was a student of expectation. That is, a student of baseball.

Baseball offers us pleasure and insight at so many levels and in so many forms that, when we try to grasp the whole sport in our two hands, we end up with nothing. The game, because it is no one thing but, rather, dozens of things, has slipped through our fingers again.

As each season begins, we always feel the desire to capsulize and define the source of the sharp anticipation that we feel as opening day approaches. We know that something fine, almost wonderful, is about to begin, but we can't quite say why baseball seems so valuable, almost indispensable, to us. The game, which remains one of our broadest sources of metaphor, changes with our angle of vision, our mood; there seems to be no end to our succession of lucky discoveries.

When opening day arrives, think how many baseball worlds begin revolving for seven months.

As history, baseball has given us an annual chapter each year since 1869. Each team will add a page to its franchise's epic. Countless questions that attach themselves to the baseball continuum will be answered. Will Pete Rose find a way to break Ty Cobb's record for hits? Will Reggie Jackson get his five hundredth home run? Will Terry Felton—oh-for-sixteen in his career and back in the minors again—ever win a game? Yes, we walk with giants.

As living theater and physical poetry, the game will be available in twenty-six ballparks on more than two thousand occasions. Baseball is always there when we want it—seven days a week, seven months a year. All the tactile pleasures of the park are ready when the proper mood strikes us: evening twilights, sundowns, hot summer Sunday afternoons, the cool of the dark late innings of night games, quiet drives home as we decompress and digest.

Then, just when we think the game is essentially mellow and reflective, we find ourselves looped in the twists and coils of a 5–4 barn burner between two contenders. When the centerfielder jumps above the fence in the bottom of the ninth and comes down with the ball and the game in his hand, we realize that two to three hours is just the proper amount of time to tighten the mainspring of tension before letting us explode in one, final cheer. We leave with a glowing tiredness, delighted by the memories of this impromptu and virile ballet, all choreographed by the capricious flight of a ball.

Despite all this, baseball may give us more pleasure, more gentle, unobtrusive sustenance, away from the park than it does inside it.

With breakfast, we have our ten minutes of box scores—enough to travel to thirteen cities, see thirteen games in our mind's eye, note at a glance what five hundred players did or failed to do. Dave Righetti, five walks in four innings, still can't get his delivery in synch. Tony Armas, three for four, out of his latest slump, will probably go right into a streak and hit five homers by next Friday.

On Sunday, the breakfast process takes an extra ten minutes, since The Averages must be consumed. We imagine the state of mind of dozens of players and their teammates. (Who ever thought Seaver had another good season in him? Kingman's down to .196; bet that bum's a prince to be around.)

Then, in odd parts of the day, the game drifts into the mind. Who's pitching tonight? Is it on TV? At worst, the home team is on the radio; catch the last few innings. "Double-play grounder to Ozzie Smith deep in the hole, Billy Russell's chugging toward first, Steve Sax trying to take out Tommy Herr."

Why, it doesn't even have to happen to be real.

The ways that baseball insinuates itself into the empty corners, cheering up the odd hour, are almost too ingrained to notice. Tape at eleven, the scores before bed, the Monday and Saturday games of the week. Into how many conversations does George Steinbrenner's name creep, so that we may gauge the judgments of

our friends, catch a glimpse of their values on the sly? The amateur statistician and the armchair strategist in us is roused. What
fan doesn't have a new system for grading relief pitchers, or a
theory on why the Expos never win?

Sure, opening day is baseball's bandwagon. Pundits and politicians and every prose poet on the continent jumps on board for a
few days. But they're gone soon, off in search of some other windy
event worthy of their attention. Then, once more, all those long,
slow months of baseball are left to us. And our time can begin
again.